# CALVERT VAUX
## ARCHITECT & PLANNER

Calvert Vaux (1824–1895)

# CALVERT VAUX

## ARCHITECT & PLANNER

William Alex

*with an Introduction by* George B. Tatum

INK, INC. NEW YORK: 1994

*for Joan Davidson*

© COPYRIGHT 1994 WILLIAM ALEX

INK, INC. 821 BROADWAY, NEW YORK 10003

ISBN 0-964065-0-2

# Contents

Calvert Vaux's field drafting set.

# Acknowledgments

THE GENESIS of this publication occurred in August of 1980, when the architectural scholar Dennis Steadman Francis visited the office of the Olmsted Association to open discussion on several subjects of interest to us. Primary among these was Calvert Vaux, on whom Francis had been conducting research toward a monograph for some years past. Francis had just completed the monumental *Architects in Practice, New York City 1840–1900* for the Committee for the Preservation of Architectural Records. During the meeting it was agreed that the Olmsted Association would support his work on Vaux as best it could in that recognition for Olmsted's partner was very long overdue.

One month after this meeting Dennis Francis died. The idea of a Vaux monograph languished for several years although we sporadically tried to free his research material and documentation for publication. To help gain the recognition so richly deserved of Vaux's contribution to architectural thought and practice, we decided to bring together a group of scholars whose interests related in some way to an understanding of Vaux's accomplishments, each of whom agreed to contribute an essay on a particular aspect of his work. Although most of these were not forthcoming, by 1988, George B. Tatum completed a comprehensive narrative of Vaux's career for this introductory volume, which, it is hoped, will be the first step in a process of further study, discovery, and understanding.

Acknowledgment and appreciation is due to many people and institutions who over the years have provided materials and encouragement for this publication. Professor Tatum has kindly made available picture material from his own collections. Dr. Arthur Channing Downs, who is at this time preparing a detailed study on Vaux that may one day serve as a companion volume to this publication, has provided picture material and information on Vaux's early years in England, a subject in which Dr. J. M. L. Booker, archivist of Lloyds Bank, London, has also been most helpful. The exchange of materials, information and opinions with Dr. Downs has been of mutual benefit. Special credit is due to inhabitants or, more properly, curators of Vaux edifices, keepers of original drawings and institutions that have made available photographs and reproductions: Katherine Delano Ryan Aldrich, Barrytown, N. Y.; Ray Armater, Margaret Partridge, and Joanne Lukacher, Wilderstein Preservation, Rhinebeck, N. Y.; Elizabeth Banks, Frederick Law Olmsted National Historic Site, Brookline, Mass.; Phyllis Barr, Trinity Church, New York, N. Y.; Mary F. Bell and Clyde H. Eller, Buffalo and Erie County Historical Society, Buffalo, N. Y.; Richard L. Champlin, Redwood Library and Athenaeum, Newport, R. I.; Kenneth R. Cobb and Evelyn Gonzalez, Municipal Archives of the City of New York, N. Y.; Thomas Daley, Gardner, N. Y.; Suzanne Davis, J. M. Kaplan Fund, New York, N. Y.; Robert Elwall, British Architectural Library, Royal Institute of British Architects, London, U. K.; Stephen Garmey, New York, N. Y.; Dr. Robert W. Gibson, Sheppard and Enoch Pratt Hospital, Baltimore, Md.; Edmund V. Gillon, Jr., New York, N. Y.; M. M. Graff, Brooklyn, N. Y.; Janet Graham, Rhinebeck, N. Y.; Christopher Gray, Office of Metropolitan History, New York, N. Y.; Jonathan P. Harding, The Century Association,

New York, N. Y.; Mrs. Gregory Henderson, West Medford, Mass.; James S. Hodgson, Harvard Graduate School of Design, Cambridge, Mass.; Marguerite B. Hubbard, Franklin D. Roosevelt Library, Hyde Park, N. Y.; James P. Hurley, Landmarks Preservation Commission, New York, N. Y.; Prof. James L. Kettlewell, Skidmore College, Saratoga Springs, N. Y.; John A. Kouwenhoven, Dorset, Vt.; Thomas Kyle, Historical Society of Newburgh Bay and the Highlands, Newburgh, N. Y.; Ethel Lambert, Children's Aid Society, New York, N. Y.; Bertram Lippincott III, Newport Historical Society, Newport, R. I.; Nancy S. McKechnie, Vassar College Library, Poughkeepsie, N. Y.; Suzanne Noel, Takoma Park, Md.; Jane W. Rehl, Museum of the Historical Society of Saratoga Springs, Saratoga Springs, N. Y.; H. Merrill Roenke, Jr., and Eleanor R. Clise, Geneva Historical Society, Geneva, N. Y.; Lu W. Rose, Reeves-Reed Arboretum, Summit, N. J.; James Ryan, Olana State Historic Site, Hudson, N. Y.; Janet St. Louis, Ashcroft, Geneva, N. Y.; Helen Scollon, Arnot-Ogden Memorial Hospital, Elmira, N. Y.; Edward P. Straka and Dorothy Unger, Riverside Historical Commission, Riverside, Ill.; Dorothy Lee Tatum, Ammadelle, Oxford, Miss.; Mary Wall, Architectural Association, London, U. K.; Elizabeth White, Brooklyn Public Library; Allis Wolfe, The Bank of New York, N. Y.; and Frederic C. Zanetti, Newburgh, N. Y.

Special thanks are due the officials and staff of the New-York Historical Society, the New York Public Library, Astor, Lenox and Tilden Foundations and the Library of Congress for material assistance provided from their rich and important collections. Substantial basic research was conducted by Esther Brumberg; photographer Peter Goldberg transformed indifferent images into good ones; Paula Porter transcribed much of the text material; and Elaine Desautels was kind enough to review the manuscript material. This publication is supported by a grant from the National Endowment for the Arts in Washington, D.C., a federal agency.

Contributions have been received as well from the Graham Foundation for Advanced Studies in the Fine Arts, Chicago, Ill., the Eva Gebhard-Gourgaud Foundation, New York, N. Y. and Joseph E. Seagram and Sons, Inc., New York, N. Y.

Appreciation is due The J. M. Kaplan Fund, an abiding force in the cultural life of New York, which provided the initial impetus and support some twenty years ago for what has become the giant presence of Frederick Law Olmsted in our midst, and now again has substantially implemented the revelation of Calvert Vaux's contribution to the historic patrimony of New York and the nation. These things would not have been possible but for the Kaplan Fund.

William Alex, *President*
Frederick Law Olmsted Association
New York, N. Y.

# Preface

THE NAME CALVERT VAUX is about to emerge from the shadows of American history just as did the name Frederick Law Olmsted some years ago. Vaux, the one professional in nineteenth-century America who combined in himself the talents of landscape designer, architect and planner, was directly responsible for initiating the process that resulted in the two seminal park designs of this nation, designs that became of crucial importance in forming the urban face of American cities. Central Park in New York and Prospect Park in Brooklyn, the great prototypical country parks in the city, and the interconnecting parkways that Olmsted and Vaux proposed for them, became the focus for related planning concepts and methods basic to the future of city building in the United States.

It was Vaux who succeeded in getting the Central Park commissioners to set aside the mediocre plan for Central Park, convincing them to establish a competition for its design. He then persuaded Olmsted to join him in creating their winning "Greensward" plan. It was Vaux who devised the preliminary plan for Prospect Park and persuaded Olmsted to return from California so that together they could perfect and execute the plan. The result in Brooklyn is probably the most admired of their creations. And finally, Vaux convinced Olmsted that he was not merely an administrator or manager of men in a species of public works, but that he was an artist, the two combining literally to create vast green earth sculptures in the midst of the city grid.

Vaux would have gained direct experience in landscape work in England as an apprentice to Lewis Nockalls Cottingham who, although noted for his restoration work on Gothic cathedrals, also designed country manor estates. In 1851, when President Fillmore asked A. J. Downing, for whom Vaux was now working in the United States, to lay out the public grounds in Washington between the Capitol and White House, Vaux, already assisting Downing in the planning of estate grounds along the Hudson Highlands, would now gain valuable experience in landscape design on a larger scale. In the Downing and Vaux domestic architecture designs, as Professor Tatum shows in his narrative, the architecture is strengthened, conception and plan are clearly rationalized, details are surer and elements of European form are more apparent, presumably due to a combination of Vaux's English training and Downing's visits to Europe.

Vaux was fully committed to his adopted country. The year after he became an American citizen, he was moved to write in his *Villas and Cottages,* "There has not, indeed, been, from the commencement of the world till this moment, an opportunity for the advance of the fine arts so replete with the material of true success as now exists in America; this advance is a question of choice, not time; of purpose, not ability; of direction, not force; there is *capacity* enough spread over all the country, and being wasted daily: it is *conviction* and *will* that is needed."

Conviction and will were indeed qualities Vaux demonstrated in his successful campaign to overturn the existing Central Park plan. Following their competition victory, Vaux and Olmsted proceeded to implement the "Greensward" plan, inspiring *Harper's Monthly* to write in 1862, "The Central Park is the finest work of art ever executed in this country . . . the exquisite forms of the ground in every direction—the perfection of the roadwork and gardening—the picturesque and beautiful bridges—the lovely sweeps of water contrasted with lawn banks—the pictorial effect of the terrace upon the water, so that you drive out of the city into the landscape. . . ."

While many important commissions followed, the Olmsted-Vaux relationship was not always a smooth one, even as Vaux embellished their parks with bridges, buildings, terraces, rustic shelters, boathouses, refectories and other necessary amenities. A state of inequity was established just after they won the Central Park competition when Olmsted, already serving as park superintendent, was, with a certain illogic, appointed architect-in-chief of the work, while Vaux, the professional, assumed what he understood to be a temporary secondary position. Despite supervisory experience of his own in site planning and architecture, Vaux accepted this arrangement in the belief that strong individual leadership was necessary for the success of the effort. But with Olmsted generally serving as spokesman and publicist then, and later in joint work as Olmsted, Vaux and Company, the public impression that Olmsted was primary in the partnership was one that Vaux came to resent deeply, despite the fact that Olmsted continually maintained their coequality. In the writing of their various reports, Olmsted clearly depended on Vaux as intricate points at issue were resolved or clarified—both spending much time in this sort of discussion, according to their associate at the time, the architect A. J. Bloor.

Early in his career Vaux had enunciated principles and beliefs by which he abided until the end, long after society in America took pathways he could or would not follow. An early sign of his determination was one of the reasons for his resignation from the American Institute of Architects, of which he was a founding member; the institute insisted on architectural exclusivity, while Vaux felt that certain new categories of membership might recognize associated arts and crafts he believed were inseparable from the creative building effort.

In his book *Villas and Cottages* Vaux observed the driving force in America toward "money-making" for its own sake, regrettably noting that the fruits of wealth were not directed toward the increase of excellence in "literature, science and art" for the general benefit of a democratic society. Whether or not Vaux anticipated the achievement of a "higher national excellence" in his adopted country, he was motivated by his beliefs and convinced of the basic validity of his principles which he strongly maintained in his fields of endeavor. Writing in 1865 to Olmsted, who was preparing to return to New York to join him in the Prospect Park job, Vaux characterized him as a vital partner "in regard to the main point,—the translation of the republican art idea into the acres we want to control." The art idea had many things within it, including the concept of uplifting social reform. A short time later Vaux writes again as they are both reappointed landscape architects to Central Park, in the belief that they might actually exercise control over its construction and management. "You are, and I am, and several other people are necessary to this work, and it can be successfully carried through in an artistic spirit to a real end, both as a constructed work and as a vital organism; but it depends on you—and the spirit in which you now approach it—whether this result is to be arrived at or not. I am willing to contribute all I can. Are you content to do the same?"

Most of the local New York politicians had little inkling of "artistic spirit" or indeed of any art in their parks at all. Vaux was to spend most of his time thereafter in New York battling to protect his and Olmsted's parks against shortsighted and venal municipal officials intent on misusing city parklands. His creative energies were being vitiated, but his idealism kept him going. Apart from his professional work, he participated in the civic, artistic and cultural life of the city. As a member of the Century Association and as clubman, he mixed with the intellectual elite of New York. He was closely involved with *The Fraternity Papers,* a literary publication that he and Mrs. Vaux helped edit and to which he contributed essays, poems and drawings.

Vaux's early years were perhaps his most satisfying, when he designed Hudson Valley residences for the urban rich who preferred to travel up to country estates that were named, in reflection of a certain Victorian sentiment of the times, Algonac, Springside, Idlewild and Olana or elsewhere Ammadelle and Ashcroft. Vaux's comfortable use of the Rural Gothic and Italianate villa styles in his early domestic architecture evolved into the Victorian High Gothic when it came to his large urban commissions, but at a time when others had taken up expedient, eclectic ideals and were producing the kind of classic, imperial architecture that better represented the success and pride of the money-makers. Vaux, although respected for his artistic, technological and sociological achievements, was not called on in later years. In 1895, the same year that Olmsted, his mind failing, retired from active practice, Vaux's career ended in death. His legacy, soon forgotten as was the case with Olmsted, is nevertheless secure, and here introduced, can begin to be understood and appreciated in our time.

In the illustrative material that follows Professor Tatum's narrative, the reader will find that the extended text captions occasionally elaborate on statements in the narrative in order to provide a more complete understanding of the specific pictures they accompany. The illustrations of Vaux's work are presented, not in a chronological mix, but separated into the major aspects of his professionalism so that each may be more easily apprehended: architecture, planning and landscape architecture. Each of these sections is introduced by a short general introduction. Beyond these design preoccupations, Vaux found time to work closely with the best heating and ventilation engineer of the day, Louis W. Leeds, with whom he took out patents for advanced systems of this sort.

THE PICTURE of Calvert Vaux's drafting set at the beginning of this book is a poignant reminder of the loss of his papers and records. Apart from the hundred or so items donated in 1929 to the New York Public Library by his daughter-in-law, Mrs. Calvert Bowyer Vaux—letters, newspaper clippings, a few park documents and several handwritten pages of lists of his works that Vaux compiled toward the end of his life—almost everything that relates to Vaux's life and career is dispersed or lost. The acquisition of his drafting set by the Museum of the City New York is the result of an unusual and unfortunate circumstance. It was donated to the museum by Leonard Grime, an actor in the Shakespearean troupe led by James L. Hendrickson of New York, who was married to Vaux's daughter Marian. Grime lived in the same West 49th Street Manhattan apartment building as the Hendricksons. Hendrickson died suddenly; Marian was in a nursing home at the time. Relatives and lawyers came to remove the contents of the apartment, which had to be vacated. Except for the drafting set, which no one seemed to want and which Grime brought to the museum, all of the Vaux-related items in his daughter's possession were scattered without record.

Hopefully, works by Vaux as yet unknown can be revealed as a result of this publication. One such tantalizing possibility arises from an entry by Vaux's brother-in-law, Jervis McEntee, in his diary entry for April 3, 1886: "Went to the Century [Association] monthly meeting . . . Calvert's model of the Great Monument was there and elicited a good deal of interest. . . ." Another vanished project is mentioned by Vaux's son Downing in an article in the 1906 *Transactions of the American Society of Landscape Architects*: "the Port Morris plan for the 1883 exhibition in New York City, by Vaux and Radford, my father's firm (and on which I did some work myself), laid great stress on the waterfront. . . ." Still another unknown work is mentioned in passing by Vaux's friend James Morse, who visited the family in New Jersey where Vaux had moved to undertake what was clearly a major town planning project. In his diary entry for October 31, 1875, Morse not only mentions the project, but also gives us a rare glimpse of the Vauxes at home.

"A week ago yesterday, it being Saturday, I went up to spend Sunday with the Vauxes in their experiment home on the Palisades. . . .  I reached an opening sloping down to the edge of the Palisades, where a magnificent scene lay under the eye—the river, the hills beyond, and, if it had not been the late twilight hour, a glimpse of the sound and of far-off Long Island. Here in the midst of the opening in a semi-wild region, was the house which Mr. Vaux has hired for three years, repaired, renewed, almost made over, and already furnished and adorned with the accumulated luxuries of his city home. Here were delicate vases, rich hangings, quaint woodwork and bronze furniture, landscapes by our dearest American artists, books and all the objects of taste and refinement which made the country the city and the city the suburb of heaven. Miss Marian was at the door holding the horse which was to be sent down to the ferry to fetch Bowyer and his father. They arrived late and it was after dark when we sat down to dinner. Next morning . . . all sallied out into the woods . . . keeping along the cliff, to whose projecting points we were frequently summoned by Mr. Vaux to note some unusually beautiful opening. Under his supervision a boulevard is being constructed a thousand feet behind the front of the plateau, from which boulevard will radiate walks and equestrian paths toward the finer points over the river. The land will be drained and laid out in sections, and probably built up with gentlemen's country houses. At least this is the expectation of the company that owns the property, and this is the point of view that brings the V's here. Certainly a more picturesque scenery than that formed by the gigantic rocks with these fine forests and a more beautiful view than is to be had from the pinnacled front could not be found with[in] a circle of fifty miles from the city. We spent the entire afternoon in rambling about, picking autumn leaves and fringed gentian which grew in abundance, while Mr. V. was keeping an eye on the landscape features over which his mind is always mulling. It was quite dinner time when we returned

to the house, laden with gorgeous things. At five o'clock I took leave and rowed with
Bowyer across the river to Yonkers."*

In his work with Olmsted, Vaux had expected recognition to come equally to
himself, but this was not the case. Their association over the years was characterized
by a mixture of bitterness and affection, of misunderstanding as well as extraordinary
accomplishment. A great part of their correspondence is preserved in the Olmsted
Papers collection at the Library of Congress, however, and study of this material will
ultimately provide a better understanding of the relationship between the two. After
the dissolution of his partnership with Olmsted, Vaux was to continue for almost a
generation longer in architecture and with occasional landscape architecture work,
alone or in partnership with his various associates, but not on the scale as with Olmsted. This body of later work waits to be examined in depth.

W. A.

---

* Diary of James H. Morse (1866–1911), Manuscript Department, The New-York Historical Society.

*Design for a Rustic Shelter.—C. Vaux, Architect.*

"Restawhile [on] the Palisades, C V July 11,
18[67]." Design for a Rustic Shelter.—C. Vaux,
Architect.

# Introduction

CALVERT VAUX'S numerous and varied contributions to the domestic, institutional, and landscape architecture of the United States deserve to be better known. His introduction to his adopted country was as the architectural assistant, and later as the partner, of Andrew Jackson Downing, probably the most personable, popular and influential arbiter of taste America has produced. His greatest successes as a designer of parks were achieved in partnership with Frederick Law Olmsted, whose commanding figure dominates the second half of the nineteenth century. And from time to time throughout his career Vaux's fortunes were inextricably linked with such talented, if less well-known, contemporaries as Frederick Clarke Withers, Jacob Wrey Mould, Thomas Wisedell, George Kent Radford and Samuel Parsons, Jr. For much of the twentieth century Vaux not only shared in the general disapproval with which one period is apt to regard the accomplishments of its immediate predecessors, but in this case his reputation also suffered from the greater visibility of a number of those with whom he collaborated. Fortunately, history teaches that in matters of taste what was once valued is likely to find favor again in due course. The 1989 exhibition "Calvert Vaux: Architect and Planner," held at the Museum of the City of New York, began such a reassessment of Vaux's career, a function this monograph continues and to which it now gives more permanent form.

EARLY YEARS: VAUX IN ENGLAND

35*

VAUX was born December 20, 1824, at his parents' home on Pudding Lane, a short, narrow street leading to the Thames near London Bridge. Although of French origin, the Vaux family had long before established itself in England and anglicized the pronunciation of its name (pronounced like "Vawks"). Calvert shared his given name with his father, Calvert Bowyer Vaux, who followed his forebears into the medical profession. His father's death when he was only nine might easily have jeopardized young Calvert's education had it not proved possible for his family to secure places for both him and his younger brother Alfred at the well-endowed Merchant Taylors' School nearby. In an age when only a small minority of school graduates went on to university, young Calvert chose a career in architecture, and at

38–41

the age of fifteen was articled to Lewis Nockalls Cottingham (1787–1847), a respected London architect more often remembered for his scholarly knowledge of the Gothic style than for the originality of his designs.

During the nineteenth century long hours and little pay characterized the lot of the average apprentice, who was usually indentured for from five to seven years, and so, while in Cottingham's office, Vaux sought to augment his income by lettering railroad maps in his free time. Besides providing good training, this paid sufficiently well that by the mid 1840s he could contemplate a walking and sketching tour

39

through France and Germany. His companion in this adventure was George Truefitt (1824–1902), a young architect only a few months his senior, whom he had come to know when they were both apprentices in Cottingham's office. In later years numerous sketches served as a reminder of this European odyssey from which both men derived continuing benefit in a variety of ill-defined but nonetheless enduring ways.[1]

At this point Vaux's career seemed likely to develop as much as did that of True-fitt, who went on to establish a solid reputation as a Gothicist in the tradition of their teacher, Cottingham. But then, quite suddenly, in the summer of 1850 Vaux was offered a new opportunity from a totally unexpected quarter. Through the good offices of the secretary of the recently formed Architectural Association, he was introduced to Andrew Jackson Downing (1815–1852), the American landscape gardener and writer on architectural and gardening subjects, who had come to London in search of a competent architect who would join him in the professional office he was in the process of establishing at his home in Newburgh, New York. Through his books, as well as through his essays in *The Horticulturist*, for which he had served as editor since 1846, Downing had already achieved a national reputation. Now, with a notable improvement in the American economy under way, Downing saw an opportunity to garner for himself some of the commissions he had earlier passed along to his friend and informal collaborator, the talented New York architect Alexander J. Davis (1803–1892).[2] When Davis had not taken up his suggestion that they form a "closer alliance," Downing had decided to look for a competent architect in Europe to assist him in an expanded practice. Almost from the moment of their meeting in London, Downing and Vaux realized they could work well together. "I was in a settled position surrounded by friends," Vaux later recalled, "but I liked him [Downing] so much, his thoughts and observations were so apparent . . . that without a fear I relinquished all and accompanied him. . . ."[3] Downing was then approaching his 35th birthday, and Vaux would not turn 26 for another five months.

For valuable aid and criticism the coauthor is indebted to William Alex, president of the Frederick Law Olmsted Association, and to David Schuyler, professor of American studies at Franklin and Marshall College and one of the editors of *The Papers of Frederick Law Olmsted*.

1. Before his untimely death, Dennis Steadman Francis had projected a much needed monograph on Vaux, for which he is understood to have collected a wealth of material, some of which was used by Joy M. Kestenbaum for a brief article in the *Macmillan Encyclopedia of Architects* (New York, 1982). Other details of Vaux's career are supplied by David W. Matzdorf, "Calvert Vaux: 1824–1895," unpublished thesis, Architectural Association School of Architecture, London, 1977; and by John David Sigle, "Calvert Vaux: An American Architect," unpublished thesis, School of Architecture, University of Virginia, 1967. Also by Sigle is the "Bibliography of the Life and Works of Calvert Vaux" published in vol. 5 of the *Papers* of the American Association of Architectural Bibliographers, William B. O'Neal, ed., Charlottesville, 1968. Several of the details of Vaux's early life in England are based on the unpublished research of Arthur Channing Downs, Jr., and are included here with his permission. Vaux's own biographical notes, which include a list of his commissions, are in the Rare Books and Manuscripts Division of the New York Public Library, Astor, Lenox and Tilden Foundations, New York City, together with various miscellaneous items relating to his career.

2. The most complete discussion of Downing's career is that provided by the papers presented at the two-part symposium sponsored by the Athenaeum of Philadelphia and Dumbarton Oaks, Washington, D. C., in the spring of 1987 and published by Dumbarton Oaks in 1989 under the title *Prophet with Honor* (George B. Tatum and Elisabeth Blair MacDougall, eds.). In his own time Downing would have been called a "landscape gardener;" as explained more fully in note 22, below, the modern title of "landscape architect" did not become current until after the Civil War.

3. Memorandum prepared by Vaux at the request of Marshall P. Wilder, president of the Massa-

## DOWNING AND VAUX'S DOMESTIC ARCHITECTURE

A. J. Downing

OWNING'S AMBITIOUS PLANS for his "Bureau of Architecture" proved well founded. In fact, so numerous were the clients that in little more than a year it became necessary to add another trained architect to the staff. Through an advertisement placed in one of the English periodicals, Downing engaged Frederick Clarke Withers (1828–1901), who was currently employed in the London office of Thomas Henry Wyatt (1807–1880), brother of Matthew Digby Wyatt and himself a prolific practitioner of the Victorian Gothic style.[4] When Withers arrived in New York in February 1852, his future and that of his employer appeared promising indeed. But just five months later Downing was dead, a victim of the burning of the Hudson River steamer *Henry Clay*.

Most of the principal commissions received while Downing was still active in the Newburgh office—about a dozen in all—are identified in the so-called "pattern book" that Vaux brought out in 1857 with Harper and Brothers as publishers. This was titled *Villas and Cottages* and offered designs that ranged from a local plumber's "Simple Suburban Cottage," to cost about $1,500, to an unnamed client's "Villa on a Large Scale," to cost at least $60,000. Its dedication to Downing and to his wife, Caroline, was the more appropriate because Vaux's book so clearly represented an effort to continue the form and character of Downing's earlier publications. In being addressed to the client as well as to the craftsman, and in providing not only plans and details but also complete elevations shown in their appropriate landscape settings, Downing's *Cottage Residences* (1842) and *The Architecture of Country Houses* (1850) had marked a clear departure from the previous "builders' guides." Of course Vaux was not alone in following Downing's lead in this regard; the English emigrants Richard Upjohn (1802–1878) and Gervase Wheeler (ca. 1815–1870)—both of whose designs Downing had praised and illustrated—were among his most notable competitors. But despite such competition, after seven years there was still sufficient demand for *Villas and Cottages* to justify a second, somewhat enlarged edition, and this, in turn, was reprinted at least four times within the next ten years.[5]

chusetts Horticultural Society, who was planning a memorial address on Downing to be delivered before the American Pomological Congress, of which he was president; Collection of the Library Company of Philadelphia, now on deposit at the Historical Society of Pennsylvania.

4. For an account of Withers' life and work, see Francis R. Kowsky, *The Architecture of Frederick Clarke Withers and the Progress of the Gothic Revival in America after 1850*, Middletown, 1980.

5. Henry-Russell Hitchcock, *American Architectural Books,* Minneapolis, 1962, 108–109. A condensed version of the text of *Villas and Cottages*, with a foreword by Edward Steese, was published in one of the early numbers of the *Journal of the Society of Architectural Historians,* vi (1947) 1–12. Modern reprints include one of the second edition by Dover (1991) and that of the first edition by Da Capo (1968), for which Henry Hope Reed, then curator of Central Park, contributed an introduction. In the second edition of *Villas and Cottages* the long introduction remains essentially unchanged, but there is a second preface, seven new numbered designs are added (nos. 11, 12, 27, 28, 29, 36, 38) and three vignettes from the first edition are dropped and ten are added. As a frontispiece for the second edition, "A Family Cottage in the Mountains" is substituted for the view of the N. P. Willis residence, which is moved to the text. In the present account, when two figures are given for a numbered design the first refers to the 1857 edition of *Villas and Cottages* and the second to the 1864 edition. In the Table of Contents of the first edition Vaux identifies a number of clients whose names are omitted from the second edition.

In bringing out a new architectural pattern book Vaux enlarged upon the article he had written in 1855 for *Harper's New Monthly Magazine* as well as two articles in *The Horticulturist* in which may be found many of the ideas developed in greater detail in the introduction to *Villas and Cottages*.[6] And though some criticized Vaux for including a discreet advertisement on one of the back pages to call attention to his practice, most of his readers were pleased to be informed about the charges that could be expected were they to engage an architect, a profession then in its infancy, in addition to, or in lieu of, a builder. Certainly modern historians can be grateful for such clear evidence of the fees a successful American architect might expect to receive on the eve of the Civil War: 2½ percent of the cost of construction for plans and specifications; 1 percent for drawings of details; 1½ percent for supervision of construction. For all services, this made a total of 5 percent, but supervision of construction was customarily provided for only the largest commissions. In many instances, after preparing the drawings—usually limited to floor plans, elevations and a few details—many nineteenth-century architects had no further association with domestic structures they designed.

Of the thirty-two houses featured in the first edition of *Villas and Cottages*, ten bear the designation "D & V," indicating they were produced by Downing and Vaux in collaboration. As in the case of the "Picturesque Square House" (Design 16/18)[7] the partners designed for David Moore of Newburgh, many of these employed a repertory of decorative features—bargeboards, window hoods, brackets, bay windows and the like—and were less innovative in their style than in their "modern improvements." These might include gas, running water, speaking tubes, a hot air furnace, ventilators and in the case of the Moore house an "outhouse, and necessary" concealed beneath the pavement of the side entrance and approached from the basement. The last was a feature described at some length in the introduction to *Villas and Cottages* and apparently used in several of the firm's commissions. About half the designs identified as by Downing and Vaux are related in varying degrees to those Downing had favored earlier; the remainder are sufficiently unlike anything he had published before that they may be assumed to reflect either the hand of Vaux or the influence of Downing's recent European visit—perhaps both. And of course all differ from a majority of the models Downing had advanced previously in having been commissioned by actual clients for erection on a specific site. For a variety of

6. Calvert Vaux, "Should a Republic Encourage the Arts?," *The Horticulturist,* vii (1852) 73–77; "American Architecture," *The Horticulturist,* viii (1853) 168–172; "Hints for Country House Builders," *Harper's New Monthly Magazine,* xi (1855) 763–778.

7. Originally, the word "picturesque" had meant simply "like or suitable for a picture," but in answer to the question of what, exactly, makes an object or a landscape appeal to picture makers, late in the 18th century Sir Uvedale Price (1747–1829) and others identified those qualities that are "rough, irregular" and marked by "sudden variation" (Uvedale Price, *Essays on the Picturesque*, London, 1810, i, 50–51; first published 1794). By this more limited definition, any house that had a free plan and an irregular silhouette might be described as "picturesque" and was thought to be especially suited to sites similarly characterized by roughness and irregularity. Among Americans, Downing had taken the lead in promoting awareness of the specific qualities of things picturesque, and it was in this later and more precise sense that Vaux and his contemporaries usually employed the word.

reasons, only six of the ten designs prepared by Downing and Vaux were executed, and of these five survive at last count.[8]

Continuity with Downing's earlier architecture is best evidenced by the new firm's designs in three different styles. First are the nearly identical houses for Francis and Robert Dodge (Design 17/19), two brothers who planned to live near each other in Georgetown, District of Columbia, and the design for Algonac, the house originally about two miles north of Newburgh that was remodeled in 1851 for Warren Delano, who had made a large fortune in the Oriental export trade.[9] With their towers, bracketed eaves, loggias, arched openings, and asymmetrical plans, all three houses are more ambitious and assured versions of the Italian villa style to which Downing had introduced American readers in his earlier books.[10]

Another design in *Villas and Cottages* for which antecedents may be found in Downing's previous work is the Newburgh residence erected for W. L. Findlay (Design 12/14), which was fortunately well photographed before its demolition in the mid-twentieth century. This belonged to a type of Gothic villa made popular by

54–55
52–53
70–73

8. The five are: Design 16/18 for David Moore, 55 Broad Street, Newburgh; Design 17/19, two similar houses for the brothers Robert and Francis Dodge at 28th and Q streets and at 30th and Q streets, Georgetown, District of Columbia (both now considerably altered); Design 20/22 for Dr. W. A. M. Culbert, 120 Grand Street, Newburgh (later enlarged to serve the City Club and badly damaged by fire in 1981); and Design 30/35 for Daniel Parish, Bellevue Ave., Newport, R.I. (burned 1855 and rebuilt by Vaux on the same site but closer to the sea). In counting ten as the total of the numbered designs by Downing and Vaux illustrated in *Villas and Cottages*, Design 17/19, which includes a similar but not identical house for each of the two Dodge brothers, is given double weight. In his text Vaux associates with Francis Dodge the design in fact executed for his brother Robert. Daniel D. Reiff (*Washington Architecture 1791–1861: Problems in Development*, U. S. Commission of Fine Arts, Washington, D. C., 1971, 122–130) discusses the Dodge houses in relation to the Washington scene and in that context mentions as contemporary and almost certainly by Downing and Vaux the more symmetrical Italian villa of Cornelius Barber, which until its demolition about 1890 stood on the west slope of Observatory Hill in the District of Columbia. In addition to the thirty-two numbered designs in the first edition of *Villas and Cottages*, there are several vignettes that need to be taken into account in assessing the art of Downing and Vaux in partnership.

9. Algonac, which burned early in the 20th century, is not mentioned in *Villas and Cottages*, but is discussed briefly by Matzdorf (pp. 18–19), who refers his readers to Kenneth S. Davis, *FDR: The Beckoning Destiny, 1882–1928*, New York, 1971, 39–40, and to Clara and Hardy Steeholm, *The House in Hyde Park*, New York, 1950, 10.

10. Its low, squat tower, stuccoed walls and free plan, mark Algonac as belonging to a type of Italian villa sometimes referred to as "Tuscan." Of this the first American example is usually considered the house, no longer standing, that was erected in 1839 from designs of John Notman for Bishop George Washington Doane at Burlington, N. J. (Constance M. Greiff, *John Notman, Architect, 1810–1865*, The Athenaeum of Philadelphia, 1979, 63–68). Called Riverside, Doane's villa was illustrated and described at some length in all editions of Downing's *Treatise on the Theory and Practice of Landscape Gardening Adapted to North America* published during the author's lifetime. With their somewhat higher and more slender towers placed in the corner formed by the meeting at right angles of their two principal axes, the Dodge houses belong to a distinctive type of Italian villa that Downing appears to have been the first to publish in America. Although not without English antecedents, Design VI in his *Cottage Residences* seems to have been, in fact, peculiarly the work of Downing without, in this case, any substantive assistance from Davis.

the New Bedford house Davis designed for William J. Rotch in 1845 and illustrated, in turn, by Downing in *Country Houses*, along with several variants of his and Davis's devising.[11] In common with other of the new firm's designs, the Findlay house betrayed its mid-Victorian date in the striped pattern of its slate roof and in the increased sense of verticality created by the steeper roofs and raised foundations then coming into vogue. The hand of Vaux may perhaps be seen in the concave profile of the roofs, the turreted ventilator (proposed but not executed) and in the bargeboards that appear to emphasize their solid plane, the pattern being produced either by perforations or by applied ornament—details not found to the same degree in Downing's earlier work, but which Vaux favored both in his introduction to *Villas and Cottages* and elsewhere.[12]

　　Yet a third style treated earlier by Downing and still recognizable among the designs produced by the new firm is that which the period somewhat loosely termed "Elizabethan."[13] While warning against the "confused melange" to which their use might all too easily contribute, Downing had occasionally favored the multi-curved gables that are the most prominent features of a style still too medieval to be called Renaissance and too classical to be considered medieval. Although not so identified in the descriptive text, here surely is the inspiration for Matthew Vassar's villa (Design 25/30)[14] as well as two other unexecuted designs: that for a Mr.

48–51

11. In all houses of this type the details are clearly intended to be Gothic, and it would appear, in fact, that the architect needed to do little more than add verandas to adapt for American use a late Tudor residence like that illustrated in P. F. Robinson's *Rural Architecture* (London, 1823), a point first made by Edna Donnell in her seminal article, "A. J. Davis and the Gothic Revival," *Metropolitan Museum Studies,* v (1934–36) 210. The Findlay residence (Design 12/14) stood at 379 Powell Avenue, Newburgh, and is No. 878 in the collection of architectural subjects photographed by the late Wayne Andrews. Vaux illustrates a simple "Rustic Outbuilding" designed for W. L. Findlay in both the first (p. 132) and second (p. 144) editions of *Villas and Cottages*.

12. Downing does use curving roofs for one of the last designs in *Country Houses,* an illustration (no. XXXI in the first edition and in the Da Capo reprint; no. XXXII in later editions and in the Dover reprint) that also bears the initials "AJD," presumably identifying it as one of the comparatively rare published examples of Downing's draftsmanship, unaided by Davis. Vaux preferred to speak of "verge-boards" rather than "bargeboards," to designate the ornamental board placed along the projecting rafters of a gable, a feature that originated during the late Middle Ages.

13. Downing's own Newburgh residence was occasionally, if incorrectly, called "Elizabethan," and he himself so labeled the architectural example he first published as figure 55 in the second edition of his *Treatise on the Theory and Practice of Landscape Gardening* (New York, 1844). Because there was no easily defined or generally recognized Elizabethan style of architecture, in the course of the 19th century both English and American authors felt free to use the word in describing structures of widely differing character. Moreover, insofar as architecture is concerned, the reign of the first Elizabeth (1558–1603) slipped so easily into that of the first James (1603–1625) that modern historians have coined the adjective "Jacobethan" to refer to the period as a whole. Although perhaps not a "revival," as that word is customarily applied to architecture of the 19th century, Anthony Salvin's spectacular use of Jacobethan forms for the designs of Harlaxton (begun 1834) in Lincolnshire must have attracted widespread notice, including perhaps that of Downing and Vaux. For a discussion of Jacobethan forms and Salvin's use of them, see Henry-Russell Hitchcock, *Early Victorian Architecture in Britain,* New Haven, 1954, 18.

14. His increasing commitment to the college that bears his name as well as to the Civil War and

S. D. Dakin (Design 31/37) and the enormous pile that serves as the final illustration in both editions of *Villas and Cottages*.

Of the designs in *Villas and Cottages* that appear to have little in common with either Downing's earlier taste or Vaux's later work, several must owe a good deal to contemporary European practice. Although labeled simply a "Suburban House with Curved Roof," its small scale, distinctive roof and classical details give the combined office and residence the firm designed for Dr. W. A. M. Culbert (Design 20/22) a decidedly "French" air, while Daniel Parish's "Marine Villa" (Design 30/35) is clearly in the Italian Renaissance style made popular in England by Charles Barry (1795–1860). Probably never again would historical sources be so clearly evident in architectural designs with which Vaux was closely involved. Neither the Romanesque we associate with H. H. Richardson (1838–1886) nor the Second Empire forms favored by such architects as Alfred B. Mullett (1834–1890) and John McArthur, Jr. (1823–1890), seem to have held much appeal for him. And if the "Design for a Church" that serves as a tailpiece for the introduction to *Villas and Cottages* is fair evidence of his skill in this category, he was well advised to leave ecclesiastical designs to Withers, who over the next two decades would emerge as one of the most talented designers of churches.[15] In common with numerous other architects of his generation, Vaux usually avoided references to a specific style, preferring instead a blend of motifs inspired by the past but imaginatively reinterpreted to create a distinctive style that he believed to be peculiarly adapted to contemporary American use and which later generations have found it convenient to call "Victorian."

### LATER DOMESTIC ARCHITECTURE

DOWNING'S UNTIMELY DEATH brought to an end the first phase of Vaux's American career. For about ten months, or until he was ready to begin extensive alterations, the purchaser of Downing's residence permitted Vaux and Withers to carry on their practice in the offices that had been added for that purpose. A notice published in *The Horticulturist* for June 1853 not only gives Broadway as the firm's Newburgh address but also suggests by its failure to mention Withers that at this point he was still serving as a draftsman and assistant rather than as a full partner. However that may be, it is significant that the new owner of Downing's Tudor villa passed over Vaux and Withers in favor of A. J. Davis as architect for the extensive alterations he had in mind; and to judge from the designs in *Villas and Cot-*

---

the inflation that followed it doubtless contributed to Vassar's decision not to build the large mansion he had earlier contemplated and which may still be studied in the architects' drawings now preserved in the Vassar College Library. Among these are conceptual sketches that appear to be by Downing, as well as finished drawings that are clearly the work of a trained draftsman, presumably Vaux or Withers. A later design for Vassar's villa incorporates a number of features that have been identified as characteristic of Vaux's work.

15. The wood engraving in *Villas and Cottages* appears to represent Vaux's only surviving attempt at church design. An engraving of Withers' handsome design for the First Presbyterian Church, which still stands at 210 Grand Street in Newburgh, was included in the second edition of *Villas and Cottages* at the end of the table of contents. In 1873 A. J. Bicknell & Co. published Withers' *Church Architecture*, which contained 51 plates illustrating 21 churches and two schoolhouses.

*tages*, the commissions of the successor firm were somewhat less ambitious than those received while Downing was the senior partner.

Of the nine principal designs identified in *Villas and Cottages* as products of the partnership of Vaux and Withers, only two survive: the simple "Suburban House" designed for the Rev. E. J. O'Reilly at 55 Grand Street (Design 5/5) and the "Suburban House with Attics" for Halsey R. Stevens at 182 Grand Street (Design 10/10). In each case the bargeboards are of a type mentioned earlier as characteristic of Vaux, but the relative simplicity of both designs may have as much to do with a restricted budget as with what has been seen by some as the restraining hand of Withers.[16] Because architectural drawings taken to the building site have a way of being worn out in use, the survival at the New-York Historical Society of a clean set suggests that the brick villa Vaux and Withers designed for J. W. Fowler (Design 13/15) was 58–59 never built. Nor, apparently, were Daniel Ryan's cottage (Design 1/1) and the "Irregular Brick Villa" for Nathan Reeve (Design 22/24), both intended for sites in Newburgh. Further afield, clients in the vicinity of Worcester, Massachusetts, seemed to have looked with particular favor on the work of the new firm: the "Suburban House with Curvilinear Roof" (Design 23/25) for an unnamed client in that city may never have been built, but though no longer standing, the "Picturesque Villa with Wings and Attics" (Design 28/33) for Thomas Earle probably was. And until its demolition in 1966 the "Irregular Wooden Country House" (Design 19/21) for H. H. Chamberlain served as the residence of the president of Clark University.[17] 82–83

For about two dozen designs in *Villas and Cottages*, Vaux acknowledges no association with either Downing or Withers, and these must therefore be assumed to represent his individual style when practicing alone. Of the houses in this category, one of the most successful—as well as one of the very few to survive in essentially its original form—is that built about 1857 for W. E. Warren at 196 Montgomery Street, 84–85 Newburgh (Design 14/16).[18] Although the general form of the Warren house may be

16. Kowsky, *Withers*, 30. The facade of the Stevens house is not unlike that of the house at 264 Grand Street, Newburgh, that Withers designed in 1865 for Eugene Brewster. In addition to the numbered designs that are offered as the work of Vaux and Withers in collaboration, about eight of the incidental vignettes in *Villas and Cottages* bear the initials "V & W" and must therefore be counted as part of the total production of the partnership, which seems to have been dissolved sometime in 1855–56 (Kowsky, *Withers*, 164), only to be reestablished in later years.

17. The Chamberlain house stood at 160 Woodland Street (earlier numbered 96), now the site of the Robert H. Goddard Library. When constructed about 1855, Chamberlain's residence lay outside the more thickly settled portions of Worcester and was surrounded by extensive gardens. According to Kowsky (*Withers*, 203) when the house was demolished miscellaneous fixtures were preserved by the Worcester Historical Society and the Smithsonian Institution in Washington, D. C.

18. Another of Vaux's early designs is the Rural Gothic house (Design 26/31) commissioned by Lydig and Geraldine Hoyt for a site overlooking the Hudson, near Staatsburg. Together with its extensive grounds, the Hoyt house was acquired by New York State in 1962 for a park that has not yet 80–81 materialized. Despite years of neglect, the grounds of The Point, as the Hoyt estate is known, retain much of their picturesque character, while the house designed by Vaux about 1853 was in poor but stable condition when last seen in early 1990. The author is indebted to the landscape architect Robert Toole for information concerning the more recent history of The Point.

late Gothic in inspiration, the prominent balcony over the central doorway appears to owe most to Italianate sources—a reminder that the Gothic and Italian were the two styles Vaux believed most adaptable to American use, as well as further evidence of the willingness of mid-Victorian architects to seek a contemporary style through the imaginative combination of architectural elements chosen from several different cultures and periods.[19] In this case the flaring eaves, projecting central gable, hooded windows, truncated gables and distinctive bargeboards, when used in combination, are vintage Vaux and so appealing that they survived the earlier 20th-century aversion to ornament that caused the R. L. Case house (Design 8/8) at 333 Grand Street to be stripped of its Victorian details. At the rear of the Warren house the sloping site permitted verandas on three levels from which to enjoy spectacular views of the river.

74–77  Among commissions that gave Vaux most satisfaction was the picturesque cottage he designed for the prominent American author Nathaniel Parker Willis. Idlewild—as Willis called his estate at nearby Cornwall—serves as the frontispiece for the first edition of *Villas and Cottages* and was discussed at some length as Design 21 in the text that followed. Now altered almost beyond recognition, Willis' cottage was described in contemporary accounts as being of brick painted a quiet yellow. Immediately behind was a deep ravine through which ran a fast flowing stream, while in front beyond a broad meadow lay Newburgh Bay with Storm King Mountain in the distance. Predictably, for so picturesque a site Vaux turned to the Rural Gothic style, which Downing—in association with Davis—had helped to popularize and of which a simpler version had been used for the Findlay house, noted previously. But whereas the latter had been rigidly symmetrical, Vaux here and in other contemporary designs seeks greater picturesque asymmetry through the use of bays and verandas. The better to accommodate the house to its site, the kitchen at Idlewild was placed in the basement, an arrangement Vaux occasionally favored despite its apparent inconvenience. And as with a number of Vaux's designs, here considerations of expense again led the owner to omit his architect's favorite ventilator disguised as a turret or cupola.

MARRIAGE, NEW YORK
AND THE MOVE INTO LANDSCAPE ARCHITECTURE

VAUX ADAPTED readily and happily to life in America. In 1854 he married Mary Swan McEntee, sister of the landscape painter Jervis McEntee, and two years later he became an American citizen. Increasingly he found his attention turning from Newburgh to New York City. There the success of the partners' design for 94–95 the Fifth Avenue house of John A. C. Gray (Design 29/34) led to a commission for 184 the Bank of New York, of which Gray was a director.[20] In late 1856 Vaux, by now the father of two boys, moved permanently to New York, initially to a house on 18th

19. *Villas and Cottages*, 1st. ed., 34; 2d ed., 46.
20. Demolished long ago, the Gray house stood at 40 Fifth Avenue and is pictured as Design 29/34 in *Villas and Cottages*. Essentially Renaissance in style, the Bank of New York was located at Wall and Williams Streets, and although ostensibly designed in 1856 under the firm's name, Kowsky

Street, and later to Stuyvesant Apartments, which had been built in 1869 from designs of Richard Morris Hunt (1827–1895). Although Stuyvesant Apartments is usually considered the first building of its kind in the United States, twelve years earlier Vaux had himself proposed such a multistoried city dwelling based on European practice, the "Parisian Buildings for City Residents." This was in a paper read in 1857 before the newly formed American Institute of Architects, which he and Withers had been among the first of their profession invited to join.[21]

92–93

Vaux's move to New York effectively ended his first partnership with Withers, but unfinished commissions had to be seen through to completion, and the firm continued to be listed in the New York City directory until at least 1858. One such commission was certainly for the Bank of New York, noted earlier; another was for John W. Burt, who proposed to build the first house in Llewellyn Park (called Mountain Park in the first edition of *Villas and Cottages*) in what is now West Orange, New Jersey. No longer standing, the Burt house was described by its architects as being of wood, with simple, unpretentious lines and a picturesque exterior. In 1858 Vaux and Withers were also architects for a stone mansion that until its demolition in 1948 must have been among the most imposing residences in West Medford, Massachusetts. Designed in a simplified Italianate style, Point of Rocks was commissioned by Peter Chardon Brooks, Jr., whose father was reputedly the richest man in New England. Withers, for his part, elected to remain a British subject for the rest of his life, and his decision to continue to practice in Newburgh after the dissolution of his partnership with Vaux may well have been influenced by his marriage in 1856 to Emily DeWint, youngest of Caroline Downing's numerous sisters and a member of a prominent Hudson Valley family.

64–67

In several respects, 1857 proved pivotal for Vaux's career. Not only did it see the publication of the first edition of *Villas and Cottages* and the ending of its author's formal ties to Withers and to Newburgh, it also marked new opportunities in a profession he was the first to call "landscape architecture."[22] The story of how Vaux invited Frederick Law Olmsted to join him in developing the winning design for New York's Central Park is well documented but has often been overlooked by a generation that has usually credited Olmsted with the leading role.[23] Beginning as early as July 1844,

(*Withers*, 164–165) considers it to be entirely the work of Vaux. So pleased were the clients with the design of the bank, they increased the architects' regular fee by $1,500 (Arthur Channing Downs, Jr., "Correspondence," *Journal of the Society of Architectural Historians*, i [1977] 61).

21. Under the title "Parisian Buildings for City Residents," Vaux's paper, illustrated with a front elevation, a section, and two floor plans, was published in *Harper's Weekly*, December 19, 1857, 809–810.

22. As early as April 7, 1860, when the New York State Legislature created a commission to lay out Manhattan streets north of 155th, Vaux and his partner, Frederick Law Olmsted, were referred to as "Landscape Architects & designers" (*The Papers of Frederick Law Olmsted*, Charles Capen McLaughlin, editor in chief; iii, *Creating Central Park 1857–1861*, Charles E. Beveridge and David Schuyler, eds., Baltimore, 1983, 257 [4]). Later, on June 3, 1865, Vaux wrote Olmsted: "I felt that L[andscape] A[rchitect] must be the title I must fight under if I fought at all" (Matzdorf, "Calvert Vaux," 139 [69], quoting a letter from Frederick Law Olmsted, Jr., to C. Bowyer Vaux, February 18, 1921, and now among the Vaux Papers in the New York Public Library). Olmsted was never comfortable with the term.

23. Although the son of a well-to-do Hartford merchant, Frederick Law Olmsted (1822–1903) had

William Cullen Bryant, editor of the *New York Evening Post*, had repeatedly stressed the need for a large public park in New York City, a cause that Downing enthusiastically supported in *The Horticulturist*. In an editorial written a year before his death, Downing had not only heaped scorn on those who thought a park of less than 500 acres would be sufficient for a city the potential size of New York, he also envisaged for it the site between 39th Street and the Harlem River. Moreover, Downing proposed many features later incorporated in the final plan. Prominent among these were "the breadth and beauty of green fields," the large distributing reservoirs "formed into lovely lakes of limpid water" and an opportunity for "excursions in carriages and on horseback;" in short he envisioned the park as a place where "pedestrians would find quiet and secluded walks when they wished to be solitary and broad alleys full of happy faces, when they wished to be gay."[24] Had Downing lived, it is likely that he would have been commissioned to design the New York park as a matter of course.

As it turned out, when the 1856 plan prepared by Egbert Viele, chief engineer of the park, was perceived as inadequate, Vaux was prominent among those who urged that an open competition be held to select a better one; and when on October 13, 1857, the park commissioners announced such a competition, he was quick to recognize the opportunity.[25] Not only was Vaux one of the few Americans who could claim any training in landscape design, he doubtless expected some advantage to accrue from his former association with Downing, as well as from his friendship with John A. C. Gray, for whom he had recently designed a house and who was currently serving as vice president of the Park Commission. Olmsted, too, brought important strengths to their collaboration. His friends on the Park Commission included Charles Wyllys Elliott, who earlier had studied with Downing and who is

---

been obliged to forgo a college education when a bout of sumac poisoning had threatened his eyesight. After a brief stint as a surveyor and a voyage to the Orient as a seaman, he had turned to farming—first in Connecticut and later on Staten Island—and to writing. His first book, *Walks and Talks of an American Farmer in England* (1852), was sufficiently well received that he agreed to undertake further travels through the Southern states as a correspondent for *The New York Times*. *A Journey in the Seaboard Slave States* appeared in 1856, followed the next year by *A Journey through Texas*. Encouraged by the success of these literary ventures, Olmsted entered into a partnership with Dix, Edwards and Company, publishers of his books, and when this failed, was left with burdensome debts he felt morally obligated to repay. Vaux had first met Olmsted at Downing's house in 1851 *(Papers of FLO,* iii, 65; Vaux Papers, New York Public Library).

24. A. J. Downing, "The New York Park," *The Horticulturist*, vi (1851) 345–349. For a public park for New York City, Bryant had in mind a picturesque tract of about 160 acres that extended along the East River in the area variously described as between 64th and 75th streets and between 68th and 77th streets, then known as Jones Wood. For a fuller discussion of the circumstances that led up to the creation of Central Park, see David Schuyler, *The New Urban Landscape*, Baltimore, 1986.

25. *Papers of FLO*, iii, 116 (4). Concerning his part in promoting an open competition as a means of selecting a design for the New York park, Vaux later recalled: "I pointed out, whenever I had a chance, that it would be a disgrace to the City and to the memory of Mr. Downing . . . to have [Viele's] plan carried out. I was also familiar with the advantages offered by a public competition and I discussed the subject not only with [the] commissioners but with any other interested persons who cared to listen to my remarks" (Vaux Papers, New York Public Library).

thought to have been the person who persuaded Olmsted to initiate his successful application for the position of superintendent of the park, a post to which he had been appointed the preceding September. As superintendent, Olmsted could be expected to have a greater familiarity than most with the 776 acres that then comprised the site selected for development.[26]

For several months after each working day Olmsted and Vaux met at the latter's house and there, with the help of a few friends, delineated their scheme for the park in time to meet the April first deadline.

CENTRAL PARK

ON APRIL 28, 1858, it was announced that "Greensward"—as Vaux and Olmsted called their plan—had received the first of the four prizes offered, and the following month Olmsted was promoted from his position as superintendent to that of architect-in-chief. Vaux was named as his "assistant"—a designation that laid the foundation for the persistent but erroneous belief that Olmsted was principally, if not solely, responsible for the design of Central Park. The truth, as Olmsted himself was later at some pains to point out, was very different.[27] In fact, those commissioners who earlier had opposed Olmsted's appointment as superintendent had done so largely on the grounds that he was a popular literary figure without practical experience, and certainly at the outset he viewed his new post as an administrative challenge rather than as a problem in the design of open space. In their analysis of the events surrounding the creation of Central Park, the editors of Olmsted's papers

108–111

Frederick Law Olmsted

26. As described by Olmsted in the article on the "Park" he wrote for the *New American Cyclopaedia*, Central Park originally contained 776 acres, to which were added approximately 68 acres when the park was extended to 110th Street in 1863 (*Papers of FLO*, iii, 178 [2], 354).

27. On May 17, 1858, Olmsted was appointed "Architect-in-Chief" of the park (*Papers of FLO*, iii, 192), and in January 1859 Vaux was named "Consulting Architect." Four years later, Olmsted put in writing his estimate of the part contributed by each of the partners to the creation of the park:

There are several properties in the park held or properly belonging to us. 1st the general design, in which our property is mutual, equal and indivisible. 2d Detail of General design from which can not be separated something of "superintendence" and in which also there is equality of property between us. 3d Architectural design & superintendence in which I have no appreciable property—which is wholly yours. 4th Organization & management of construction force in which you have very little property, though more than I have in the last. 5th Administration & management of the public introduction to and use of the park, in which you have very little property and which I hold to be my most valuable property in it (Olmsted to Vaux, November 26, 1863, Vaux Papers, New York Public Library).

Vaux appears to have endorsed readily enough this estimate of his role, but from time to time others continued to ascribe to Olmsted sole responsibility for the design of Central Park. A letter implying this and published in the New York *Daily Tribune* for January 11, 1878, brought an angry reply from Vaux (Laura Wood Roper, *FLO: A Biography of Frederick Law Olmsted*, Baltimore, 1973, 361). To his credit, on more than one occasion Olmsted went out of his way to ensure that his partner received the recognition due him: "I hope you will not fail to do justice to Vaux," he admonished one admirer, "and to consider that he and I were one. I should have been nowhere but for his professional training" (Roper, *FLO*, 291). Oh this same point, see also Olmsted's letter to *The American Architect and Building News*, ii (1877) 175.

have concluded that "not until 1865 did Calvert Vaux convince Olmsted to consider himself as much an artist as an administrator."[28] Even then Vaux was obliged to admit that it was more for his administrative experience than for his skill in landscape design that he sought to have Olmsted join in the planning of Brooklyn's Prospect Park, begun in that year. Olmsted's chief interest was the park's potential as an agent for social reform. His earlier travels in monarchical Europe and in the slaveholding states of the South had served to reinforce his own republican views; now he saw the park, in which Americans from all walks of life might share equally, as a "democratic development of the highest significance."[29]

108–129
To create a serene oasis in the midst of a city they correctly anticipated would one day be among the largest in the world, the designers of Greensward planned a barrier of trees and plants around the periphery of the park, while a series of ingenious cuts and tunnels prevented the four roads required to carry crosstown traffic from interfering with the interior walks and drives. Groves of trees judiciously dispersed on gently rolling terrain gave the area above the new reservoir and the 97th Street transverse road much the character of an English landscape park and provided a portion of the greensward from which the winning design took its name. In contrast, the uneven terrain and outcroppings of the lower or southern portion of the park suggested lusher vegetation and more picturesque effects. Here, along with a pond and lake, Vaux and Olmsted placed the popular Ramble—"a series of walks carried, in constantly changing grades and directions, through 80 acres of ground of very diversified character"—as well as the play areas and the parade ground required by the conditions of the competition.[30] Creation of such features represented a formidable undertaking that called for extensive blasting and the moving of over four million cubic yards of earth and stone. And to supply the drainage necessary for the park to be used in all seasons of the year, work crews installed over sixty miles of terra-cotta pipe, the need for which Olmsted had been introduced in the course of his European travels. Time has amply proved the wisdom of this provision.

At the outset, both Vaux and Olmsted agreed that natural scenery should domi-

28. Beveridge and Schuyler, *Papers of FLO*, iii, 11.

29. Ibid., 200-201. Although Vaux was always anxious to stress the importance of the park as a work of art, he also recognized fully its social implications. In the introduction to *Villas and Cottages* he had written: "even here [in America] the man of small means may be almost on the same footing as the millionaire, for public baths, gymnasiums, theaters, music halls, libraries, lecture-rooms, parks, gardens, picture-galleries, museums, schools, and everything that is needed for the liberal education of an intelligent freeman's children, can be easily obtained by the genuine republican if he will only take the trouble to want them."

30. F. L. Olmsted, "Park," *New American Cyclopaedia*, 1861, as quoted in the *Papers of FLO*, iii, 355. As to the originator of the distinctive and much praised plan to isolate the crosstown traffic from the roads and drives of the park, Vaux wrote: "The idea of keeping the transverse roads for city traffic clear of the Park roads designed for pleasure driving was gradually developed by a close study of the actual topography and of the imperative future needs of the City, and its importance as an elemental feature being recognized before the plan was completed, it was tacitly agreed between the two partners that no individual claim should be made by either designer in regard to that particular feature" (Vaux Papers, New York Public Library).

nate their design and that any artifacts introduced should be as unobtrusive as possible. This principle applied to the more than 40 bridges Vaux designed—or the design of which he supervised—that were eventually required to keep the many miles of walks, carriage drives and bridle paths from interfering with each other, as well as to such structures as the "prospect tower," called for by the terms of the competition. 115 The better to blend with their surroundings, many of the first bridges, shelters and benches were conceived as being fashioned from rough logs, but as the concept of the park developed, so did the importance of its architectural components. As pictured in the presentation drawings, such structures as Glade Arch, designed for a site 122 west of Fifth Avenue at 77th Street, or Denesmouth Bridge, which was intended to 123 carry the 65th Street Transverse, appeared so effective as works of art and so well suited to their function that it is easy to understand why neither their monumental form nor their costly materials deterred the commissioners from accepting them.[31] But perhaps most surprising was the extent to which such designs favored the Renaissance canons then championed by the French Ecole des Beaux-Arts instead of the Victorian Gothic usually associated with Vaux. Both Glade Arch and Denesmouth Bridge were built of cut stone, but at the southern end of the play area (Ball Field) the designers of Greensward introduced a delightful iron bridge—its structural features wrought and its decorative details cast—that until its demolition in 1934 was one of the picturesque features most often selected for comment in descriptions of the park. Completed in 1862 and named for the outcropping of schist to which one side was anchored, the Spur Rock span's destruction was a serious loss, although the contemporary Bow Bridge, which leads into the Ramble, and Pine Bank, near 126 the Columbus Circle entrance, are notable as two of the earliest surviving iron bridges in the country.

But no architectural element in Central Park—or perhaps in any public park—was so ambitious as the stone terrace that at its upper end terminates the Promenade (Mall), the most formal element in the Greensward design and one that had been 116–117 introduced in the southern portion of the park as a kind of foil for its more picturesque surroundings. A major function of the Terrace is to permit the footpath at the northern end of the Promenade to pass under one of the principal carriage drives, but instead of a simple underpass, Vaux's design called for a broad flight of stone 114 steps leading to a large chamber located under the carriage drive and overlaid on floor and ceiling with Minton tiles in a variety of colors. Beyond the underground hall and connected to it lies the lower terrace, which can be reached from the north side of the same carriage drive mentioned earlier by two flights of stone steps, the balustrades of which are richly ornamented with carved decoration. Concerning this aspect of the Terrace, Clarence Cook observed in his 1869 guide to the park: "On no public building in America has there yet been placed any sculpture so rich in design

31. Some 1,400 drawings relating to Central Park are now preserved in the Municipal Archives of New York City. For color illustrations of several of the best of these, together with a brief account of their discovery and subsequent conservation, see *The Central Park: An Historic Preservation Project of the Frederick Law Olmsted Association*, text by William Alex, published by the Frederick Law Olmsted Association, 1980.

. . . or so exquisitely delicate in execution. . . . All the sculpture on the walls of the new Houses of Parliament in London is not worth . . . these four ramps of the great stairs of the Terrace."[32] Later critics have generally agreed that Vaux was justified in considering the Terrace his most successful design, but its decoration was largely the work of Jacob Wrey Mould, a young architect who had recently emigrated from England and who now became the fourth talented designer whose professional career was closely linked with that of Vaux.[33]

Mould's arrival in New York in the spring of 1853 was at the invitation of Moses Hicks Grinnell, a wealthy New Yorker who hoped thereby to obtain a suitable design for All Souls' Unitarian Church, of which he was a prominent member. Mould claimed to have been a pupil and later an assistant of Owen Jones, the English designer whose theories concerning the use of color had brought him appointment as superintendent of the works for the Great Exhibition of the Industry of All Nations held in London in 1851, an assignment with which Mould is also thought to have been associated.[34] In one of the few quotations attributed to him, Mould described himself as being "hell on color," and if his design for All Souls' introduced Americans to constructional polychromy, its alternating horizontal bands of yellow Caen stone and the reddest of red brick inevitably led to the irreverent nickname "Church of the Holy Zebra."[35]

Perhaps through the good offices of clients such as Moses Grinnell or John A. C. Gray, who were either members of the park commission or in a position to influence it, in December 1858, Mould began a 30-year association with the New York City Department of Parks, first as assistant to Vaux and later in a variety of other capaci-

32. Clarence C. Cook, *A Description of the New York Central Park,* New York, 1869; reprinted by Benjamin Blom, New York, 1972, 55. Cook was an influential art critic and journalist.

33. A year younger than Vaux, Jacob Wrey Mould (1825–1886) was not only an architect but also a successful designer of interiors, a song writer and an opera translator. While admitting that he was something of a "universal genius," the diarist George Templeton Strong described Mould as "ugly and uncouth" with an unfortunate propensity for shady business dealings. For these and other details of Mould's career, see David T. Van Zanten, "Jacob Wrey Mould: Echoes of Gwen Jones and the High Victorian Styles in New York, 1853–1865," *Journal of the Society of Architectural Historians,* xxviii, (1969) 41–57. Except for the Terrace and most of the bridges, the majority of the park structures on which Vaux and Mould collaborated have been demolished.

34. Born in London, Owen Jones (1807–1874) was educated privately before being apprenticed to the architect Lewis Vulliamy (1791–1871). In the course of extensive travels in the Mediterranean area, Jones applied the same careful study to the Alhambra in Spain as had hitherto been accorded the antiquities of Greece and in the process identified what he considered to be certain universal laws of form and color. Among other strong opinions, Jones held that, instead of being applied, the color of buildings should result from the inherent character of their materials, a principle that came to be referred to as "constructional polychromy." The notice accorded his *Plans, Elevations, Sections, and Details of the Alhambra (1836–1845),* produced jointly with the French architect Jules Goury (d. 1834), led to Jones' appointment as superintendent of works for the international exhibition of 1851. In 1856 he published his *Grammar of Ornament,* for which he is best known. David T. Van Zanten, *Macmillan Encyclopedia of Architects,* New York, 1982, ii, 513–515.

35. Van Zanten, *JSAH,* 45.

ties, including briefly, from 1870 to 1871, as architect-in-chief.[36] A superb draftsman and gifted designer of ornament, Mould signed many of the surviving drawings related to the park and has been credited with the design of the fanciful Music Stand that originally stood at the northern terminus of the Promenade. Like similar structures elsewhere, this was intended to be vaguely Moorish, a style with which Mould must have been especially familiar, if, as he claimed, he had earlier assisted Owen Jones with his publication of the Alhambra. Mould also designed the Sheepfold, which now serves as the Tavern on the Green restaurant.

As an entity created by the state legislature in 1853 and after 1857 managed by a board of commissioners, appointed by the legislature but dependent upon the Common Council of the city for its funding, it was inevitable that the new park would soon become embroiled in politics. When it came time to select the winning design from among 33 submitted, the board had voted largely along party lines, and all prizes but the fourth went to persons who, like Olmsted, were already in the employ of the commission.[37] In fact, to many it appeared that service as a Republican or a Democrat, rather than experience or skill, should decide who was hired to work on the project—a perception that was only aggravated by the severe financial panic of 1857. Undoubtedly conflicts with the commission delayed the progress of construction, markedly increased its cost, and on several occasions seriously affected Olmsted's health. But however viewed by politicians, from the outset the park was popular with New Yorkers; more than anything, it was their enthusiastic support that assured its continuing development in accordance with the general principles first laid down in Greensward and later modified.

## NEW COMMISSIONS AND THE COMING OF WAR

WHILE WORK on the New York park progressed, beginning about 1860 its designers sought to extend their collaboration to other commissions. Among the firm's first clients were the ship owner E. K. Collins of New Rochelle, New York, and William Cullen Bryant's son-in-law Parke Godwin, whose country seat was at Roslyn, Long Island. But in some ways the two most interesting commissions were for the grounds of the Hartford Retreat for the Insane in Connecticut and the Bloomingdale Asylum in New York City, both reflections of the growing humanitarian concerns of a period firmly committed to an environmental interpretation of human behavior. Of all environments the most deleterious was considered to be that of the city, widely regarded as a cause of mental disorder.[38] Well before the physical

190–191

36. *Minutes*, New York City Board of Commissioners of the Department of Public Parks, May 19, 1870, 34.

37. *Papers of FLO*, iii, 27.

38. Ibid., 31–32. When the Connecticut state asylum was opened in 1868, Vaux and Withers were engaged to remodel extensively the Hartford Retreat (Kowsky, *Withers*, 175 [45]),which as the Institute of Living still stands at 400 Washington Street. As part of his illustration of the design of "Retreat Park" (plate XVIII), Jacob Weidenmann, in his *Beautifying Country Homes* (New York, 1870; reprinted, with an introduction by David Schuyler, by the American Life Foundation, Watkins Glen,

or psychological basis for insanity had begun to be seriously investigated, it was proposed to help, if not cure, the insane by changing their environment. On this basis, Downing had earlier been called upon to provide landscape settings for asylums at Utica, New York, and at Trenton, New Jersey. Indeed, the desirability of offering city dwellers some of the benefits of a rural environment had helped support the arguments of Downing and others who had urged the creation of a large public park for New York City.

But before the new firm was fairly launched, on April 12, 1861, the country was plunged into war with the shelling of Fort Sumter. Though not an American citizen, Withers, who the year before had agreed to help work out the details of the park plan, promptly volunteered for the army. Olmsted, now permanently lame from a serious carriage accident the previous year, accepted the position of executive secretary of the United States Sanitary Commission, the voluntary organization charged with monitoring the health of the Union forces and the medical care accorded them. Despite the demands made on his time by the work of the Sanitary Commission, Olmsted retained nominal supervision of the park, while leaving its day-to-day direction to Vaux, whose 4 ft. 10 in. height rendered him unsuited for military service. On May 14, 1863, the commissioners finally adopted the additional plan that Olmsted and Vaux had developed for the upper park and its extension above 106th Street. At the same time Vaux, unhappy in his relationship with the board, resigned on behalf of the firm.[39] After 1865 both Olmsted and Vaux again served the park commission in a number of capacities, but their later efforts were principally directed at preserving or executing as much of their earlier designs as the exigencies of New York City politics would permit.

While supervising work on the New York park, Vaux also undertook a number of architectural commissions elsewhere. To the period 1859–1860 belongs the Rural Gothic house erected for Levi P. Stone at Llewellyn Park, New Jersey, as well as the Italian villa designed for Thomas Pegues of Oxford, Mississippi. Other commissions conformed essentially to prototypes introduced by Downing and later developed further in the designs illustrated in *Villas and Cottages*. Much the same thing might be said of the remodeling of Ashcroft, the Rural Gothic house in Geneva, New York, for which Vaux's plans are dated 1862.[40] Not only are the bargeboards and turret (here not a ventilator) of a type noted previously as especially favored by Vaux, but the studied asymmetry of its numerous bays, gables, chimneys and verandas give Ashcroft a more varied and picturesque silhouette than had most of Downing's earlier designs, which in most respects may be considered its predecessors. Here again, as with the Warren house, noted earlier, the overall design of Ashcroft may be said to be in the Rural Gothic vein, but the use of Italianate forms—specifically the

56

86–89

---

1978), also includes a sketch of Vaux's design for a small museum on that site. Swiss by birth, Jacob Weidenmann (1829–1893) had emigrated to the United States in 1856 and thereafter played an important role in the development of American landscape architecture in the second half of the 19 century.

39. *Minutes*, Board of Commissioners of the Central Park, May 14, 1863, 5.

40. The author is indebted to Michele D. DeAngelus for first bringing Ashcroft to his attention.

round-topped windows—is consistent with mid-Victorian architects' deliberate disregard of historic or regional consistency.

Because of his English training, throughout his career Vaux preferred masonry construction over that in wood, a preference Downing also stressed when cost was not the determining factor. As a consequence, neither Downing nor Vaux took any interest in the new balloon frame that was beginning to play so large a part in the burgeoning cities of the Midwest. And in common with their English predecessors, Vaux also shared with Downing an aversion to white houses, especially when accompanied by green blinds. At Ashcroft the smooth brick walls are said to have originally been painted an ochre hue that would effectively complement brown wooden trim and darker brown blinds, while above the cornice the red brick of numerous chimneys formed a pleasant contrast to the gray of the slate roofs. Old photographs show the gardens at Ashcroft to have been in the mid-Victorian style— sometimes called "gardenesque"—that depended for its effect on an asymmetrical arrangement of flower beds, garden ornaments and specimen plantings. Possibly because the grounds of the private residences he designed were often of limited extent, Vaux appears to have been more willing to accept gardenesque elements than was Olmsted, who seldom wavered in his preference for plant materials arranged so as to create deceptively natural effects that, in the idiom of the day, were considered to be either "pastoral" or "picturesque."

89

In the same year he planned the remodeling of Ashcroft, Vaux also designed the Moses Sheppard Asylum (now The Sheppard and Enoch Pratt Hospital) in Baltimore. Olmsted and Withers were both engaged with the Union war effort at the time, but for this commission Vaux had yet another collaborator, the superintendent, Dr. D. Tilden Brown, whose views on asylum architecture had been formed in the course of a recent European trip.[41] To this period belongs also the symmetrical red-brick mansion on fashionable Bellevue Avenue in Newport, Rhode Island, that Vaux designed for Federico L. Barreda, the Peruvian ambassador, and illustrated as Design 38 in the second edition of *Villas and Cottages*.[42] Set on a high balustraded terrace, Beaulieu betrays its Italian sources by its central tower, round-topped windows and bracketed eaves, but the steep slope of the roof is evidence of the growing popularity of French Second Empire forms and specifically of the revival of the distinctive type of roof associated with the work of the French architect François Mansart (1598–1666).[43] With Vaux what one critic called the "mansard madness" seems to have passed quietly enough but not before it left its mark on a number of his domestic designs, including the house commissioned by Francis Tomes in Greenwich, Connecticut, and illustrated in the second edition of *Villas and Cottages* as Design

182, 186–189

60–63

41. Kowsky, *Withers*, 176 (46).

42. Antoinette F. Downing and Vincent J. Scully, Jr., *The Architectural Heritage of Newport, Rhode Island: 1640–1915*, Cambridge (Mass.), 1952; reprinted 1967, 138–139. Scully dates the house to 1856–1859, but does not name the architect. Vaux also designed the additions Barreda made to his New York City residence at the corner of Fifth Avenue and 31st Street (*Papers of FLO*, iii, 321 [25]).

43. John Maass, "The Mansardic Era," *The Gingerbread Age*, New York, 1957, 117–134.

184   29.[44] A mansard roof was also a prominent feature of the two-story addition that in 1879 Vaux and Radford provided for the Bank of New York, a building that, together with the John Gray house, may be said to have launched Vaux's New York career some twenty years earlier.

## PROSPECT PARK AND OTHER POSTWAR COMMISSIONS

MEANWHILE, by dint of long days and little sleep, Olmsted succeeded in improving the sanitary conditions of the Union forces and the delivery of medical assistance to them. Finally, however, what the diarist George Templeton Strong called his "monomania for system and organization on paper (elaborate, laboriously thought out and generally impracticable)"[45] led to conflicts that could only be resolved by his own resignation from the Sanitary Commission. This was in the winter of 1863, and a few months later, worn out and low on funds, Olmsted was glad to accept the position as resident manager of the Mariposa Mines in California. But any hope that his work there might prove financially rewarding was soon dashed when it became apparent that the worth of the mines had been misrepresented to the new owners. At this point Olmsted considered returning to a career in journalism and might well have done so had he not received word from Vaux that they had been offered reappointment as landscape architects of Central Park and that Brooklyn was planning a large park worthy of his interest, on the design of which his collaboration would be welcome. In November 1865 Olmsted returned to New York and to his association with Vaux, the person who had first introduced him to landscape architecture and who was now responsible, at a time when he was moving in a wholly different direction, for inducing him to make it his life's work.

The popular success of New York's Central Park inevitably encouraged similar projects in other American cities, including nearby Brooklyn (then an entirely separate municipality), where James S. T. Stranahan, one of its richest and most influential citizens, had for some years been agitating for a system of parks and parkways.
131   Once again the civil engineer Egbert L. Viele was first approached to plan a park for somewhat more than 300 acres adjacent to Mount Prospect, whereon was located the city reservoir, and which were bisected by Flatbush Avenue. Recognizing the shortcomings of Viele's proposal, on June 13, 1865, Stranahan and his associates
131–132 retained Vaux to draw up an alternate plan. By the time Olmsted returned from California, Vaux had persuaded the commissioners to exchange the land north-east of Flatbush Avenue for a large tract on the southwest in order that the prospective park could be treated as a unit without being cut in half by a public highway. Olmsted had earlier concurred in the wisdom of this change, which now enabled the two partners to design promptly the coherent plan they presented to the board in January 1866,

44. After narrowly escaping sale to developers about 1980, the 22-room Tomes-Higgins house on East Putnam Avenue in Greenwich today serves as the rectory of Christ Church, its owner. The house is surrounded by three acres of fine gardens, which some would attribute to Vaux.

45. As quoted in *Frederick Law Olmsted's New York*, text by Elizabeth Barlow, illustrative portfolio by William Alex, New York, 1972, 28.

and which earned the firm of Olmsted, Vaux & Co. appointment as landscape architects of the new park the following May.[46]

When it came time to summarize the principal features of the park they were proposing for the Brooklyn Common Council, the commissioners singled out three for special comment: the large open meadow, which they believed would provide abundant space for play; the picturesque hilly area filled with shaded rambles; and the 60-acre, spring-fed lake, which would offer good opportunities for boating and skating.[47] As they had for Central Park, the architects provided for numerous rustic structures that in this case included shelters, an arbor over 100 feet long, positions from which to view the sunset over the water and of course seats of sassafras and cedar—more than fifty of them. Because of their masonry construction, a number of the distinctive and highly original bridges Vaux devised to separate the pedestrian walks from the carriage drives have survived, but less solid structures like the picturesque Dairy and the fanciful Concert Grove House (which housed a restaurant and comfort station) have been demolished. Fortunately, the Concert Grove Pavilion, with its delightful cast-iron supports in the Hindu style, escaped a similar fate. After being partially destroyed by fire while serving as a snack bar, the Pavilion was restored in the mid-1980s to something approaching its original appearance. In the design of the Pavilion, as with a number of the other structures in Prospect Park, Vaux was assisted by Thomas Wisedell (1846–1884), an English immigrant who would later establish an architectural practice in New York City.

131–141
137
138
139

As finally constituted, the Brooklyn park contained over 500 acres, but Prospect Hill, from which the park takes its name, lay outside its boundaries. Although Central Park is the better known, Prospect Park proved the more consummate work of art. For this the reasons are obvious: its designers had almost a decade of experience behind them; its compact, arrowhead shape lent itself to a coherent plan far better than did the long, narrow plot with which the designers of Greensward were obliged to contend; and finally, the Brooklyn park commission under Stranahan was much more understanding and sympathetic than had been its New York counterpart.

While engaged in working out the details and supervising the construction of both the New York and Brooklyn parks, Olmsted and Vaux found time to undertake a number of other projects. Moreover Vaux, doubtless wishing to place himself in a favorable position to accept major architectural commissions, once again established a partnership with Frederick Clarke Withers, who had moved from Newburgh to New York in 1864, his first wife having died the previous year. Since his earlier association with Vaux, Withers had been won over to many of the views of John Ruskin, the popular English architectural critic whose writings had served to shift attention from the drab Gothic forms of northern Europe to the more polychromatic ones of Italy.[48] When he designed the Dutch Reformed Church for Fishkill Landing (now Beacon,

46. For a discussion of the circumstances leading to the appointment of Vaux and Olmsted as landscape architects for Prospect Park, see Schuyler, *New Urban Landscape*, 115–117.

47. Clay Lancaster, *Prospect Park Handbook*, New York, 1967, 28.

48. Inasmuch as John Ruskin (1817–1900) was essentially a critic and theorist, it remained for such

New York) in 1859, Withers was among the first architects practicing in America to use contrasting materials—light and dark brick in this case—for the banding of walls and to mark alternating voussoirs in the arches, but soon Ruskin's views were enthusiastically endorsed by numerous others. The zebra striping of Mould's All Souls' Unitarian Church of 1853 was remarked upon earlier, and, it seems to have been the lively polychromy of its Italian Gothic forms that led the judges to prefer the design of the relatively unknown Peter B. Wight over such established architects as Leopold Eidlitz (1823–1908) and Richard Morris Hunt in 1861 when it came time to select the architect for the new building of the National Academy of Design.[49] Now, in partnership with Vaux, Withers adapted the Ruskinian Gothic style—hitherto used largely for churches and public buildings—for the Brooklyn townhouse of Charles Kimball, designed in 1865 and no longer standing. Some would also find a part for Vaux in such commissions of the mid-1860s as the Brewster house in Newburgh (1865), the Newburgh Savings Bank (1866–1868), the Monell house in Beacon (1867), and the Hudson River State Hospital for the Insane at Poughkeepsie (1867–1872); but the Ruskinian Gothic features of each point to Withers as the principal designer.[50] And though perhaps no longer representative of the latest architectural fashion, Venetian Gothic was still sufficiently popular in the early '70s that Vaux and Withers felt free to use a particularly uncompromising version for the Hall Building that still stands on River and First Streets in Troy, New York. Indeed the insistent banding of the Rice Building (as the Hall Building is now known) makes it in some respects a kind of commercial counterpart to Mould's All Souls.'

Of the principal projects in which Vaux, Olmsted and Withers all had some part during the 1860s, two are of special interest: the plan and public buildings of Riverside, a new suburb being planned for a tract along the Des Plaines River nine miles west of Chicago; and the campus and buildings for the Columbia Institution for the Deaf and Dumb in Washington, D. C., now known as Gallaudet University. The latter commission was undertaken in the spring of 1866 at the request of Olmsted's friend Edward Miner Gallaudet, the youthful president of the college. But despite the importance of Vaux's role as the apparent link between Olmsted and Withers, the six Ruskinian Gothic buildings erected at Gallaudet in the course of the next 20 are usually considered principally the work of Withers and to be, in fact, among the

191

193

162

171

---

contemporary English architects as William Butterfield (1814–1900), George Edmund Street (1824–1881), and George Gilbert Scott (1811–1878) to translate his theories into brick and stone.

49. Sarah Bradford Landau, *P. B. Wight: Architect, Contractor and Critic, 1838–1925*, The Art Institute of Chicago, 1981, 16. The National Academy building, which stood on the northwest corner of 23rd Street and Fourth (now Park) Avenue in New York City, was demolished in 1901. Although the style of the whole was more Renaissance than Gothic, as early as 1856 Vaux and Withers had used alternating bands of brownstone and brick in their design for the principal floor of John Gray's New York residence (*Villas and Cottages*, 29/34).

50. In their article for the *Macmillan Encyclopedia of Architects*, Francis and Kestenbaum mention Vaux in connection with several of these commissions; Kowsky *(Withers, 60, 61, 64, 71–73)* gives all four exclusively to Withers.

most successful of his designs.[51] Vaux's part in the final design of Riverside is, if anything, even more ambiguous. In 1868, when Olmsted was approached by the Riverside Improvement Company, Vaux was in Europe, and although he is the architect
for several of the delightful Gothic and Swiss cottages pictured in the promotional         163
literature on Riverside, the Ruskinian Gothic block of stores and offices that serves
to anchor the commercial area is thought to be largely the work of Withers, who
was certainly responsible for the community chapel nearby.[52] Unfortunately the new
suburb encountered financial problems from the outset, and in the fall of 1870 Olmsted and Vaux terminated their association with its promoters. Later, the Chicago
fire of 1871 and the economic panic of 1873 further delayed development, but today
its park along the river, its effectively placed Long Common, and its rows of houses
set well back along tree-lined streets make Riverside an outstanding example of
many of the principles its designers were among the first to introduce and for which
they fought so hard.[53]

   But if in the short term their association with the Riverside Improvement Society proved unrewarding, Olmsted and Vaux could take more satisfaction in other
commissions undertaken about the same time, especially their work for Chicago
and Buffalo. For the latter, beginning in 1868, they developed Delaware Park,                152
which—together with the parkways that connect it to a series of outlying squares
and circles—forms one of the principal attractions of the modern city. Alas, a less
congenial fate awaited other contributions of the partners. As with the flamboyant
pavilions he and Withers provided Saratoga Springs in time for the centennial cele-         158–161
bration of 1876, the large wooden boathouse and the festive refectory Vaux designed         154–155
for Buffalo in 1874 have unfortunately fallen prey to fire, decay and the vagaries of
public taste.

   In Chicago on business associated with Riverside, during the fall of 1869 Vaux
was approached concerning a plan for what was known as South Park, an area that         165–169
had Lake Michigan as its principal natural feature. Realizing that the growing city
would surround any park they could devise, Olmsted and Vaux sought to provide
Chicago with many of the advantages they had earlier secured for New York and
Brooklyn. Accordingly, their plan called for an open green space of 100 acres—then
the largest of its kind in the country—a more formal mall where groups might
assemble, and of course a Ramble with rustic seats and arbors. For those who
sought active recreation there would be swimming and boating; for more passive
visitors there would be concerts and appropriate places to picnic. In the end, not all

   51. Kowsky, *Withers*, 75–86. Incorporated in 1857, the Columbia Institution for the Deaf and Dumb
was renamed Gallaudet College to honor Thomas Hopkins Gallaudet (1787–1851), a pioneer in education for the deaf in America and the father of Edward Minor Gallaudet (1837–1917), president of the
college from 1864 to 1911.
   52. Kowsky (*Withers*, 95) cites parallels with another of Wither's designs in support of the view
that he was the principal architect of the business block at Riverside. Withers appears to have served
as the representative of Olmsted, Vaux & Co. at Riverside.
   53. For a fuller account of Riverside and its relationship to other suburban developments of the
period, see Schuyler, *New Urban Landscape*, 149–166.

the amenities their designers envisioned were realized, of course, but today Jackson and Washington Parks, together with the Midway, Drexel Boulevard and South Parkway (now Martin Luther King Drive), are counted among Olmsted and Vaux's most successful and enduring contributions.[54]

## COLLABORATIONS WITH WITHERS

WHATEVER part Vaux may have had in the design of Riverside or in the buildings of Gallaudet College, while the latter were under construction, he and Withers were associated on several other projects. During 1870 they provided professional assistance for the painter Frederic Edwin Church in the planning of Olana, his spectacular Oriental villa overlooking the Hudson River, near Hudson, New York.[55] And although the firm of Vaux, Withers and Co. is not listed in the New York City directory after 1871–72,[56] the design of the Jefferson Market Courthouse, begun in 1874 on a triangular site at the corner of Sixth Avenue and West Tenth Street, was credited in contemporary accounts to both men. Admittedly the "Study for a City Prison and Courts," published in *The New-York Sketch-Book of Architecture* for April 1874 and there identified as by "Messrs. C. Vaux, and F. C. Withers," does not much resemble the combined market and courthouse as finally built, but a later illustration in the *Sketch-Book* is much closer to the executed design, and for this the authors—now with a significant reversal in the order of their names—are given as "Messrs. Frederick C. Withers and C. Vaux, Architects."[57] Although Withers may have had the major role in the final design, modern historians are not being entirely fair to Vaux when they omit his name from their discussion of what by common consent has been judged among the country's most successful Victorian buildings.

## THE METROPOLITAN MUSEUM OF ART
## AND THE AMERICAN MUSEUM OF NATURAL HISTORY

TO PREVENT them from intruding on the pastoral or picturesque moods they sought to create for Central Park, Olmsted and Vaux proposed to place any concert halls or museums mandated by the commissioners along its eastern perimeter. A decade passed before anything of this kind was undertaken, but in the winter of 1869 a group of influential citizens began a series of discussions that eventually led to the location of the Metropolitan Museum of Art at its present site on the edge of Central Park at 82nd Street and the American Museum of Natural Histo-

---

54. Victoria Post Ranney, *Olmsted in Chicago*, Chicago, 1972, 25–31.

55. Kowsky, *Withers*, 180 (101). The Frederic Church Papers at Olana contain records of two payments to Vaux, Withers and Co., each for $300, and dated December 8, 1870, and September 21, 1871. On January 7, 1873, Church made a similar payment to Olmsted, Vaux & Co., presumably for professional services in connection with landscaping the grounds. In 1966 New York State purchased Olana for a museum and park.

56. Dennis Steadman Francis, *Architects in Practice, New York City, 1840–1900*, Committee for the Preservation of Architectural Records, [1979], 78; Kowsky, *Withers*, 180 (101).

57. *The New-York Sketch-Book of Architecture II* (June 1875). Handsomely restored, the Jefferson Market Courthouse now houses a branch of the New York Public Library.

ry on land immediately west of Eighth Avenue, facing the park at 77th Street. In the summer of 1872 Vaux was asked to work with Jacob Wrey Mould, who was then serving as architect of the New York City Department of Public Parks, in preparing a suitable master plan for an art museum and detailed drawings for a single block to be erected immediately.[58]

With this and other important architectural commissions in sight, Vaux and Olmsted decided to terminate their partnership as landscape architects in 1872, but not before they had provided Brooklyn with Washington Park (Fort Greene) on the     144–145 heights above New York harbor and Tompkins Park, a leafy oasis in a residential neighborhood. Both also shared in the creation of Morningside Park in New York     148–149 (1873–1887) as well as in the drafting of the General Plan for the Improvement of the Niagara Reservation (1887), which succeeded in reclaiming from commercial     178–179 exploitation the scenic area adjacent to the Falls. Appropriately, among their last joint endeavors was a small park in Newburgh, for which in 1889 they agreed to     176–177 waive their fee on condition that the area they designed be dedicated to the memory of Andrew Jackson Downing.

The Metropolitan Museum of Art was opened March 30, 1880, to mixed reviews.     206–209 Although some found the new building impressive or even magnificent, many agreed with the critic who likened the great hall to a railroad station.[59] Inasmuch as no art museum of this size had previously been built in America, and since the future needs of this one were anything but clear, it was inevitable that the original design would later prove deficient in a number of respects. In any case, there was little disposition to continue with Vaux and Mould's plan, and subsequent additions to the museum so concealed the Victorian Gothic original that almost nothing of it is visible today.

As in the case of the art museum, the building that Vaux and Mould designed for the natural history museum again favored the type of Venetian Gothic made popu-     202–205 lar by the writings of John Ruskin. The comparatively modest structure completed in 1877 was only intended to be the interior unit between four courtyards that were to be eventually enclosed by 12 galleries. For its time, the design of the natural history museum made effective use of light and space, but funds for additional construction were not available until the 1890s and by then the trustees had come to prefer the bolder forms of Richardsonian Romanesque over the lively polychromy produced by the contrasting stone and brick of the original.[60]

INSTITUTIONS: COLLABORATION WITH RADFORD

ALTHOUGH none of the pertinent drawings appear to have survived, one of the first commissions Vaux must have received after the dissolution of his partnership with Olmsted was for the grounds of the Canadian Parliament Buildings in     180–181

---

58. *Minutes*, New York City Board of Commissioners of the Department of Public Parks, July 17, 1872, 455–456.

59. Matzdorf, "Vaux," 93.

60. Jay Cantor, "Temples of the Art: Museum Architecture in Nineteenth Century America," *The Metropolitan Museum of Art Bulletin*, April 1970, 331–354.

Ottawa.[61] This was in 1873, about the same time he established a professional relationship with yet another English emigrant. Vaux's partner in this case was the civil engineer George Kent Radford, who earlier had assisted Olmsted, Vaux & Co. on the commissions for South Park in Chicago and for the new park in Buffalo, where he served for a time as superintendent. During the 18 years that Vaux and Radford were associated, their professional practice included a variety of commissions, ranging from the Arnot-Ogden Memorial Hospital at Elmira, New York, to the suspension bridge (demolished 1911) across upper Broadway in New York City for the trustees of Trinity Church, but much of their time and attention was occupied with projects for New York citizens engaged in public service. The same humanitarian interest that led some 19th-century reformers to demand more compassionate treatment for the insane caused others to seek better housing for the urban poor, especially children. One such group was the Improved Dwellings Association for which Vaux and Radford designed the block of tenements erected in 1880 between 71st and 72nd Streets on First Avenue. Composed of 200 two to four-room units grouped around a central court, the new "improved dwelling" was praised in one contemporary account for its "pleasant location, the unusual number of windows, the arrangements for ventilation and draft, the fire-proof stairways, secluded [water] closets, shoots for ashes, [and the] public laundries," which combined to make the new structure, in the opinion of the author, "the most attractive and wholesome residence for laboring people in the city."[62]

At about the same time they were planning their model tenement, Vaux and Radford began the first of more than a dozen buildings they designed between 1879 and 1892 for the Children's Aid Society, an organization founded some years earlier under the leadership of the prominent welfare worker Charles Loring Brace (1826–1890) to educate and care for homeless children. In addition to living quarters and appropriate provision for an "industrial school," a number of the houses erected by the society had spaces that could be made to serve as a gymnasium, as a large gathering room and even as a conservatory. Each of the society's buildings was given by a private donor and each was of a different architectural design, although in deference to the Dutch origins of the city a number were characterized by a prominent stepped gable. Other features such as the segmental arch, diminutive columns that seemed too slight to support the load they were asked to carry, contrasting panels of lavish ornament, stone corbels and the like suggest that Vaux and Radford had been favorably impressed by the distinctive interpretation of the northern Gothic style made popular by the writings of Eugène Emanuel Violet-le-Duc (1814–1879), the influential French architect, and most particularly by its principal American exponent, the talented Frank Furness (1839–1912) of Philadelphia.[63]

230–231

196–197

210–213

215–227

Charles Loring Brace

61. John J. Stewart, "Notes on Calvert Vaux's 1873 Design for the Public Grounds of the Parliament Buildings in Ottawa," *Bulletin of the Association for Preservation Technology*, viii (1976) 1–28.

62. *Twenty-ninth Annual Report of the Children's Aid Society*, New York, 1881, 7.

63. James F. O'Gorman, *The Architecture of Frank Furness*, Philadelphia Museum of Art, 1973. Furness shared his love of rich ornament with Jacob Wrey Mould, to whose work he may have been

The majority of buildings for the Children's Aid Society were located in New York City and all were competent designs in the High Victorian style, but historians are most likely to associate Vaux and Radford with their entry in the 1873 competition for a building to house the Centennial Exhibition that was to open in Philadelphia in 1876. Called by one modern critic "a Xanadu of bewildering scale,"[64] the exterior elevation of the Vaux and Radford entry is known only through contemporary drawings, but that of the interior presented a building so arresting in concept and so beautifully rendered that it was selected for preservation when a majority of the other drawings were discarded or left uncared for.[65] Because it failed to conform to the conditions of the competition, Vaux and Radford's entry was not premiated, but the jury nonetheless recommended its adoption for the gigantic structure that would be required to house the projected international exhibition. In the end, however, considerations of time and expense led the commissioners to abandon plans for a single building in favor of a number of smaller ones that could be designed by local architects and engineers and that could be erected simultaneously.[66]

199–201

## LATER WORK

BECAUSE of the structural problems involved, Radford's knowledge of civil engineering must have figured prominently in the design he and Vaux entered in the Philadelphia competition. His contribution was not apt to be so important for the domestic commissions the firm undertook during the 1870s and 1880s, however, and occasionally Vaux may even have accepted commissions on his own account, as he had earlier while in partnership with both Withers and Olmsted. Presumably this was the case when about 1880 he produced for Raphael Pumpelly, a geologist and entrepreneur, one of his rare designs in wood. As befitted the holiday mood of a vacation retreat at Newport, the lacy decorations of the verandas of Pumpelly's "cottage" may have had a vaguely Moorish cast, as the profiles of the dormers certainly did an Elizabethan one, but the exterior expression of its wooden frame linked the whole design with what modern historians have elected to call the "stick style."[67] The practice of emphasizing the wooden members—whether structural or essentially decorative—doubtless had its origins in such earlier forms as the so-called Swiss cottage and the half-timber structures of the late Middle Ages, the latter involving a type of construction Vaux had just finished adapting for the pretentious house and outbuildings erected for Henry Baldwin Hyde at Islip, Long Island, between 1876 and 1878. Because as a peculiarly American expression the stick style had reached the height of its popularity during the 1870s, Vaux could hardly claim to be in the van-

90

———

introduced through his father, William Henry Furness, a Unitarian minister undoubtedly familiar with All Souls' Unitarian Church, the commission that is said to have brought Mould to New York.

64. Cantor, "Temples," 345.

65. For a full description of the Vaux and Radford entry, see *The New-York Sketch-Book of Architecture* (September 1874) 1–5. In this account the perspective drawings are described as the work of "Thomas Wisedell, principal assistant to Messrs. Vaux and Radford."

66. John Maass, *The Glorious Enterprise*, Watkins Glen, 1973, 32–33.

67. Vincent J. Scully, Jr., *The Shingle and the Stick Style*, New Haven, 1955; rev. ed., 1971.

guard of taste when about 1885 he used it to such good advantage for the residence he designed for R. S. Bowne at Flushing, Long Island.[68]

The idiosyncratic interpretation of medieval forms often associated with the work of Frank Furness and mentioned earlier in connection with several of the designs for the Children's Aid Society was again employed by Vaux for the combined house and office planned about 1875 for George T. Bull of Worcester, Massachusetts.[69] In this case constructural polychromy was achieved through the use of red granite for the walls and contrasting gray granite for the banding, window trim and other decorative details. But the incised ornament around the doorway and the sharp and linear character of the metal decoration of the Bull residence owe less to John Ruskin or Frank Furness than to another contemporary approach to the arts that went by the name Neo-Grec.[70] Much as Violet-le-Duc had been intent on demonstrating that medieval principles of design could be used to solve architectural problems of his own day, other Frenchmen sought inspiration in what they believed to be the spirit—as opposed to the specific forms—of Greek art. Occasionally furnishings might be produced in what passed for the pure Neo-Grec idiom, but in the hands of Victorian architects its forms were likely to be combined with those of the neo-Gothic, a style with which, after all, it shared a somewhat similar philosophical basis.

Dr. Bull's house must be counted among Vaux's most satisfactory designs, but the commission that attracted the most attention from contemporaries was the remodeling of the house at 15 Gramercy Park South for Samuel J. Tilden, for whom Vaux had earlier designed the grounds of Greystone, Tilden's country estate in Yonkers, north of New York City. As a successful corporation lawyer, a power in the Democratic Party and a former governor and candidate for president, Tilden had the means to permit his architect considerable latitude in the selection of materials, and the resulting color harmonies and contrasts established by the use of red sandstone, darker brownstone and polished black granite were praised as "admirable" by no less an architectural critic than Montgomery Schuyler.[71] On the interior, a number of the rooms remodeled earlier by the New York architect Griffith Thomas (1820–1879) were

91

96–99

100–105

68. *Building*, iv (1886) 78. Although the firm of Vaux and Radford was the architect of record for the Bowne house, it seems doubtful that Radford contributed much to the final design. At the same time, he must have played the major role in developing other designs like that which figured in the firm's unsuccessful bid to be the designers of the Harlem River Bridge (*Building*, v [1886] 49–41).

69. *American Architect and Building News*, i (1876) 117, as noted by Matzdorf, "Vaux," 106.

70. Kenneth L. Ames, "What Is the Neo-Grec?"in *Nineteenth Century*, Summer 1976, 13–21. Vaux's contemporaries, Detlef Lienau (1818–1887) and Richard Morris Hunt, both of whom had French training, helped to popularize Neo-Grec forms in America. Because it was economical to incise, the characteristic hard, linear Neo-Grec ornament, based on abstract floral motifs, was widely used for speculative housing in New York and Boston. Other motifs associated with the style include rondells, parallel channels ("Neo-Grec fluting"), akroteria and pediments.

71. Schuyler was contrasting favorably the High Victorian work of men like Vaux with the popular "Queen Anne" style, which he suggested that "analysis finds absurd and Vitruvius condemns . . . as incorrect." Schuyler's comments were first published in "Recent Building in New York," *Harper's Magazine*, 67 (1883) 557–578, and more recently reprinted in *American Architecture and Other Writings by Montgomery Schuyler*, William H. Jordy and Ralph Coe, eds., Cambridge (Mass.), 1961, ii, 453–487.

left more or less intact; it was on Tilden's new library and dining room that Vaux concentrated his major efforts. To house his client's extensive collection of books and manuscripts, he devised a handsome room covered by a stained glass dome that could be illuminated at night by a series of gas jets. Even richer in its detailing, the dining room was praised in contemporary accounts for its wainscotting of black walnut and its walls of satinwood ornamented with carved birds amid foliage; the ceiling—some 31 feet square—glowed with blue tiles framed in satinwood.[72]

105

While engaged in architectural practice, either alone or in partnership with Radford, Vaux also accepted landscape commissions under the name "Vaux and Company." During this phase of his work, which occupied the period from about 1880 until his death, he was associated with Samuel Parsons, Jr. (1845–1923), who had previously supervised the planting in Central Park, and toward the end of his career with his son Downing Vaux (1856–1926). Although called upon to design nothing of the size and complexity of the earlier parks in New York or Brooklyn, Vaux and Company was responsible for a number of university campuses, cemeteries, private estates, and the like—most reflecting the English landscape style Vaux had learned with Downing which he and Olmsted had developed and refined.[73] Nor did Vaux sever completely his ties with the New York Department of Public Parks. From late in 1881 until early 1883, and again from 1888 until his death, he held the post of landscape architect. In this capacity, beginning about 1889, many of his efforts were directed at turning the long, narrow strip of land along the Hudson River into Riverside Park, a project he and Olmsted had begun during the 1870s.

146–147

## RENEWING YEAR BY YEAR

VAUX died November 19, 1895. In some respects his death was surrounded by many of the uncertainties and ambiguities that had marked much of his professional career. When he failed to return from his morning walk, his elder son Bowyer, whom he had been visiting in Bensonhurst, Brooklyn, notified the police. Two days later his body was found in Gravesend Bay, and for want of any evidence to the contrary, the coroner's jury ruled his death an accidental drowning. The fog

---

Montgomery Schuyler (1843–1914) served on the staff of *The New York Times* and was one of the founders of the *Architectural Record*.

72. Vaux' s remodeling of Tilden's house—really two contiguous houses—was carried out between 1881 and 1884. After Tilden's death in 1886, his will was successfully contested by collateral heirs, but in 1895 his books and a considerable portion of his estate were combined with the Astor and Lenox libraries to form the New York Public Library. After doing duty for a few years as a rooming house, in 1906 the mansion on Gramercy Park was acquired as the headquarters of the National Arts Club, a function it continues to serve. When Tilden's dining room was enlarged to provide an exhibition gallery, Vaux's decorations were removed, but the library with its glass dome survives. Stephen Garney, *Gramercy Park: An Illustrated History of a New York Neighborhood,* New York, 1984, 93–103.

73. Among the notable commissions of Vaux and Company were the grounds of Grace Church, New York (1886); Trinity Cemetery grounds in Upper Manhattan (1881–1889); grounds of Wilderstein, Rhinebeck, N. Y. (1890–1891); Isaac Gale Johnson grounds (1891); New York University grounds (1894); and the New York Botanical Garden (1895). Matzdorf, "Vaux," iii; Francis and Kestenbaum, *Macmillan Encyclopedia*, 304.

on the morning of the 19th was shown to have been unusually dense, so dense, in fact, that it might possibly have caused a man past 70 and unfamiliar with his surroundings to have blundered off the end of one of the piers.[74] On the day following the inquest Vaux was buried at Kingston, New York, not many miles from where he began his life in America and near the river wherein his first American partner, Downing, had met his death by drowning.

Vaux's last years cannot have been entirely happy. There were aspects of his personal life, to be sure, that must have brought him satisfaction. His two sons, Bowyer and Downing, became landscape architects like their father; his two daughters married well and had children of their own. Although for some obscure reason back in 1869 both Vaux and Withers had resigned their memberships in the American Institute of Architects,[75] Vaux continued his regular visits to the Century Association, a citadel of the arts, of which he had long been a member. And while his architectural and landscape practice had declined, there is no reason to suppose that finances were a matter for serious concern.[76]

Vaux's professional life, however, presented quite a different picture. The general public was clearly coming to prefer the Beaux Arts classicism of such architects as Stanford White (1853–1906) and Richard Morris Hunt to the High Victorian style for which Vaux was known. Had he lived another six years he would have seen Downing's picturesque park in Washington give way to the straight *allée* (the present Mall) we know today, and elsewhere the growing popularity of the formal over the pastoral and the picturesque was all too obvious. For George W. Vanderbilt, Olmsted himself had designed the grandiose gardens of Biltmore (begun 1888) in the formal French style. What Vaux thought of this or of Olmsted's acclaimed classical design for the Columbian Exposition of 1893 we can only guess; we do know that in his later years many of his own efforts as landscape architect for the New York Department of Public Parks had been directed at preventing unsuitable intrusions—many of them classical—that he believed would endanger the integrity of the Greensward plan.[77] In Brooklyn, too, the political tide had turned against James Stranahan, who for so long had championed the original goals of Prospect Park; in his place were new leaders like Frank Squires, president of the Brooklyn Park Commission, who spoke disparagingly of "that peculiar style of architecture which

74. *The New York Times*, xlv (November 21, 1895) 1; xlv (November 22, 1895) 1.

75. Kowsky, *Withers*, 90–91. Leopold Eidlitz also resigned from the AIA at the same time. Vaux's wife had predeceased him by several years.

76. Matzdorf, "Vaux," 118–119.

77. It is perhaps worth noting in this context that Frederick Law Olmsted, Jr.,was a prominent member of the McMillan Commission that in 1901 recommended the abandonment of what remained of Downing's Washington Park and in its place the return to L'Enfant's concept of the mall or esplanade we know today. The late-19th-century shift in taste from the medieval and the picturesque toward the classical and the formal is discussed by Schuyler, *New Urban Landscape,* 180–195. Vaux's specific objections to the monumentality and the classical style of Hunt's proposed additions to the park are the subject of Francis R. Kowsky's "The Central Park Gateways: Harbingers of French Urbanism Confront the American Landscape Tradition" in Susan R. Stein, ed., *The Architecture of Richard Morris Hunt,* Chicago, 1986, 79–89.

was in vogue in the days of Mr. Vaux."[78] Nor was Riverside Park free from interference from Tammany Hall. Not content with locating Grant's tomb within its boundaries, the park had hardly been completed when a group of politicians sought to promote legislation authorizing a speedway along the river's edge. Predictably Vaux's opposition to this, as to all proposals likely to subvert the original purpose of the New York parks, only confirmed several of the park commissioners in their desire to dispense with the services of their troublesome landscape architect. In reply, Olmsted, anxious to defend Vaux against those who sought his dismissal, was quick to recall his former partner as "absolutely the most ingenious, industrious, and indefatigable man in his profession of all [he had] known for the study of plans to meet complicated requirements"[79]—praise any architect might envy.

If modern historians have difficulty identifying Vaux the artist, perhaps it is because they have been looking in the wrong places and asking the wrong questions. By definition, surely the most successful collaborations are those in which the contributions of the individual participants are submerged in the unity of the whole. Unlike so many in his profession, Vaux seems to have preferred to work with others and to have been fortunate in finding others to work with him over an extended period of time. Toward the end, Radford may have criticized his partner's qualifications—at least in private—but his harsh words concerning Vaux are called into question by his willingness to continue their professional affiliation for nearly 20 years, and Mould and Vaux were associated, off and on, for a similar period. To be sure, in the collaborative projects he undertook with Vaux, Withers would appear to have contributed rather more than he received, yet even he was willing to preserve an alliance that extended, in one form or another, over a quarter of a century. And if Vaux never evolved a distinctive personal style like that of H. H. Richardson or Frank Furness, it was perhaps not so much from a lack of professional conviction as because he believed that different problems demanded different solutions.

Both physically and philosophically, Vaux provided the link between Downing, the first American-born landscape gardener to achieve an international reputation, and Olmsted, whose name has become virtually synonymous with American park design in the second half of the 19th century. It was Vaux who named the profession we know as "landscape architecture," and without him Olmsted would be remembered—when he was remembered at all—as a journalist and author. In his park structures Vaux gave Americans their first glimpse of what recreational architecture could be and in so doing set a standard that his successors have rarely equaled and probably never surpassed.

Even when allowance is made for the practice of speaking well of the dead, the recollections of Vaux's friends at the Century Association form a moving tribute:

78. Letter to Paul Dana, March 12, 1891, quoted in the *Papers of FLO*, iii, 65. The son of Charles A. Dana (1819–1897), owner-editor of the *New York Sun*, Paul Dana was the park commissioner appointed by the mayor to evaluate Vaux's competence.

79. Quoted by Roper, *FLO*, 440.

. . . nothing could have induced him to degrade his art or misuse the reputation which secured his employment by consenting to modify his criticism or give sanction of his name to a plan he could not approve. He was a modest and unassuming gentleman, a most genial companion, a loyal and incorruptible public servant. . . .[80]

But the words Clarence Cook used to close his guide to Central Park may have said it best:

. . . if it be pleasant to man to know that he will not be wholly forgotten, let those who conceived the idea of this pleasure-ground, those who designed its beauties, and those whose public spirit and untired zeal have brought it to perfection, be sure that their memory will not pass away, but will renew itself year by year with the waving trees and blossoming flowers.

As one who had wished to be remembered as a designer of landscapes, Vaux could scarcely have asked for more.

George B. Tatum
Old Lyme, Connecticut

80. Henry E. Howland, "Calvert Vaux," *Reports, Constitution, By-Laws, and List of Members of the Century Association for the Year 1895,* New York, 1896, 18–19.

## Vaux in England

W̲ITH FAIR CERTAINTY, the Vaux family in England can be traced back to the mid-16th century and most probably before then to a Robert de Vaux, Lord of Catterlen, Cumberland and Pentney, Norfolk. Later descendants of this branch of the family are recorded to have been physicians and surgeons, as was Calvert Bowyer Vaux, the father of Calvert. Thirty-six Pudding Lane in London, where Calvert was born, housed his father's practice as "Surgeon and Apothecary" plus a large, growing family. Calvert Bowyer was supporting a wife and five children—another on the way—under the increasing strain of a declining medical practice, when in 1831 he suffered a paralyzing stroke, dying soon afterward. Although young Calvert did well in the Merchant Taylors' School where he had been enrolled, he seemed less interested as the years passed and decided not to complete the final schedule of forms for graduation. He left at the age of 14, beginning his architectural apprenticeship a year later in the office of Lewis Nockalls Cottingham. The years seem to have passed uneventfully except for his sketching trip on the Continent with fellow apprentice George Truefitt, both young men 21 years of age at that time. On Cottingham's death, Vaux worked with Cottingham's son, a situation of declining promise until the moment A. J. Downing came to see his drawings exhibited in the galleries of the Architectural Association in London.

*Harwood's Map of London,* 1813. Map shows the district just north of London Bridge, now the financial center known as "the City."

1. 36 Pudding Lane, birthplace of Calvert Vaux.
2. 7 Jerusalem Court, where Vaux lived when he was registered at the Merchant Taylors' School.
3. Suffolk Lane, site of the Merchant Taylors' School.

*Pudding Lane, Seen from Lower Thames Street.*

Vaux was born in a house just beyond the upper curve of the lane, at number 36, the
second house on the right, south of Little Eastcheap Street, which marked the
northern end of Pudding Lane. The photograph dates from about 1900 and shows
the street as it appeared from at least the 1820s.

*Robert Hooke, Merchant Taylors' School, Suffolk Lane.* Built in 1675, demolished in 1875.

*Merchant Taylors' School.* Schoolroom.

Calvert Vaux entered the Merchant Taylors' School in December 1833 at the age of nine, a few months after the death of his father. Endowed by the Merchant Taylors' Company of London, the school accepted 100 worthy boys without charge and about 150 others at a very small charge. It was characterized by the usual strict educational environment, and included in its curriculum Latin, Greek, geography and writing, but was stronger, however, in mathematics than other similarly endowed schools. In 1838 Calvert was rewarded for the excellence of his studies with a copy of James Rennie's *The Architecture of Birds*. He did not graduate, but left in late 1838 or early 1839. About a year later he was apprenticed to the architect Lewis Nockalls Cottingham.

*Lewis Nockalls Cottingham, House-Museum, Waterloo Bridge Road, ca. 1825.*
The house-museum was the building at the end of the block, at the far left of the photograph. Its main entrance was around the corner on Boyce Street. Cottingham had designed the entire block—which no longer exists—as part of his work of laying out the extensive Waterloo estate of John Fields.

Calvert Vaux served his architectural apprenticeship with Lewis Nockalls Cottingham in the house-museum Cottingham built for himself on Waterloo Bridge Road, London. Noted and appreciated as a medievalist, Cottingham had a successful career primarily as a restorationist architect of Gothic churches, while occasionally designing secular buildings and country estates in the Gothic style. He published several books on his restoration plans and on Gothic details and ornamentation. The building contained Cottingham's extensive collection of Gothic artifacts: casts of details from demolished buildings including statuary,

furniture, altarpieces, reliquaries, casts of high tombs with recumbent figures and several entire elaborately carved ceilings. In this environment Vaux worked for some 10 or 11 years, occasionally being taken as field assistant to the sites where Cottingham worked. After Cottingham's death in 1847, Vaux continued with his son, Nockalls Johnson Cottingham, an association that lasted until 1850 when Vaux sailed for America. In 1851 the entire Cottingham collection was sold at auction and Nockalls Johnson moved from Waterloo Bridge Road. He was also on his way to America in 1854 when he was lost at sea in the wreck of the steamer *Arctic*.

*Cottingham's House-Museum.* Ceiling.

*George Truefitt (1824–1902).*

Truefitt was apprenticed to Cottingham at the same time as Vaux. The two took their walking-sketching trip to the Continent in about 1845. After concluding a successful architectural practice in England and Scotland, Truefitt, according to *The Building News* of August 1, 1890, retired to his home in Worthing, "which is filled with choice curiosities which he has been collecting since he was first a pupil." Truefitt, in friendship, according to an account by Vaux's son Downing, presented his book of sketches to Vaux.

Cottingham designed Snelston Hall for John Harrison, Esq., lord of the manor, in 1827 and provided additional furniture designs for it in 1844. He also designed the grounds, interiors and ornamentation, plus the gates, lodges, farm buildings and other necessary structures. Cottingham designed or improved other estates of this kind, work in which Vaux undoubtedly assisted. Snelston Hall was demolished in 1951.

*Lewis Nockalls Cottingham, Snelston Hall, Ashbourne, Derbyshire, 1827.*

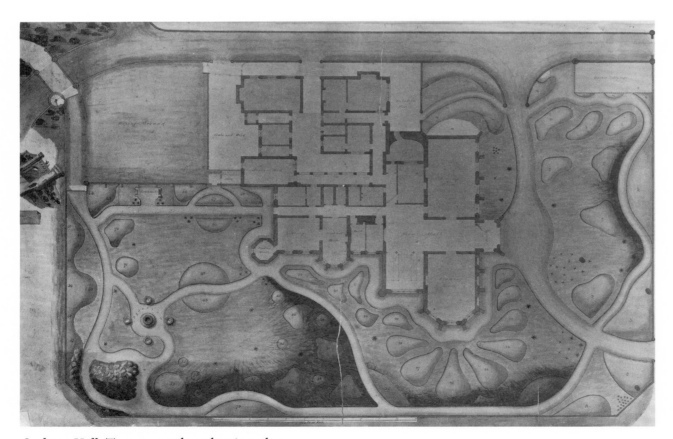

*Snelston Hall.* Terrace garden planting plan.

Plants and trees specified by Cottingham included cedars of Lebanon, standard rose trees, yucca *Gloriosa filamentosa,* variegated *Aloe ugare* and choice evergreen trees, arranged in a picturesque plan.

*Snelston Hall.* Library.

The Gothic penchant for elaborately carved and decorated interior surfaces carried over into Vaux's work when he was provided with this kind of design opportunity. Examples are the Central Park Mineral Springs Pavilion (p. 121) and especially Samuel Tilden's Gramercy Park residence (pp. 104–105). The carved heads over the library bookcases may relate to the medallion busts in the Tilden house facade.

DESIGN FOR AN ARTIST'S STUDIO.

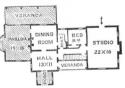

PLAN OF PRINCIPAL FLOOR.

N.E. VIEW.
SHOWING THE COTTAGE COMPLETED.

## Domestic Architecture

MANY OF THE EXAMPLES of Vaux's domestic architecture that follow are described and illustrated in his *Villas and Cottages*, first published in 1857. Vaux's first works were of course in collaboration with Downing. Beginning as Downing's assistant, or "pencil," he soon began superintending construction and corresponding with clients of the "bureau of architecture." After Downing's death he worked to finish the commissions on hand, continuing afterward with Frederick Withers, who for a time remained junior to him. Later he worked in partnership with Withers in Newburgh, New York, and then in New York City. Although Vaux designed houses throughout his professional career, his early major accomplishments in the Hudson Valley were clearly the most influential of his designs.

While the majority of house designs in *Villas and Cottages* are in the Hudson Valley, examples are shown elsewhere in New York State as well as in Connecticut, Rhode Island, Massachusetts and the District of Columbia, the distant sites due to the widespread influence of Downing. Photographs of several houses that follow are shown together with their engravings, which are reproduced in the same size as they appear in *Villas and Cottages*. The somber appearance of the engravings is belied by the quality of the original working drawings, which were rendered in fine line and color (p. 80), or the finished appearance of the house itself (p. 81). Various artists or delineators have made the engravings, but just one engraving is signed by Vaux, the vignette "Design for an Artist's Studio," where the overlapping initials C and V are seen in the lower left corner. The drawing for the vignette "N. E. View" shows the initials FCW for Frederick Clarke Withers (see opposite). The studio design was for the Hudson River School painter Jervis McEntee, Vaux's brother-in-law.

The engravings are reproduced from the second, 1864 edition of *Villas and Cottages*. Vaux indicated design credit with initials over the engravings: (D. & V.) for Downing and Vaux, (V. & W.) for Vaux and Withers and no credit when the design is his alone. (The exception is the Chamberlain house, Design 21, which is not marked but is V. & W.)

While the designs of all three have been studied and are discussed in this work, their individual contributions will doubtless be the subject of scholarly concern in the future. Apart from his pertinent observations on art and life in America, Vaux's domestic designs, together with his lessons on practical construction techniques, his architectural detailing and his all-round professionalism, have been influential and extensive, producing offshoots and copies throughout the East Coast and as far as California.

*Highland Gardens, Home of A. J. Downing, Newburgh, New York.*

The highly respected and successful writer, horticulturist and estate planner Andrew Jackson Downing came to England in 1850, where he engaged Vaux as an architectural assistant for his Newburgh-on-Hudson office. Downing inquired at the Architectural Association in London where the secretary recommended Vaux, whose work was then on exhibition in the association's gallery. Downing and Vaux together went to the gallery where Downing hired Vaux on the spot. Both men sailed for the United States in September of that year.

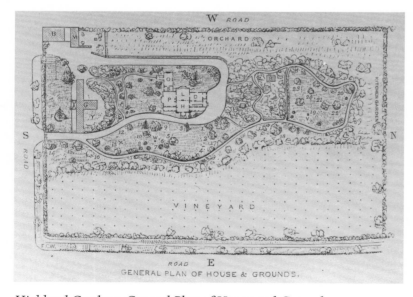

*Highland Gardens, General Plan of House and Grounds.*

*"Bureau of Architecture" Wing, Drawn by Vaux.*

Downing added a small wing to his Highland Gardens residence to house the "Bureau of Architecture" he had established with the arrival of Vaux. Also hired from England came the young architect Frederick Clarke Withers, in 1852. Downing unfortunately died later that year in the destruction by fire of the *Henry Clay* on the Hudson River.

*Highland Gardens, Grounds, ca.* 1870. From a rare stereographic view showing the grounds after ownership of the estate had been transferred. The rustic seat appears to date from Downing's time.

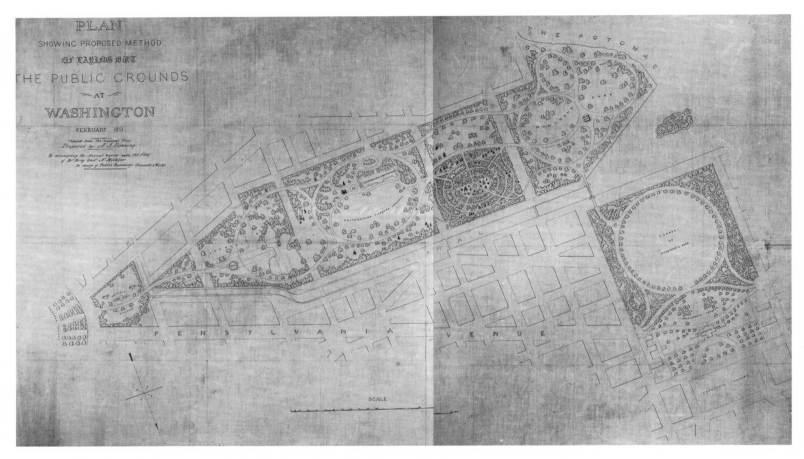

*A. J. Downing, Plan for Laying Out the Public Grounds at Washington, D.C., 1851.*

Recognizing in 1850 that Downing was the only person then capable of designing a large-scale landscape park for the nation's capital, President Millard Fillmore commissioned him to prepare a plan for the improvement of the public grounds between the Capitol, the Smithsonian Institution and the White House. Downing's design was never fully realized, although portions are still recognizable despite having been basically supplanted by the formal McMillan Plan of 1901. Vaux appears to have assisted in the preparation of the plan and of the accompanying two sketches for the suspension bridge over the canal and the arch for the entrance to the White House grounds, sketches, he noted, "we prepared."

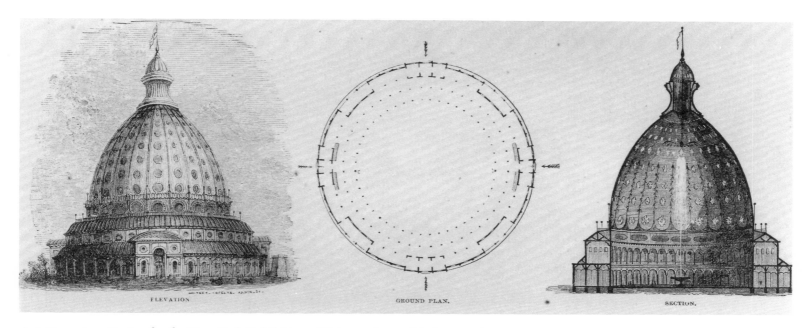

*A. J. Downing, Design for the New York Exhibition of Science, Art and Industry, 1852.*

Downing's submission for the building to house the first international exhibition of science, art and industry in the United States was to be a structure of wood and canvas, despite the requirement for one of iron and glass. The book of the New York exhibition noted, "The late A. J. Downing also presented for the consideration of the Association a plan of great novelty and bold conception. We are indebted to the kindness of Calvert Vaux, Esq. of Newburgh, New York for drawings of the exterior and interior views, and the ground plan of this design." The colossal outer dome of wood was to be supported by thin wooden ribs, while the inner lining of canvas was to be colored pearl gray at the dome's springing line, gradually shading to intense blue at the crown. A smaller version of Joseph Paxton's London Crystal Palace was eventually built in what is now Bryant Park.

DESIGN No. 30.—(D. & V.)

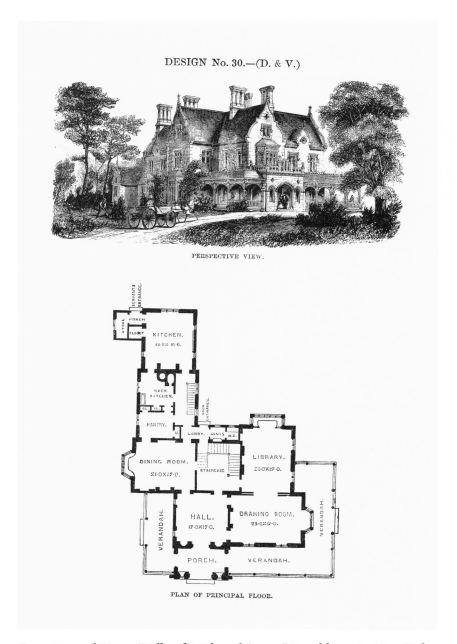

PERSPECTIVE VIEW.

PLAN OF PRINCIPAL FLOOR.

*Downing and Vaux, "Villa of Brick and Stone," Poughkeepsie, New York, 1850.*

*Matthew Vassar Residence.* Pencil sketch.

Springside, the extensive country estate of the wealthy Poughkeepsie, New York, brewer Matthew Vassar, had its full complement of accessory structures, such as a coach house–stable, farmer's and gardener's cottages, summerhouse, conservatory, arbor, vinery, pagoda and much more. What these were to be accessory to was, however, lacking, a house for Vassar himself.

In 1850 a design for his residence was sketched in pencil, probably by Downing, then rendered in a full set of drawings by Vaux, but which carry Downing's initials. The building was not built. The curved gable, one of the principal design elements, tends to characterize the style of the house as Elizabethan or Northern European, which Downing considered not inappropriate for the countryside.

*Matthew Vassar Residence.* Principal elevation.

*Matthew Vassar Residence.* East elevation.

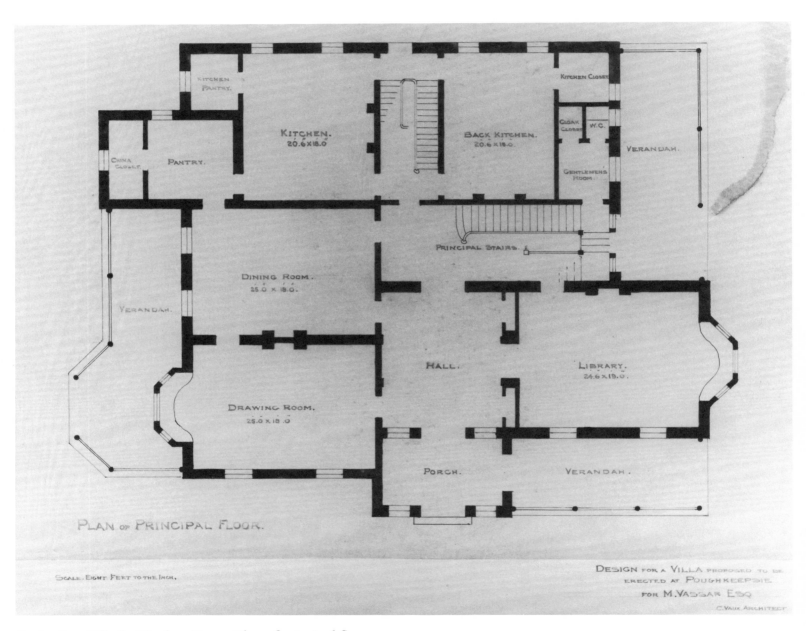

*Design for a Villa for Matthew Vassar.* Plan of principal floor.

*Calvert Vaux, "Design for a Villa Proposed to Be Erected at Poughkeepsie for M. Vassar, Esq.," 1854.*

Four years after the first Vassar design, Vaux produced a rather more elaborately detailed exterior in a design that also was not built, nor did Vaux include it in his extended article the next year, "Hints for Country House Builders," in *Harper's New Monthly Magazine*. When at Springside, Vassar stayed in the gardener's cottage.

*"Algonac 1851 by Vaux."*

Under the rendering appears the notation "Algonac 1851 by Vaux," no doubt
referring to the making of the drawing rather than the design, which is clearly
Downing's developed Italian villa style, here confidently expressed in Vaux's hand.
The "half moon" upper margin is seen frequently in later drawings by Vaux or
drawings supervised by him. Warren Delano wrote at the time to his brother, "Mr.
Downing and his assistant Mr. Vaux are at work devising plans for the
improvement." The "improvement" ultimately resulted in a house of about 40
rooms for the wealthy Delano.

*Downing and Vaux, Algonac, Residence of Warren Delano, Newburgh, New York,* 1851. Delano is seated at the left side of the veranda with his family, photo ca. 1877.

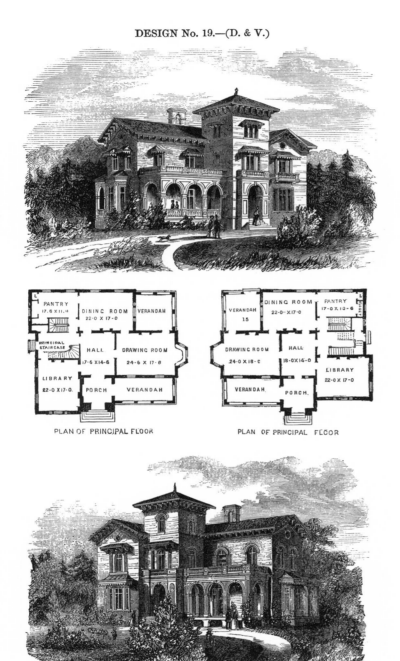

DESIGN No. 19.—(D. & V.)

PLAN OF PRINCIPAL FLOOR          PLAN OF PRINCIPAL FLOOR

*Downing and Vaux, "Suburban Villa," Georgetown, D. C., 1851.*

Downing's Italian villa style characterizes the pair of houses for Robert P. and Francis Dodge, brothers who, in Vaux's description in *Villas and Cottages*, "wished for a general similarity in the two designs, although the situations on which the buildings were to be erected differed somewhat in their local requirements. By reversing the plan, and altering the position of the library, the necessary change was made, and the details also were varied as much as possible, the windows in one design being square and covered by projecting wooden hoods, while in the other they were made with circular heads and stone label mouldings. Minor modifications were also introduced throughout the whole of the exterior and interior; and thus, although these two houses have their principal features in common, neither is a servile imitation of the other." The architects were unable to superintend construction because of the distance from Newburgh, and so Vaux wrote asking about the final cost of the houses. Francis Dodge replied, "We find the cost of our houses to be much beyond what Mr. Downing led us to expect . . . say about $15,000 each; yet we have fine houses, and very comfortable and satisfactory in every respect." Both Dodge houses still exist; the substantially remodeled Robert Dodge house was sold in 1987 for $4 million.

*Robert P. Dodge Residence.*

*Ammadelle, House for Thomas E. B. Pegues, Oxford, Mississippi,*
1860. Front facade.

PERSPECTIVE VIEW.

*"An Irregular Cottage Without Wing."*

*Thomas E. B. Pegues Residence.* Entry porch.

Vaux was architect for the Pegues house and landscape architect for its seven-acre site. Commissioned by a wealthy landowner and railroad magnate, the house, built of red brick with white Italianate details and set off by black shutters, has been properly maintained into the present day. It is considered the finest Italianate villa in Mississippi, its ambient qualities so attractive as to have made it a setting for the Hollywood film *Home from the Hills,* starring Robert Mitchum. Ammadelle's exterior closely resembles Design 27/32 in *Villas and Cottages,* "An Irregular Villa Without Wing" proposed to be erected in Middletown, Connecticut, but apparently not built. The Mississippi house was, however, built with a wing, and was completed except for a rear balcony when construction was halted by the Civil War.

"Mr. Downing knew that Newport was the great social exchange of the country, that men of wealth and taste yearly assembled there, and that a fine house of his designing there would be of the greatest service to his art." So wrote George William Curtis in the edition of Downing's *Rural Essays* he edited in 1853.

Erected in 1852, burned in 1855, and rebuilt 250 feet closer to the ocean in 1857, the house for Daniel Parish became known as Beechwood, the summer home of the Astors when they purchased it from Parish's daughter in 1880. A period of extravagant alterations followed, including the construction of a ballroom by Richard Morris Hunt. The basic Italianate front remains, although Vincent Astor stuccoed over the red brick in the early 1900s. It was also under his ownership that the original Downing and Vaux arch design for the veranda was extended around the house, forming a continuous piazza whose ocean-facing facade presented an especially felicitous appearance.

DESIGN No. 35.—(D. & V.)

ENTRANCE FRONT.

*Downing and Vaux, "Marine Villa," Newport, Rhode Island, 1852.*

*Daniel Parish Residence.*

*Daniel Parish Residence, Remodeled as Beechwood.*
View from the northwest.

### DESIGN No. 15.—(V. & W.)

PERSPECTIVE VIEW.

*Vaux and Withers, "Brick Villa with Tower, and Without Attics," Newburgh, New York, 1854.*

As part of his design justification for the James Walker Fowler house, Vaux, writing in *Villas and Cottages*, provides his usual careful analysis of the site, as he does for each design that has a specific location. The height and variety of trees concerned him, as did the slope of the land, the direction of the scenic views and, of special importance, the impression of the house itself as one approached. Pride in villa, manor or country seat is clearly evident. "Considerable judgement is needed in settling on the exact position for a house like this, so as to realize all the advantages that the site affords," he wrote. "It must not seem to overhang or descend or the effect will be crowded, and will give the idea from the road of a small, restricted property. Neither should it retreat very far from the brow of the hill, or the house will be shut out of sight, and altogether lost on a tolerably near approach to the premises. A happy medium, both in the location of the site and in the pitch of the roof, is the desirable point to aim at under such circumstances." The Fowler house appears not to have been built.

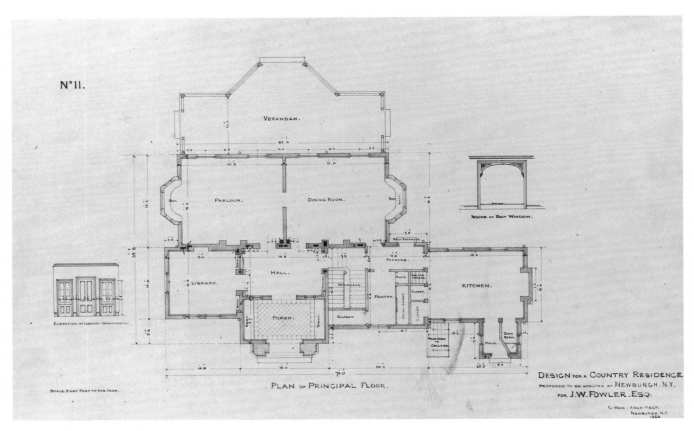

*James Walker Fowler Residence.* Plan of principal floor.

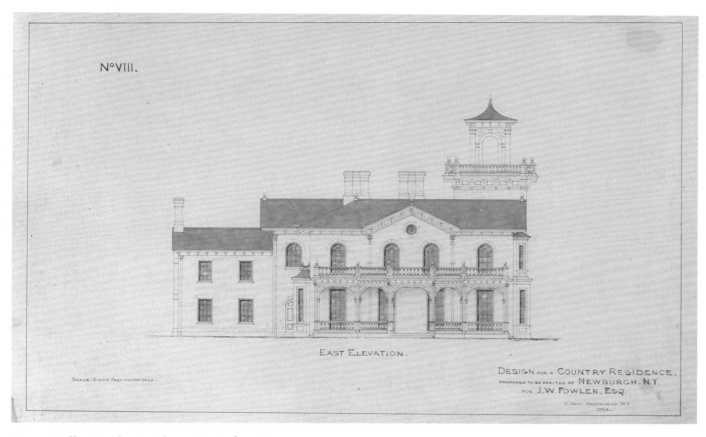

*James Walker Fowler Residence.* East elevation.

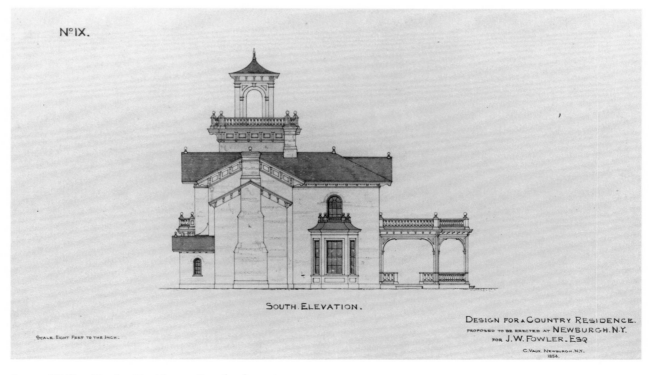

*James Walker Fowler Residence.* South elevation.

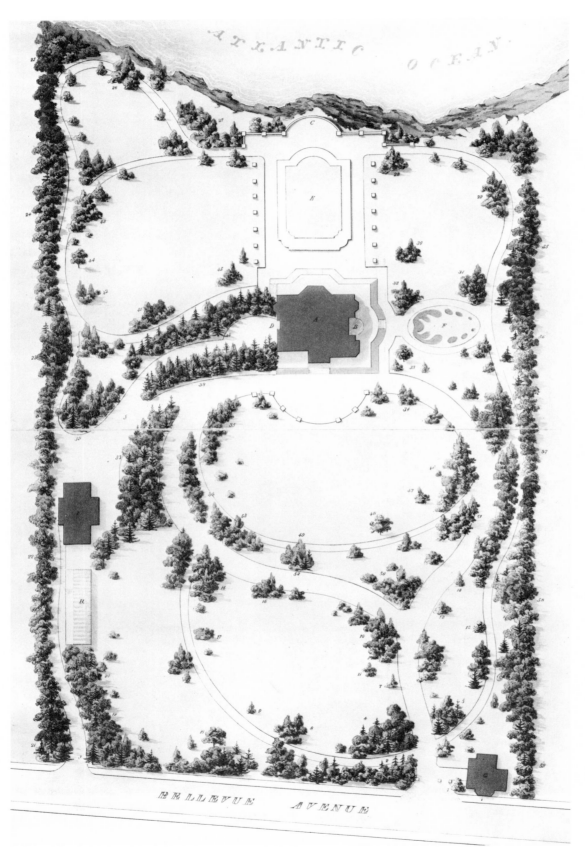

*Federico L. Barreda Residence.* Site plan.

"The terraces around the mansion and the parterre between them and the sea are very happy combinations of the natural and the artificial style of landscape gardening, and reflect great credit upon the excellent taste of Mr. Eugene A. Baumann, the landscape artist who designed and partly superintended the laying out of the grounds, and Mr. Calvert Vaux, the eminent architect of this princely residence," wrote Jacob Weidenmann in 1870 in *Beautifying Country Homes.*

In contrast to its modest description as Design 30/35 in *Villas and Cottages*, the house for Federico L. Barreda was a large villa-estate for the wealthy Peruvian businessman who also served as his country's minister to the United States. The imposing front facade, first seen by visitors, is dominated by an Italianate central tower and upswept mansard roofs, in the kind of large-scale composition appropriate for a house on Bellevue Avenue. The house was designed for an extended family, guests and servants, with generous interiors suitable for the entertainments held there. It was later owned by members of the Astor and Vanderbilt families and has through the years been one of the settings for the grand balls held at Newport.

*Federico L. Barreda Residence, now called Beaulieu.*

DESIGN No. 38.

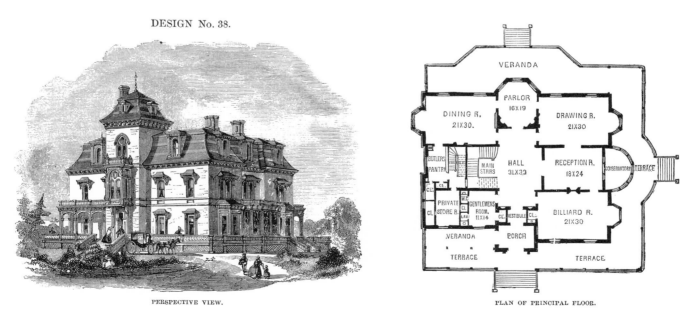

PERSPECTIVE VIEW.                                    PLAN OF PRINCIPAL FLOOR.

*Calvert Vaux, "Marine Villa with Tower," Newport, Rhode Island, 1856–1860.*

*Federico L. Barreda Residence.* View across the east lawn to the seawall.

*Federico L. Barreda Residence.* West facade detail.

*Federico L. Barreda Residence.* East facade.

The arches of the veranda, which is 30 feet wide in places, are most prominent in the east facade of the house, which faces the ocean. No fewer than 23 visits to the five-acre estate were billed by Vaux for "plans and superintendence for house, stable, lodge, terrace and gateways for Newport residence."

*Peter Chardon Brooks, Jr., Residence, West Medford, Massachusetts, 1858.*
Porte cochère, house under construction.

Point of Rocks, one of Vaux's richest and most substantial commissions, was built for Peter Chardon Brooks, Jr., whose father is said to have been New England's first millionaire. The original estate comprised some 300 acres at the West Medford–Winchester town line, northwest of Boston. The house, stable, barn and various outbuildings were built of granite. Elaborate materials were imported from Europe, including chandeliers, interior paneling and grand mantelpieces. The piazza was paved with colored tile from Italy. Inside the huge barn, built of great granite slabs, was an elevator that lifted carriages to the second floor. A stream fed three artificial ponds on the grounds, which also contained costly and exotic plants from around the world which the Brookses had collected during their travels.

*Peter Chardon Brooks, Jr., Residence.* House seen from the northeast.

*Peter Chardon Brooks, Jr., Residence.*
Peter Chardon Brooks III on the piazza.

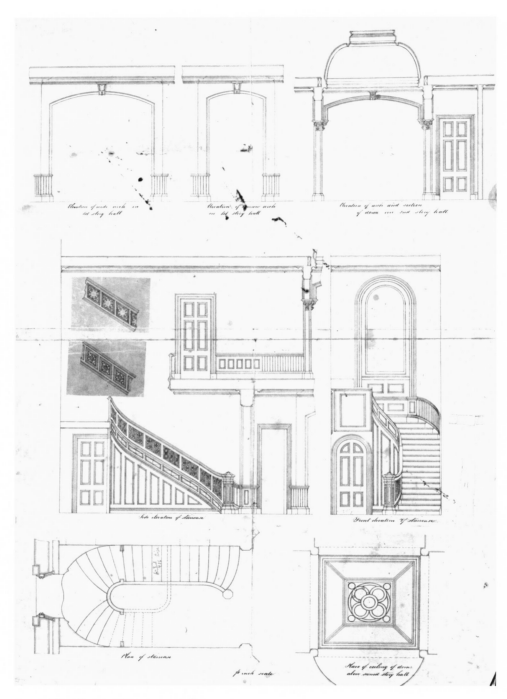

*Peter Chardon Brooks, Jr., Residence.*
Sheet of interior details drawn by Vaux.

Regrettably, almost nothing remains of this "chief crown of Italianate architecture in the Boston area." By the late 1930s the family had dispersed, and as the property was being transferred to the town of West Medford, the architecture, in its remoteness, had become defenseless, and the processes of vandalization and destruction had begun. But in a sense the house lives on. Almost all of the granite, especially the dressed stone, and entire building segments, such as tall window bays, were removed, simply cannibalized by local contractors, and can now be found incorporated in dozens of West Medford and Winchester houses.

*Peter Chardon Brooks, Jr., Residence.* View of stable from top of house.

*Peter Chardon Brooks, Jr., Residence.*
Stable detail: "Irving in cart; Eleanor, Harriette, Lawrence and Barrett."

*Vaux, Withers and Co., "Study of a House for F. E. Church, Esq're at Hudson N. Y.,"* 1870.

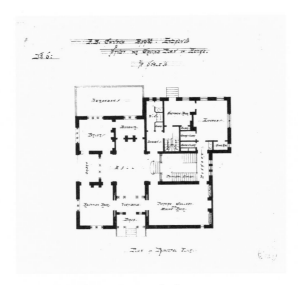

*Study for Olana.* Ground plan.

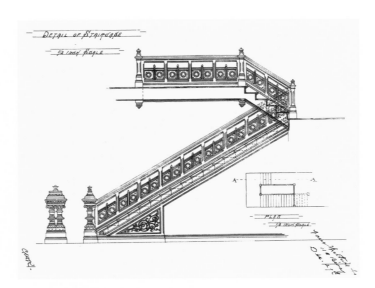

*Study for Olana.* Detail of staircase.

Before seriously undertaking the architectural enterprise that became Olana, Frederic Church asked Vaux for preliminary design advice. Church was then serving as a Central Park commissioner, an appointment suggested by Vaux. Vaux, Withers and Co. thereupon provided sketches and plans, with the initial construction stages being conducted under the firm's superintendence. Beyond that, the story of Olana is the creation of a palatial villa of Islamic-Moorish delight whose every square exterior and interior inch was subject to Church's artistic-decorative spirit.

*Olana.* Watercolor sketch by Frederic Church.

*Olana.* Payment to Vaux, Withers and Co.

Besides Vaux's preliminary design work, Church had a real need for professional architectural advice. This is shown by a telegram in the Olana archives from Vaux to Church in response to a request for a consultation. Vaux wired: "Your note received shall start Thursday ten to eleven train."

A check for $235. issued by Church to Olmsted, Vaux and Co. would suggest they rendered landscaping advice for his 125-acre estate. From the tower of his villa, Church, it is said, could see Connecticut, Rhode Island and Massachusetts. Olana is now a New York State Historic Site.

*William L. Findlay Estate.* Panoramic view showing house, orchard and, at far right, the Hudson River.

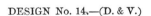

*Downing and Vaux, "A Symmetrical Country House,"
Newburgh, New York, 1852.*

In one of the last Downing and Vaux commissions, brought to completion after Downing's death, Vaux felt keenly the lack of a ventilating turret over the front gable, one of his favorite design elements, in W. L. Findlay's Rural Gothic house, "as the gentleman for whom the plan was prepared preferred to omit it." He put it in the engraving anyway, but in all respects the wishes of the client were followed in the construction of a dual-purpose house of compact plan, airy in summer and cozy in winter. The two front verandas were connected by the open brick porch to form a continuous piazza facing the river view. These rare early photographs appear to have been taken in the 1890s when the estate belonged to the Chadwick family. The house no longer exists.

Out of sight of the house to its rear and left were the outbuildings which Vaux designed. The stable, he writes, "contained accommodations for three horses, a coach-house, a harness room, a coachman's living room, with bedroom over, and a hayloft in the roof" and a ventilating turret.

*William L. Findlay Estate.* Stable and outbuildings.

*William L. Findlay Residence.* Dining room.

Vaux's plan was carefully worked out with regard to interior functioning, ventilation and vistas. For example, if seated in the library bay window seat, one could look through the entire length of the house and see the river framed in the arch of the porch. Or if one stood in the center of the house, in the hall just where the table is located in the picture, Vaux notes, "one can see clear through the house, north, south, east and west," signifying, when the house is thrown open, total crisscross ventilation. On the other hand, Vaux arranged the plan so that in winter "the first step should be to inclose the arches of the porch with glazed frames, and the next to close the sliding doors for the season." The small library was entered by conventional sliding doors, but here Vaux provided a favorite Victorian device: "two of the book-cases are hung and fitted with an inconspicuous catch, so as to swing when needed, books and all, and a private communication is thus afforded with a boudoir on one side, and a staircase-hall on the other." Findlay's secret is revealed in the section on library planning in *Villas and Cottages.*

*William L. Findlay Residence.* Hall, looking toward library.

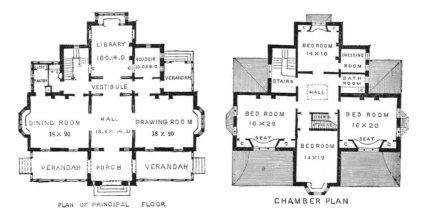

*William L. Findlay Residence.* Floor plans.

"Idlewild," Residence of the late N. P. Willis.

*Nathaniel P. Willis Residence.*

DESIGN No. 23.

PERSPECTIVE VIEW.

*"A class who can afford to let the trees grow* is getting possession of the Hudson; and it is at least safe to rejoice in this, whatever one may preach to the displacement of the laboring tiller of the soil by the luxurious idler. With the bare fields fast changing into wooded lawns, the rocky wastes into groves, the angular farmhouses into shaded villas, and the naked uplands into waving forests, our great thoroughfare will soon be seen (as it has not been for many years) in something like its natural beauty. It takes very handsome men and mountains to look well bald."

The noted journalist, writer and poet Nathaniel Parker Willis wrote the above in 1855 about those who were commissioning the country houses, villas and cottages of Downing and Vaux. And, as a member of that class, Willis engaged Calvert Vaux to design Idlewild, overlooking the Hudson. Although Vaux felt it a privilege to design the house, he hints at some discussion before Willis firmly takes over: "All the lines of the plan were set out under the special direction of Mr. Willis, who seemed to take more interest in accommodating the house to the fancies of the genius of the place than in any other part of the arrangement." Given the aura then surrounding Willis, "fancies" could be equivalent in our day to "romance."

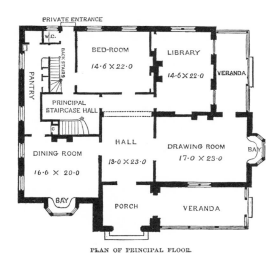

PLAN OF PRINCIPAL FLOOR.

*"Simple Picturesque Country House," Moodna, New York, 1853.*

*Nathaniel P. Willis Residence.* "The River, East from the Piazza."

*Nathaniel P. Willis Residence.* "The Cottage, from the Meadow."

And when all was said and done between the two, Vaux's Rural Gothic cottage "was so fitted among the evergreens, and adapted to every peculiarity of the site, that it appears to be almost surrounded by tall, flourishing trees, although broad stretches of distance in every direction, and extensive views of the river and mountain scenery are gained from the various windows, each view being a separated picture set in a frame of unfading foliage."

*Residence at Fordham, Highbridge, New York, ca. 1862.*

*Residence at Fordham.* Lodge for gardener.

DESIGN No. 36.

The Fordham house displays Vaux's fully developed ideas for the Rural Gothic stone villa, here located on a rise of land in a then rural area of New York, now the Bronx. The random ashlar rough stone walls, again of stone quarried on the site, are set off by finished quoins of New Brunswick stone which Vaux described as having a soft olive tint, a stone he favored for many of his Central Park bridges. For the interior of this large house Vaux provided a separate children's dining room and schoolroom. He also designed a lodge on the estate grounds for use as a gardener's cottage.

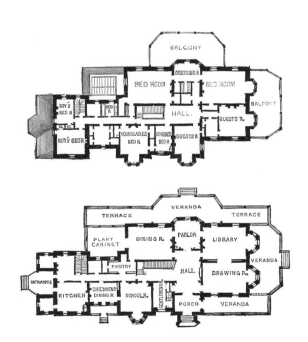

*"Irregular Stone Villa," Highbridge, New York.*

*Lydig M. Hoyt Residence, Staatsburg, New York, 1853.* South elevation.

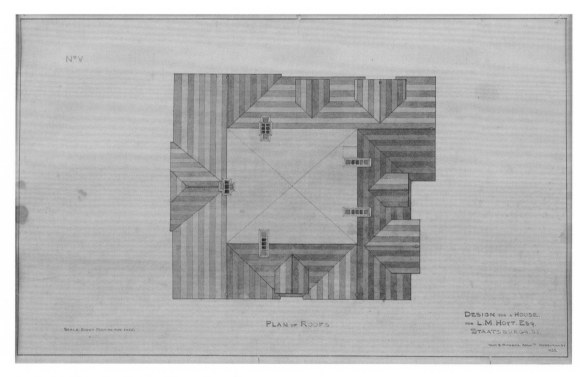

*Lydig M. Hoyt Residence.* Plan of roofs.

*Lydig M. Hoyt Residence.*

In *Villas and Cottages*, Vaux devotes the most extensive description of any of his designs to the Hoyt house. The site comprised one of the largest and finest Hudson riverfront settings, also known as The Point. In siting the house, Vaux carefully considered the approach road, beginning a third of a mile away, the preservation of the immediate landscape and the Hudson Valley views to the west and north. As to the house, characteristic of his architectural sensitivity, after opening a quarry on the site, Vaux chose a dark red pointing mortar: "In ten or twelve years this blue stone will begin to change its hue, and then every month will add new beauty to its color...after about fifteen years of exposure it assumes a delicate, luminous gray tint, each stone differing just so much from the one next to it as to give life and brilliance to the general effect in the sunlight."

The estate and house, which is in disrepair, are now part of New York State's Mills Norrie State Park facility and are currently the subject of discussion for restoration and possible adaptive reuse.

DESIGN No. 31.

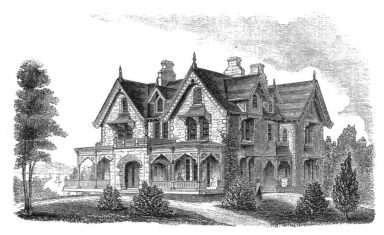

PERSPECTIVE VIEW.

*Vaux and Withers, "Picturesque Stone Country House," Staatsburg, New York, 1853.*

DESIGN No. 21.

PERSPECTIVE VIEW.

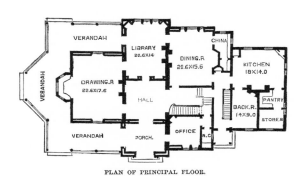

PLAN OF PRINCIPAL FLOOR.

*Vaux and Withers, "Irregular Wooden Country House," Worcester, Massachusetts, 1854.*

In his description of the Chamberlain house, Vaux took the occasion to express some thoughts at length on the place of women in architecture, inasmuch as "the leading edge of the plan was suggested by the wife of the proprietor, and the disposition of the rooms on the principal floor, with a few slight modifications, is in accordance with a pencil-sketch furnished me, as expressing her wishes on the subject." He writes further, "There can be no doubt that the study of domestic architecture…even if we allow the objections that might be raised by some against the actual practice of

architecture by women, such as the necessity for their climbing ladders, mingling with the mechanics and laborers during the progress of the work, and having frequently to attend to the superintendence of buildings during disagreeable weather…we must, nevertheless, see at once that there is nothing in the world, except want of inclination and opportunity, to prevent many of them from being thoroughly expert in architectural drawing, or from designing excellent furniture." Formerly the home of the president of Clark University, the house has been replaced by a library building.

*Henry H. Chamberlain Residence.*

*Henry H. Chamberlain Residence.*

*Henry H. Chamberlain Residence.*
Drawing room, typical Vaux bay
window design.

*William E. Warren Residence.* West, street facade.

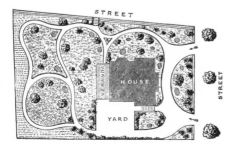

*William E. Warren Residence.* Plan of grounds.

Vaux exercised considerable care in the design of the Warren house, combining in it a goodly number of his favorite design elements. He devised a characteristic front facade of centered entryway, projecting porch above, and crowning gable with decorative bargeboards. Because the house is located on a steeply pitched corner site, he designed a rear elevation to soften the effect of multiple stories on the slope facing the Hudson. Here wide balconies and verandas afforded views of West Point and the Hudson highlands. The master bedroom's topmost balcony was arranged to be in the cooling shade of evening. It is one of the best preserved Vaux houses.

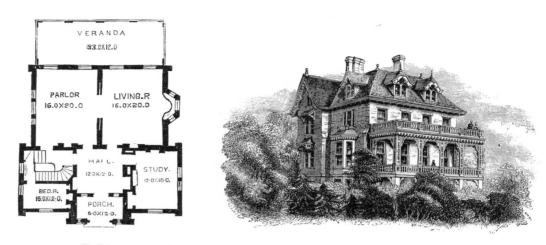

*"A Picturesque Country House,"* Newburgh, New York, 1857.

*William E. Warren Residence.* South facade.

*Ashcroft, Residence for Stephen H. Hammond, Geneva, New York, 1862.*

*Stephen H. Hammond Residence.*

Vaux was commissioned to remodel and substantially enlarge an existing cottage for Stephen Hammond, a successful New York State political figure who, after completing his legal training at Columbia University, went on to become a state senator and deputy attorney general. Ashcroft, which demonstrates a confident, generous example of Vaux's developed Rural Gothic style, appears to have been completed too late to be included in the 1864 edition of *Villas and Cottages*. The house is built of brick with a slate roof, and is consistent with the array of domestic qualities and details that he discusses in the book. One might agree with Vaux now that the turret, or bell cote tower over the front gable, purely ornamental in this case, enhances the design, imparting a proper sense of domestic monumentality for this important rural villa. It is today in need of extensive restoration.

*Stephen H. Hammond Residence.* Mrs. Hammond and her dog Tiny, 1880.

*Stephen H. Hammond Residence.* Gardens and greenhouse. A contemporary account credits Vaux with the design of the knot garden, seen in the foreground.

*Residence for Professor Raphael Pumpelly, Newport, Rhode Island, 1880.*

*Raphael Pumpelly Residence.*

Vaux was probably introduced to the remarkable Raphael Pumpelly at the Century Association in New York, where both were members. Attaining his wealth by securing a percentage of the natural resources he discovered and claimed—coal, iron ore, commercial forest lands—on assignment from Eastern financiers, Pumpelly, a geologist, explorer, scientist and sociologist among other avocations, asked Vaux to design a house for him in Newport. The result, related to stick-style domestic architecture then current, could be called "chalet" style,

*Residence for R. S. Bowne, Flushing, New York, 1885.*

a form Vaux had experimented with earlier in some of his houses and park structures. His use of the curved gable and dormer ends recalls the first Matthew Vassar villa design of 30 years before, ostensibly a properly decorative use in a resort area "cottage." Pumpelly's input in the construction may have been considerable; for example, he specified that for certain health reasons the interior walls be made of a special concrete formula which made their demolition exceedingly difficult when the last purchaser of the house decided to build anew.

The Bowne house came about five years after the Pumpelly house in a much plainer version of the "chalet" style. Although Vaux may have preferred to build in stone and brick, he was equally competent in wood construction. The drawings for both houses were made by Vaux's son Downing, a landscape architect in his own right and capable in building architecture as well.

FRONT VIEW.

*"Parisian Buildings for City Residents,"* 1857.

On moving his family to New York from Newburgh, Vaux became aware of the lack of suitable or sensible housing in the city. He therefore proposed the first design for New York City apartment dwellings, or "separate suites of rooms under the same roof" on the "European plan." This was a novel idea for New York of the 1850s where hotels, boarding houses or room rentals, whether for families or individuals, were the norm, except for crowded slum-like tenement buildings with hall or outside toilets. Vaux showed his plans and read his proposal before the June 2, 1857, meeting of the American Institute of Architects. The "Parisian Buildings" design, capped with a Hudson Valley domestic-style gable,

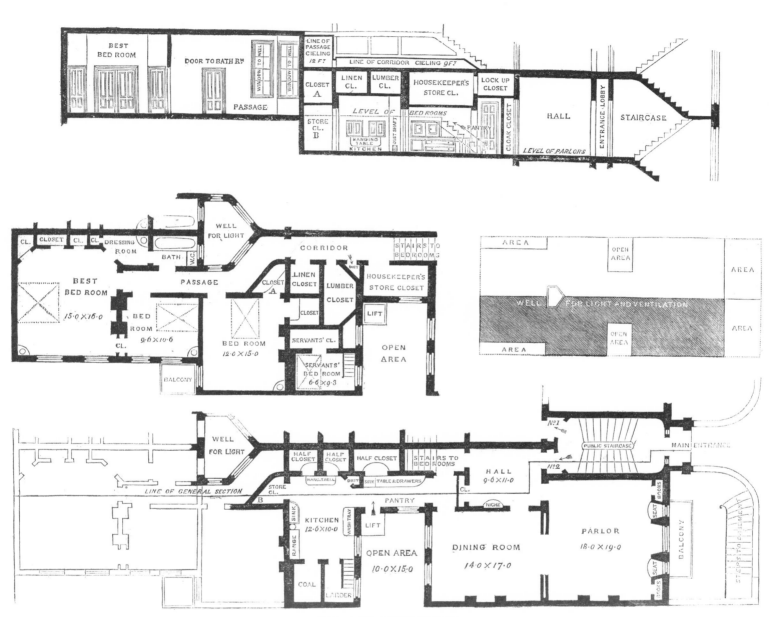

*"Plans of the Parisian Buildings."*

was a very well-thought-out semi-duplex arrangement for apartment living, albeit on a middle-class income. His full proposal (Appendix, pp. 251–254) considered economics, light, air, sanitation, fireproofing and much more in a practical design for urban living. The first apartment building in New York, however, came 12 years later, designed by Richard Morris Hunt, secretary, coincidentally, of the AIA meeting where Vaux read his paper. This was the Stuyvesant Apartments on East 18th Street in Manhattan. Vaux and his family moved into the building in 1869.

DESIGN No. 34.—(V. & W.)

PERSPECTIVE VIEW.

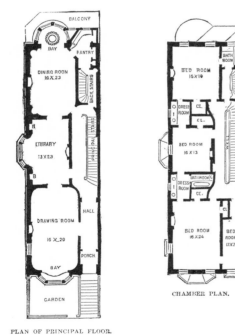

PLAN OF PRINCIPAL FLOOR.

*Vaux and Withers, "A Town House," New York, 1856.*

The drawing in *Villas and Cottages* differed from the final working drawings, according to Vaux, because the bay window for the library, overlooking the side court of the Church of the Ascension, was not built. Instead a light shaft was indented, anticipating a house alongside in the future. The original row of townhouses has been replaced by an apartment building that now abuts the church at Fifth Avenue and 10th Street in Manhattan. In a September 1858 article, the *Crayon* praised Vaux's design, especially the roof, which it compared favorably with the conventional horizontal cornices of its neighbors. John A. C. Gray, whose house this was, later secured the commission for the new Bank of New York building for Vaux and Withers. Gray also became a Central Park commissioner, which benefited Vaux and Olmsted. A *Crayon* article the next year gave very high praise to the architect Jacob Wrey Mould, Vaux's associate, for his work on the interior painting scheme for the house: "We are well aware that the building was designed by the clever hand of our friend Vaux, but when we entered this time a feeling of Mould came over us which did not originate with the weather, but with the interior painting. Bold as a lion in the selection of his colors, and grave as a judge in their combination, he dazzles with brightness, without offending the most fastidious taste; and as to design, we must pronounce it exquisite. Every line and every leaf betrays the spirit and life of a master hand." The comments seem well justified when one sees the work of Mould in the Central Park Terrace.

*John A. C. Gray Residence.*

·:-RESIDENCE OF Dᴿ BULL , WORCESTER , MASS·:- — GENERAL VIEW -·:·

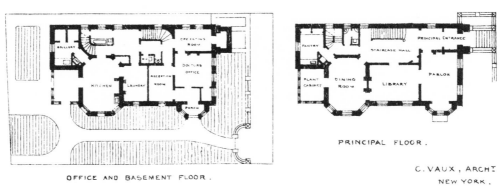

OFFICE AND BASEMENT FLOOR.

PRINCIPAL FLOOR.

C. VAUX , ARCHᵀ
NEW YORK.

*George T. Bull Residence, Worcester, Massachusetts, 1876.*

*George T. Bull Residence.*

Daniel Wesson of Smith and Wesson firearms built this house as a wedding present for his daughter Sarah when she married Dr. George Bull. For them, Vaux created one of his best urban designs, a High Victorian–style mansion. The exterior facades are of random ashlar courses of red granite from Connecticut quarries, accented with horizontal bands and trim of smooth gray granite. The detailing of the stone lintels, brackets and corbels is especially fine and craftsmanlike. Missing now are the iron corbels and roof cresting that completed the design. Despite the loss of these and some cast-iron ornamentation, the building is in very good condition. The granite fence separating the house from the street is said to have cost $10,000 alone. A portion of it was used some 40 years later in constructing the matching facade of the rear addition.

*George T. Bull Residence.* Front facade detail.

*George T. Bull Residence.*
Side entrance to medical office.

*George T. Bull Residence.* Front entrance. Formerly Post 10 of the Grand Army of the Republic, it now houses the Worcester Cultural Commission.

*Residence for Samuel J. Tilden, New York, 1881.*

Calvert Vaux's most illustrious client was perhaps Samuel J. Tilden, a wealthy corporate lawyer, former governor of New York State, and an "almost" president of the United States. In 1881 Tilden hired Vaux to remodel, and in effect combine, the two adjacent row houses he had previously purchased in the Gramercy Park area. Tilden's greatest pleasure was his collection of books, manuscripts and incunabula which he ultimately donated to the institution that is known as the New York Public Library, Astor, Lenox and Tilden Foundations. There, preserved in his personal scrapbook, is the watercolor sketch of the facade Vaux submitted for approval. It is shown precisely as built, except for details like the carved medallion heads of literary savants in the first-story decorative panel. These are of Shakespeare, Milton, Dante, Goethe and Benjamin Franklin, the latter a particular favorite of Tilden's. Decorative panels of foliage accent the facade whose Gothic quality is manifested by the arched, banded windows and pediment details at the roofline, which rises rather deliberately above the adjacent ones, as Vaux's lettering specifically notes on his watercolor sketch.

*Samuel J. Tilden Residence.* Watercolor sketch of facade.

*Samuel J. Tilden Residence, Gramercy Park South.*

When the National Arts Club purchased the Tilden house in 1906, they remodeled it to their purposes, "sacrificing" the entrance porch, a step that some have come to regret. During its demolition, the rubble was neatly assembled in front of the house on Gramercy Park South, as seen in the photograph. The elaborately carved balcony brackets are visible on the sidewalk at the right. Various interiors were changed, and although some of the Vaux decoration was dispersed, much of it was saved and reinstalled elsewhere in the building.

*Samuel J. Tilden Residence.* Front entrance.

*Samuel J. Tilden Residence.* Dining room.

While some of the house interiors were not changed, the library and dining room were entirely reconstructed to Vaux's design. They are described in contemporary accounts as two of the most spectacular, if not costly, interiors ever created for a residence in New York City. To speak only of the ceilings, if the stained glass dome of the library was extraordinary—one can see a portion of its bookcase wall through the dining room arch—the ceiling of the dining room may have been even more so. In the precisely 31-foot-square ceiling, each of the eight-inch-square, shimmering, turquoise-hue encaustic tiles, backed to an iron plate, was held in its own carved satinwood frame, the frames then held in a satinwood quadrant whose beams terminated in a half segment of an octagonal panel. The entire octagonal form comprised the carved satinwood center of the ceiling. Vaux's drawing is the merest schematic rendering for the decorative opulence of the actual thing. Below, satinwood wall panels accented with horizontal blue tile bands echoed the ceiling woods and colors. A lotus leaf motif in the ceiling cove recalled such carving in the exterior facade.

*Samuel J. Tilden Residence.* Study for dining room ceiling.
The dining room is now the gallery of the National Arts Club, but a small portion of the ceiling remains in the enlarged gallery space. Some of its wood panels have been moved to the club's ground floor.

which must be low, E. Richardson, box 138 Herald office

BOARDING—290 WEST TWENTIETH STREET.—
Rooms on second floor, unfurnished, for a family, in a house with modern improvements. References exchanged.

BOARDING—A SUIT OF ROOMS AND TWO OR three single rooms, with board, may be obtained at 1.5 West Fourteenth street; the house is strictly first class, and was leased by its present occupant last May, by whom it has been renewed and furnished with every comfort and convenience. Small children not received.

BOARDING—A PLEASANT SUIT OF FRONT ROOMS for a gentleman and his wife, and one single room for one or two single gentlemen, also, the basement, at 97 Clinton place.

BOARDING—A SMALL PRIVATE FAMILY WILL ACcommodate a single lady, or a single gentleman, or a gentleman and his wife with a handsome front or back room, on the first floor, with or without board, furnished or unfurnished. Apply at 48 Allen street.

BOARDING—TWO OR THREE FURNISHED rooms, pleasantly situated, to let, either with or without board. Apply at 12 Sixth avenue, near Amity street.

BOARDING, NO. 4 UNION SQUARE—HANDSOME rooms, with board, to be had by applying as above. References exchanged.

COMFORTABLE APARTMENTS CAN BE HAD FURnished, with or without partial board, in a first class house with modern improvements. Also an entire floor, communicating, suitable for a small respectable family or a party of gentlemen. Best of reference required. Call at 209 Greene street, near Clinton place.

FURNISHED HANDSOMELY—A SUIT OF ROOMS ON the first floor, consisting of parlor and two bedrooms to be let together or separate, with or without partial board, also two single rooms to let, at 61 Bleecker street. Bath, gas &c.

FURNISHED ROOM TO LET, WITH PARTIAL BOARD, to two gentlemen, front room, second story, on Broadway, handsomely furnished, Croton, gas, pantry, &c. Inquire at Dodworth's 806 Broadway

FURNISHED ROOMS TO LET—IN A FIRST CLASS house No. 38 Clinton place; an elegant suit of furnished parlors, with bedrooms on the same floor, kitchen, &c. Also, a single parlor and bedroom

FURNISHED ROOMS TO LET—ONE LARGE, WITH fire place and pantry, suitable for a party of three or four gentlemen; terms moderate; references exchanged. Apply at 12 Charlton street, near Varick street. The Sixth and Eighth avenue cars pass near the door.

FURNISHED ROOMS—A SMALL PRIVATE FAMILY, occupying a first class house in Ninth street a few doors west of Broadway, will let a part or the whole of their second floor, consisting of four rooms, all communicating, with every modern convenience, to a party of gentlemen of the first respectability. Apply at 113 9th street.

FURNISHED ROOMS TO LET—TWO LARGE ROOMS on second floor, with bath and gas. Hall bedroom, kitchen or basement if required. Also an unfurnished room, bedroom and kitchen, to permanent parties. Rent low. Apply at 313 Broome street.

strictly enforce the provisions of this section by its proper orders in respect thereto It shall be the duty of the said Board to prevent any booth or box for the distribution of tickets at any election to be erected or maintained within one hundred and fifty feet of any polling place within the said district.
Section 23. It shall be a misdemeanor, punishable by imprisonment in the county jail or penitentiary if there be a penitentiary in the county where the conviction is had, not less than one year nor exceeding two years, or by fine not less than two hundred and fifty dollars, for any person, without justifiable or excusable cause, to use personal violence upon any elector in the Metropolitan Police District, or upon any member of the police force thereof, when in the discharge of his duty, or for any such member to neglect making any arrest for an offence against the law of the State, committed in his presence, or for any person not a member of the police force to falsely represent himself as being such member, with a fraudulent design.
Published by order of the Board of Commissioners of the Metropolitan Police District.
F. A. TALLMADGE, Supt. of Police.

PLANS FOR THE CENTRAL PARK.—THE BOARD OF Commissioners of the Central Park offer the following premiums for the four designs for laying out the Park, which may be selected:—
For the first.....................................$2,000
For the second....................................1,000
For the third.......................................750
For the fourth......................................500
The plans to become the property of the Board
Topographical plans may be consulted and particulars obtained at the office of the Board, room 10 Bank of Commerce Building. A limited number of photographic sketches of the ground may be obtained by applying to the Clerk of the Board.
All designs must be presented to the Board by the first day of March, 1858
The Board reserve the right to reject any or all plans.
JNO A C GRAY,
CHARLES W. ELLIOTT, } Committee.
ANDREW H. GREEN.

HOUSES, ROOMS, &C., WANTED.

3 SECOND HAND TEN PIN ALLEYS WANTED.—ADdress Bowling, Herald office.

$10,000.—MERCHANDISE WANTED IN EXchange for city property and Western lands Address confidentially J. L., box 2,849 Post office.

$50,000.—WE ARE AUTHORIZED TO OFFER this amount to loan, at moderate rates, on first class stocks or bonds. W. & M. H. WARD, 47 Exchange place.

HOUSE WANTED—BY A PERSON OF EXPERIENCE. A furnished boarding house, in a genteel and convenient location. Address H. S. Broadway Post office, stating location, rent and number of boarders or lodgers in the house.

PART OF A SMALL HOUSE WANTED—ON THE WEST side of the city, for a gentleman and wife. No children. Rent must be moderate. Address for two days, stating full particulars as to price, situation, &c., Island, Herald office

PART OF A HOUSE WANTED—ON THE WEST side of the city, below Fourteenth street and above Bleecker; rent must be moderate. Address B. COLMAN, Brooklyn Post office.

TO story house, No. 20 Tenth street, between the Fifth and Sixth avenue, to a respectable family of grown persons. Gas in the house in the basement.

TO LET—FROM NOW UNTIL FIRST OF NEXT MAY— A very desirable two story and attic cottage, situated in Hanover place, Brooklyn and furnished throughout in a comfortable style. Rent low to a good tenant. Apply at 18 Hanover place, Brooklyn.

TO LET—THE UPPER PART OF HOUSE 184 at lante street, Brooklyn, L. I.

TO LET—UNFURNISHED, TO A VERY SMALL QUIET and unobtrusive family only, for $136, in advance for six months, the parlor, alcove and tea room (entire parlor floor) dormitory and attic room, on back room floor; rooms on upper floor, with privilege in kitchen, vault, etc. Hot and cold water, bell and register in each room. Occupant has no children or boarders. A rare opportunity for a suitable party desiring the exclusiveness of an entire house. Possession immediately. Apply at No. 130 West Fifteenth street, basement entrance.

TO LET—TO A SMALL, RESPECTABLE AMERICAN family (no others will be noticed), the upper part of house No. 8 First street; three rooms on second and one on third floor. Possession 1st of Nov. For particulars inquire on premises.

TO LET—A SMALL COTTAGE HOUSE, NO. 32 WEST Twenty first street, between Fifth and Sixth avenues. Apply to RONKON & BLAKEVELL, corner of Broadway and Thirty fourth street.

TO LET—A NEAT THREE STORY BRICK HOUSE, consisting 12 rooms, with bath and gas and large yard, only two blocks west of Broadway, near Prince street. Inquire at 108 Green street. Possession immediately, with furniture if required.

TO LET—PARLOR THREE BEDROOMS, KITCHEN and closets, on third floor of the first class house No. 132 West Thirty sixth street, with bath room. Rent $10 per month. Apply as above.

TO LET—STORE AND DWELLING 444 FOURTH AVEnue, near Thirty first street—Contains store and cellar, and seven or eight rooms. Rent $450 for the whole. Also, store corner of Thirty first street and Broadway. Also store and cellar corner of Twenty fourth street and Fourth avenue. Apply to R. S. RINEHIMER, 319 Fourth avenue.

TO LET—SECOND STORY, CONSISTING OF FOUR rooms, with or without basement, at No. 10 Bethune street; gas and water throughout. Rent low to a small family. Immediate possession.

TO LET—AN ENGLISH BASEMENT HOUSE NO. 129 West Twenty eighth street, near Seventh avenue; has chandeliers and gas fixtures throughout. Will be let very low till May to a good tenant. Inquire of RICHARD WALTERS & CO., auctioneers, 13 Henry street

TO LET—TO PHYSICIANS OR DENTISTS, FRONT basement office, tea room, bedroom, (with use of front parlor if required) furnished or unfurnished. No physicians in the neighborhood. Would answer a man and wife. Apply at 14 Wooster street.

TO LET—A NEW THREE STORY BROWN STONE English basement house, in one of the best locations in Brooklyn. Apply at 205 Sackett street, or to J. W. MARTINE, corner of Atlantic and Clinton streets.

*New York Herald, Friday, October 30, 1857.*

# Landscape Design and Architecture for Landscape

WHILE it was Downing's initiative that brought him to the United States, the critical event in Calvert Vaux's career came about on his own doing. It was his successful effort to force a competition for the design of Central Park. The opportunity came about first because of the influence of his mentor and partner, Downing, whose continual campaign on the need for a major public park in New York City was shared by some of its most influential citizens, especially the editor and publicist William Cullen Bryant. These two had been pushing hard for over a decade and many others had joined in. Just as he was chosen by President Fillmore to design the nation's most important public grounds in Washington, D.C., Downing, were he alive, would have been the obvious choice to design the park. Secondly, apart from his own professional training in architecture and knowledge of English and Continental parks, estates and landscapes, Vaux came from a notable tradition of architectural competitions, marked, for example, by the enormous publicity that attended that for London's Houses of Parliament, won in 1836 by Sir Charles Barry. And finally, Vaux had previously developed personal and professional relationships, some stemming from Newburgh, especially with two influential New Yorkers. One was John A. C. Gray for whom Vaux and Withers had designed a Fifth Avenue townhouse. Later, through Gray, a director of the Bank of New York, they were awarded the commission for the bank's new building. Gray also happened to be a vice chairman of the Board of Central Park Commissioners. A second commissioner was Charles W. Elliot, who also served as the board's secretary and had been a sometime landscape gardener and former student of Downing's. Vaux, attracted by an anonymously written essay on "Barns," had quoted it extensively in his book, only to discover later that Elliot was the author. This same Elliot had also suggested to Olmsted, at a chance meeting, that he apply for the job as Central Park Superintendent.

The board, lacking funds and uncertain on how to proceed with the creation of the park, had in early 1867 adopted the plan, at this point gratuitously provided, of its engineer-in-chief, Egbert L. Viele. It was based on his topographic survey of the grounds, showed little or no landscape design imagination and had been criticized in the press. Vaux campaigned against it,

citing its manifold defects, declaring that were it to be carried out "It would be a disgrace to the city and to the memory of Mr. Downing."

By August of that year the situation had changed. On the 25th of the month, the Central Park commissioners met, Gray and Elliot present, and "Mr. [James] Hogg called up his resolution in regard to advertising for plans, as follows: Resolved that the board do now advertise for plans for laying out Central Park, and that they offer for the best plan chosen $2,000; for the second, $1,000" and so forth. That Vaux had been at work here could be ascertained by the concluding sentence of the meeting, which was reported in the *New-York Daily Times* the next day: "The thanks of the Board were returned to Mr. C. Vaux for a handsome work on Rural Architecture presented some time since." He had obviously taken care to provide the commissioners with copies of his recently published *Villas and Cottages*.

Meanwhile, Olmsted had also been at work. Anxious to secure the job of superintendent, he had canvassed influential men of the day to secure their names on a petition recommending him. Washington Irving and Peter Cooper had signed; Asa Gray had written separately. Success came on September 11 when Olmsted was appointed superintendent under Viele, to begin the work of clearing out the park grounds.

Vaux and Olmsted had first met at Downing's house. Vaux was familiar with *Walks and Talks of an American Farmer in England,* in which Olmsted had demonstrated his intelligent understanding of agricultural practice and sensitivity to landscape design. Satisfied to see the competition publicly announced and the advertisement appear in the press on October 30, Vaux now sought out Olmsted to join in preparing an entry. Olmsted's workaday knowledge of the grounds would be of enormous help, if not essential. Reluctant at first, Olmsted cleared it with his boss, Viele, and agreed. The plan was prepared in Vaux's Manhattan apartment on East 18th Street. "Greensward" won, Central Park was built, and it became the nation's prototypical country park in the city, the urban-environmental focus that provoked the need for related planning concepts and methods that thereafter significantly affected the face of American cities.

*Greensward Presentation Study Number 4.*

Together with their narrative description of their Greensward plan, the designers submitted 11 studies, ten of them comprising before and after views of an area as it existed and the "effect proposed" in their design—a device used earlier to good effect by English designers, especially Humphrey Repton. The views were keyed to a miniature park plan at the top of each study. Typical of these is Number 4, a view just inside the western edge of the park at about 73rd Street. Vaux's "after" watercolor sketch faces northeast toward Vista Rock, now the site of the Belvedere, across what became the widest part of the Lake. Although the small turreted pavilion at the left, on the spit of land known as the Hernshead, was never built, Vaux bided his time and built one very much like it ten years later in Buffalo's Delaware Park (p. 155).

*Greensward Presentation Study Number 4.*
Present outlines.
Dimly seen on the left horizon is the fire watchtower on Vista Rock, the highest point in the park, the future site for the Belvedere and its structures.

*Greensward Presentation Study Number 4.* Effect proposed.

An added element in the Greensward submission was a small painting by Jervis McEntee, the Hudson River School painter who was Vaux's brother-in-law. It is inscribed "J.M.E. 1858 View from Terrace Site looking toward Vista Rock and showing proposed site for ornamental water." One of Vaux's clients, Raphael Pumpelly (p. 90), took McEntee along on one of his exploratory trips in the West in 1882 to make sketches for his reports. McEntee found subjects like Yellowstone Canyon "too savage," but did make "charming" sketches of milder scenes with Rocky Mountain backgrounds.

*Jervis McEntee,* View from Terrace Site, 1858.

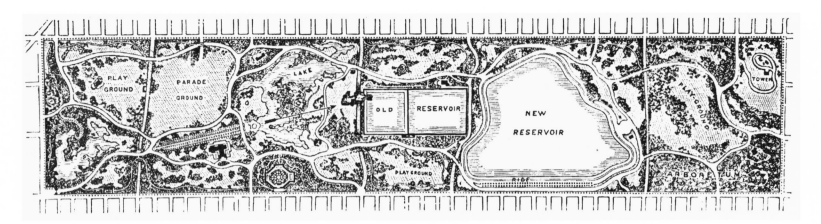

*Greensward Plan*, 1858.

This schematic version, reproduced in the press immediately after the prizes were announced, was the same as the small key plan at the top of each of the presentation studies. It showed only the few major features of the design, which was fully and richly detailed on the 12-foot-long competition drawing submitted to the commissioners.

*Greensward Plan*, 1858, *Detail*. Water Terrace.

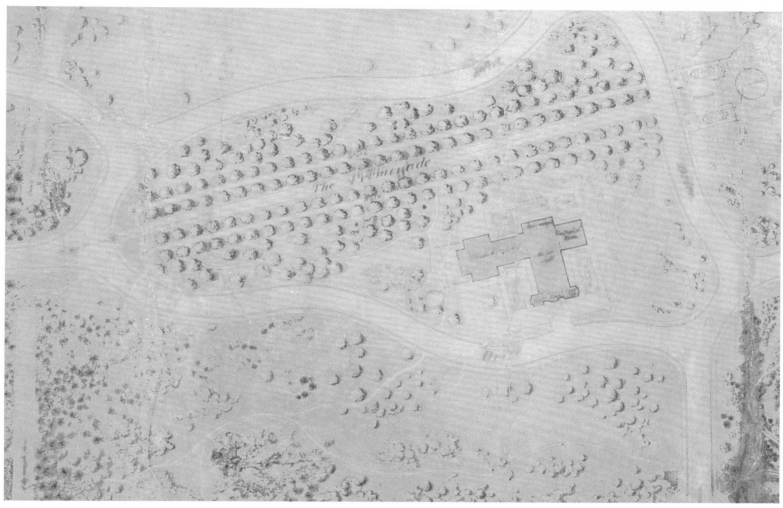

*Greensward Plan, 1858, Detail.* The Avenue, or Promenade.

These details from the original Greensward drawing of 1858 show the two major formal elements of the plan, the Promenade and Water Terrace. Straight rows of American elms line the Promenade, now called the Mall, and lead just north to the Water Terrace, now Bethesda Terrace. This strong diagonal with its line of view was deliberately created by the designers to counter the very long rectangle of the park itself. The line of view was emphasized by a dotted line drawn straight through the center of both the Promenade and Terrace, continuing directly across the Skating Pond, now the Lake, to the highest point in the park, Vista Rock. Here they proposed a martello tower be erected, on the lines of the circular stone forts built along the Irish and English coasts to counter the threat of Napoleon, perhaps a suggestion made by Vaux. In time, the structure evolved into a small castle, on Vista Rock's Belvedere platform. As for the original Water Terrace, Vaux considered its perfected result the best thing he had ever done (p. 114).

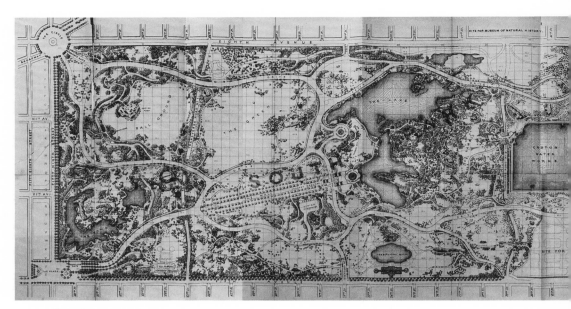

*Central Park Map, 1873.*

About three years before the park was declared to be "completed," Olmsted ordered a complete horticultural survey. The park was divided into 100-foot squares, seen above, in which every growing plant was tallied and listed. The list even included a giant sequoia (*Sequoia gigantea,* Endl. / *S. giganteum,* Buchholtz) located then at a spot just west of what is now Conservatory Garden at 105th Street. This map was precise and accurate.

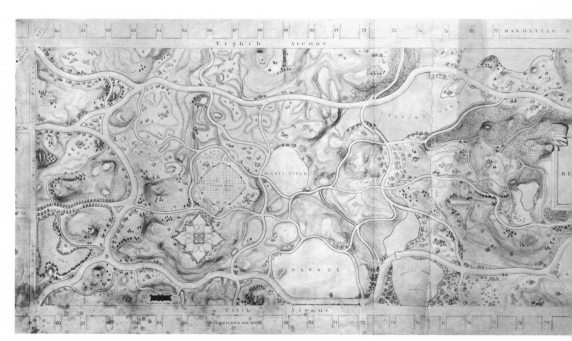

*Roswell Graves, Jr., and George E. Waring, Central Park Competition Entry Number 29, 1858.*

The only plan drawing known to be in existence, apart from Greensward, of the original 33 Central Park competition entries is Number 29, "Art the Handmaiden of Nature," by Graves and Waring. Their accompanying narrative stressed the importance of drainage, and in their wisdom Olmsted and Vaux later chose Waring to devise the drainage system for their design. Waring went on to become one of the outstanding sanitary engineers of the day.

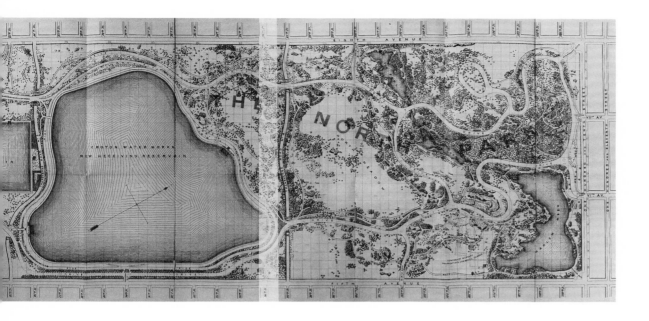

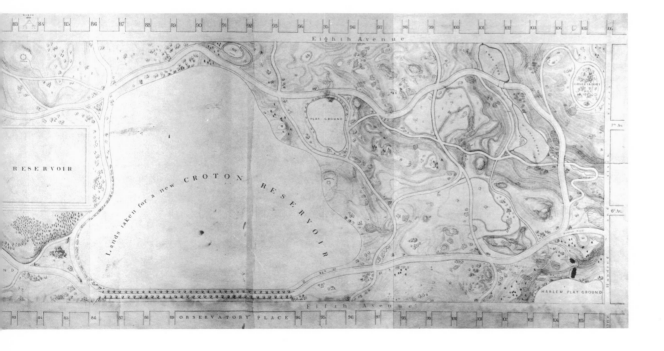

*The Water Terrace, 1864.*

With his Terrace, Vaux gave New York and America a magnificent composition. In England and the Continent he had seen the work of gardeners and architects practicing the art of transition from the formal to the gardenesque to the natural, from *rampe douce* to stairway to terrace. His Central Park solution, beginning at the termination of the Mall's *allée,* involved a combination of multiple wide stairways, a covered arcade, curving ramps, a generous terrace-esplanade with fountain, seating, a boat landing and pathways into the surrounding landscape. It was surely equivalent in conception to the finest palace, estate or garden designs in Europe. On tall poles, gonfalon pennants, fluttering overhead, completed the setting. *Harper's Monthly Magazine* declared simply: "The Central Park is the finest work of art ever executed in this country."

*John Bachmann,* View of Central Park, *1875.*

Four major works by Vaux are shown in Bachmann's bird's-eye view: Bethesda Terrace in the center, Bow Bridge at right center, the Boathouse at left center and, in the left foreground, drawn far out of place, the Belvedere platform and castle. The castle was exactly on line with the long axis of the Promenade across the Lake. A closer look shows some of Vaux's rustic structures, while an even closer look shows the silent electric boats Olmsted brought in, which circumnavigated the lake. One could embark or disembark at any of six landings.

*Central Park, The Mall,* 1906. Summer.

Olmsted and Vaux's set piece, the Mall, with its American elms, formed the majestic canopy through which sunlight filtered down on a sunny day to create lacy patterns of light and shade beneath. The Avenue was surely equal to any in Europe. The elms are now sadly decimated.

*Central Park, The Mall,* 1906. Winter.

The stone railings define the stairway leading down to the Terrace. The view faces south and shows the ornamental detailing by Jacob Wrey Mould, who also designed the Music Stand, seen at the right in both pictures.

*The Dairy, 1870.*

Designed to serve children, the Dairy was located in the "Childrens Department" of the lower park, together with the Carousel, Children's Cottage and Rustic Shelter. It provided "perfectly fresh pure milk" at "a moderate price." On the greensward in front were to be kept cows, lambs and chickens for the amusement of the children seated in the open gallery.

*The Boathouse, 1872–1876.*

Architectural assistants to Vaux in the detailing of the Boathouse were Mould and
Julius Munchwitz. The upper decks offered views over the Lake and landscape. A
silent electric boat with its passengers sits alongside the mooring.

*Mineral Springs Pavilion, 1868.*

If the Dairy was bucolic, the Spa, as it was called, for adults, was flamboyant. It was originally located within a grove of trees which the concessionaire, with the connivance of a parks commissioner, managed to have cut down.

Noteworthy in its elaborate interior detailing is the ceiling design which presages that of the Tilden house of a decade later (p. 104). In the spirit of curative recreation, 30 varieties of mineral water were served here.

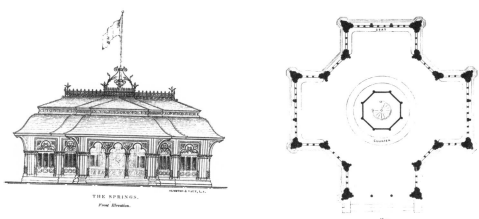

*Mineral Springs Pavilion.* Front elevation and plan.

*Mineral Springs Pavilion.* Interior.

*Glade Arch,* 1860. Constructed of New Brunswick stone except for the vault facing, which is Philadelphia pressed brick.

Forty-six bridges were ultimately built for Central Park, the great majority designed by Vaux or under his supervision. These were integral parts of four separate circulation systems: carriage roadways, pedestrian paths, bridle paths and depressed transverse roads to carry crosstown traffic under the park. They ranged from long tunnels blasted out of solid rock to rustic bridgelets over streams, and they enabled visitors to travel and concentrate on their own specific means of park enjoyment without the danger or distraction of those moving faster or slower.

*Denesmouth Bridge, 1859.* Watercolor rendering submitted to the Board of Commissioners prior to construction.

Vaux, in charge of architecture in the park, demonstrated his talent for bridge design in three modes: masonry, cast iron and wood. His arches faced with stone tended to present a formal, simplified classic appearance. Long cast-iron bridges came as elegant spans, while short ones were often fancifully decorative. Wood bridges were rustic in spirit and construction, as was an occasional boulder bridge. With Central Park the first of its kind, Vaux was highly conscious of his position and made an especially creative effort in this area.

*Rustic Bridge in Ramble, 1863.*

*Oak Bridge, 1860.*

*Bow Bridge, 1860.*

The photographs on these two and the preceding two pages are part of a special collection at the British Architectural Library of the Royal Institute of British Architects. They were among a large group of photographs brought to England in 1867 by Professor William Ware of Columbia University, representing the work of the then most notable American architects. They were part of his response to current opinions in England denigrating the artistic quality of American architecture (although praising American engineering). Vaux, among those asked to contribute examples, included these five Central Park bridge pictures as part of his group.

*Balcony Bridge, 1860.*

*Terrace Bridge, 1861.*

*Bridle Path Arch, 1864.*

*"Shaded Seat."* Vaux reproduced this as a vignette in the 1864 edition of *Villas and Cottages.*

*The Children's Shelter.*

*Prospect Park, View from the Reservoir Looking West, before 1861.*

The beginnings of Prospect Park were not auspicious. Egbert L. Viele had been
hired in 1861 by the Brooklyn Board of Park Commissioners to make a topographic
study of the intended grounds. This then had evolved into a park plan. Brooklyn,
third largest city in the nation at that time and growing in population and prosperity,
was ready to build a grand public park, matching New York's, but the Civil War
intervened and the plan was shelved. When the park idea was taken up again in 1865,
Vaux, now with some eight years of Central Park experience, was asked to resurvey
the boundaries and report on them. He walked the area, at times with the very
much concerned park board president, James S. T. Stranahan, a wealthy businessman
who had been advocating the idea for many years. When Vaux's recommendations
were reviewed, Viele's plan was set aside, as was his Central Park plan seven years
before. Its greatest and obvious fault was that it was bisected by Flatbush Avenue,
one of Brooklyn's major traffic arteries.

Vaux's plan was a single entity, containing a large greensward, a lake two and a half times larger than Central Park's, with islands, and groupings of pastoral elements enhancing the whole. Writing to Olmsted, who was now in California, Vaux sent along a sketch plan in his letter of January 9, 1865. Olmsted wrote back in March: "Your plans are excellent, of course. You go at once to the essential starting points, and I hope the Commissioners are wise enough to comprehend it." Vaux recommended that the single plot of land be extended west of Flatbush Avenue, as shown by his dotted lines, and the previously purchased property on the east be exchanged for the new land.

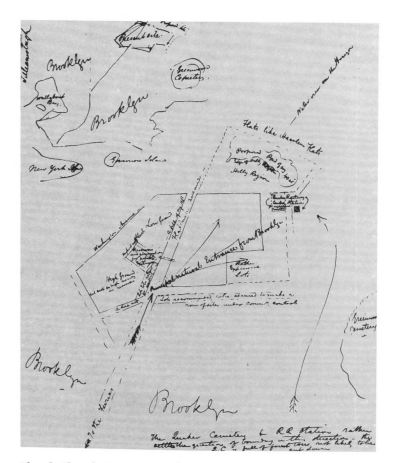

*Sketch Plan for Prospect Park, January 9, 1865.*

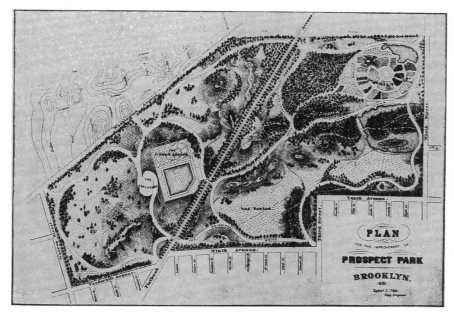

*Egbert L. Viele, "Plan for the Improvement of Prospect Park," 1861.*
Viele's plan encompassed both sides of Flatbush Avenue. The park was ultimately created on the further, western side.

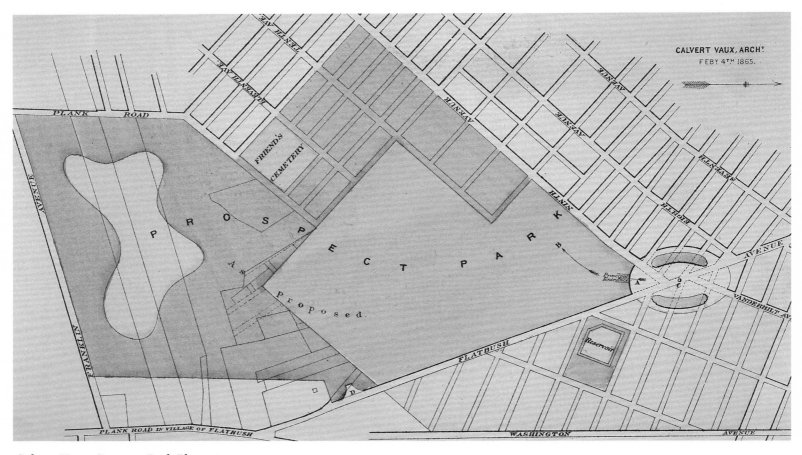

*Calvert Vaux, Prospect Park Plan, 1865.*

As Olmsted anticipated, the commissioners were wise enough to accept Vaux's plan, assisted by a clear drawing that Vaux had provided them in February 1865. Vaux now embarked on a campaign to persuade Olmsted to return to join him in carrying out the design. He was again successful, and Olmsted arrived in New York in November. In January 1866, one year after the Vaux-Stranahan walkabout, Olmsted, Vaux and Co. formally submitted their plan to the commissioners. Accepted, it was carried out, the work proceeding with relative calm under Stranahan's enlightened protection, and the result, highly satisfying to the designers, is held by many to be their finest work. Further, Vaux's plan enabled the land across Flatbush Avenue later to become Brooklyn's Botanic Garden and Parade Ground, adding substantially to the city's open space preserve.

*Olmsted, Vaux and Co., Design for Prospect Park, 1866–1867.*

*Site for Prospect Park, before 1861.*

*The Long Meadow, 1902.*

Three successive stretches of gently rolling greensward formed the Long Meadow, each area entered through a tree-landscaped "gate," each drawing the visitor along to explore the mystery beyond. The Long Meadow extended for almost a mile.

*The Dairy, 1869.*

As in Central Park, the Dairy here dispensed milk and other refreshments and
provided a private room for child care. In addition to grazing sheep, cows were
pastured nearby on the Green, assuring a fresh supply of milk. The building no
longer exists.

*Rustic Arbor, ca. 1868.*

*Swiss Thatched Cottage, Prospect Park, ca. 1867.*

The Thatched Cottage, one of the park's earliest rustic shelters, could be seen to the left of the pathway soon after entering the grounds through Meadowport Arch. It no longer exists.

*Olmsted, Vaux and Co., Concert Grove.*

*Concert Grove House, 1872.*

*Concert Grove Pavilion and House, 1906.*

Prospect Park's Concert Grove reflects the prevalence of German music societies in Brooklyn and is the one formal element reminiscent of Central Park's Mall and Music Stand. The design here focused on a music stand set on a small island off the eastern edge of the Lake. A system of walks, raised terraces and concourses fanned out from this edge in a concentric pattern. One could listen to music seated in carriages in either of the two carriage concourses, European style, or from the pedestrian concourse situated between

them. The ambient qualities of this pleasure ground were enhanced by fountains, sculptured likenesses of famous composers (Mozart, Beethoven, von Weber), decorative posts and railings and trees and plantings. Vaux designed two buildings for the far end, the Concert Grove House, containing a restaurant and comfort station, and the Concert Grove Pavilion, an imaginative "Oriental" structure where one could sit with one's refreshments. The former is gone but the latter has been restored.

*Proposed Carriage Concourse Shelter, 1869.*

*Concert Grove Pavilion, 1874.*

The Shelter is counted among the series of experimental, engineered or innovative designs Vaux came up with during his career. He felt this kind of structure was not inappropriate for the festive, relaxed atmosphere of a park setting, as was his example of Victorian orientalia in the Concert Grove Pavilion. He was able to build a smaller version of the Shelter later in Brooklyn's Fort Greene Park (p. 144).

*Meadowport Arch, 1868.*

*Endale Arch, 1867.*

Two of the series of bridges that Vaux designed for Prospect Park are located just inside the main pedestrian entrance. Endale Arch is a long, dark tunnel, Meadowport is less so; the former leads southeast into the park, the latter southwest. Both have the specific purpose of providing, just after leaving the city's urban environment, an interlude preparatory to the sudden, dramatic pastoral vista beyond of greensward, as far as one can see. This kind of apprehending experience was specifically intended by the designers. Among other major Vaux bridges are the Cleft Ridge Span,

*Cleft Ridge Span, 1871.*

*Cleft Ridge Span, View in 1911.*

*Nethermead Arches, 1868.*

Terrace Bridge and Nethermead Arches, under which converge a stream, bridle path and pedestrian way, and over which is the carriage drive. He also designed East Wood Arch, of which three drawings, now in the collection of the New York Public Library, appear to be the only known remaining original drawings of Prospect Park. Vaux's original rustic Lullwood Bridge has been replaced by a McKim, Mead and White–designed structure.

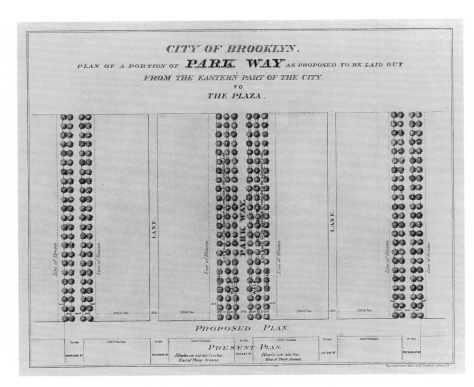

*Olmsted, Vaux & Co., Plan for Eastern Parkway, Brooklyn, 1868.*

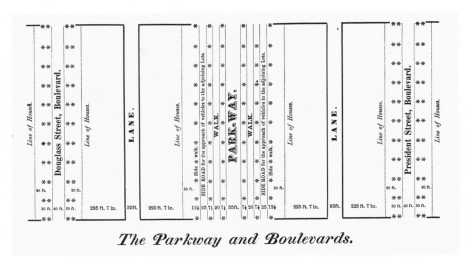

*Olmsted, Vaux and Co., Plan for the Parkway and Boulevards, Eastern Parkway, Brooklyn, 1873.*

In the idealized mid-1860s conception of Olmsted and Vaux, Prospect Park was to be one node in a system of parks with interconnected parkways that were to spread throughout the city. In Brooklyn they created two versions of their parkway, loosely based on European models, radiating out from Prospect Park. The first, Ocean Parkway, completed in 1868, ends reasonably at a recreational area, Coney Island. Eastern Parkway, the second, whose later developed plan shows it to be the basis for a linear residential community, did not end at a park but stopped at a cross street. This was as far as they got. However, almost simultaneously, Olmsted and Vaux were successfully carrying out this concept of an entire system in Buffalo (p. 151).

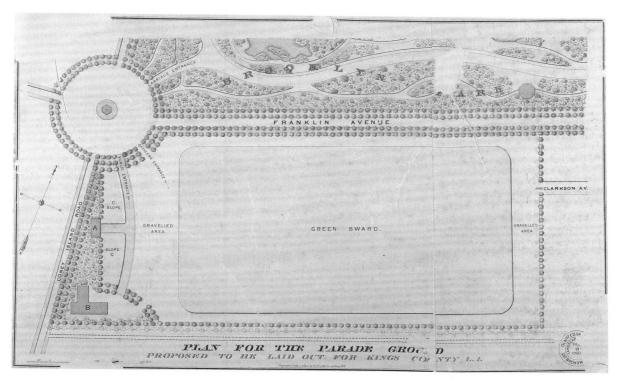

*Olmsted, Vaux and Co., Parade Ground for Kings County, Long Island, New York, 1867.*

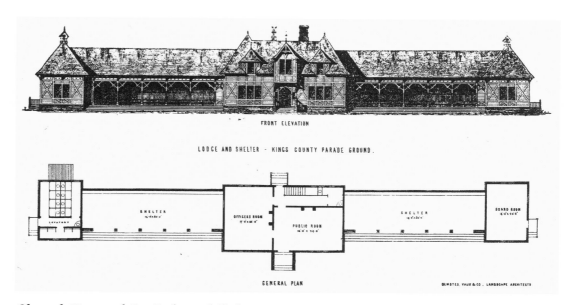

*Olmsted, Vaux and Co., Lodge and Shelter, Kings County Parade Ground, 1869.*

The parade ground, initially destined for Prospect Park but separated from it as a result of Vaux's judicious recommendation, shared, however, an inviting circular entryway with the southern end of the park. Its rectangular central greensward for drills was surrounded by gravelled areas for watchers, who could also watch from the Lodge and Shelter Vaux designed for its western end. A better spectator view could be had from the raised wings of this pavilion, which was the forerunner of a much larger version he designed for Buffalo a few years later (p. 155).

*Olmsted, Vaux and Co., Fort Greene Park, Brooklyn.* View in 1904.

Olmsted and Vaux's design for Fort Greene Park combined country elements with formal public-ceremonial areas on high ground, which afforded wide vistas across New York's waterways. The park has undergone several changes over time and is now notable as the site of the Martyrs' Memorial, an underground vault containing the remains of Revolutionary War soldiers who were taken prisoner and died aboard British prison ships in nearby Wallabout Bay. Many landscape elements are still extant, but the site of Vaux's original sheltering structure is now occupied by the memorial's symbol, erected in 1908 and purported to be the world's tallest Doric column.

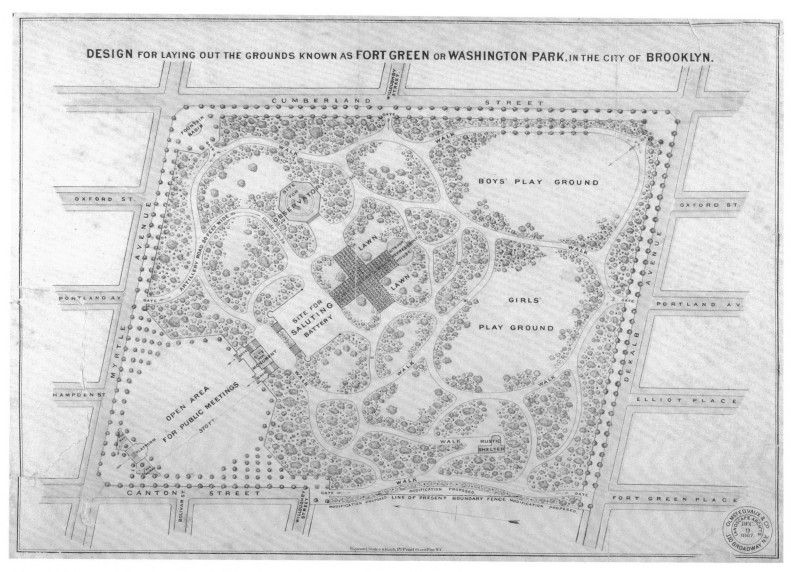

*Olmsted, Vaux and Co., Design for Laying Out Fort Greene Park, Brooklyn, 1867.*

*Frederick Law Olmsted, Calvert Vaux, Riverside Park, New York.* View in 1901.

Olmsted himself provided the initial plan for Riverside Park in 1875, three years after the cessation of his partnership with Vaux, who was then occupied with major architectural projects, especially the Metropolitan and American Natural History museums. In 1877 Vaux, also superintending architect of the Department of Public Parks, worked to complete Riverside Park as best he could, although under heavy political pressure at that time because of his efforts to protect Central Park from abuse and encroachment. Ultimately Riverside Park and Drive succeeded in attracting the residential development for which it was intended. The long curving line of apartment buildings along the Drive, following the original 1875 plan, today comprises New York City's most attractive urban face.

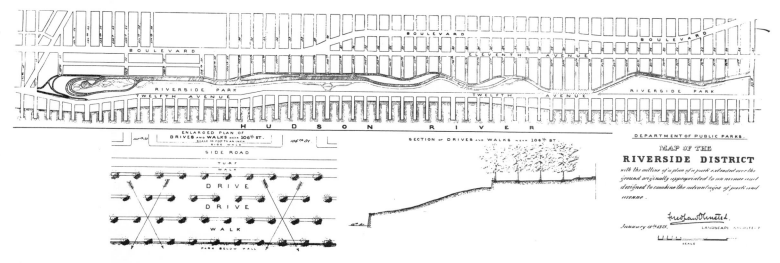

*Frederick Law Olmsted, Map of the Riverside District, New York, 1875.*

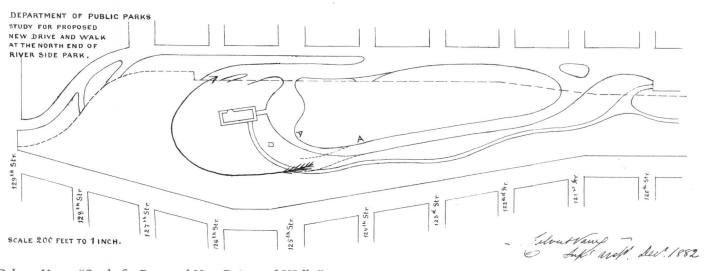

*Calvert Vaux, "Study for Proposed New Drive and Walk," 1882.*

*Olmsted, Vaux and Co., Morningside Park, New York.*

Morningside Park, characterized by one of the deepest physical clefts on Manhattan Island, separates Morningside Heights from Harlem. Rocky and precipitous, the area was not capable of being turned into real estate plots in accord with the city's grid plan and was thus turned over to the designers to be formed into a park. They made the best of it, planning an alpine garden and scenery for this "picturesque

cliff of rock." Olmsted, who wrote the park report and was ever concerned with connecting parks with parkways, noted that Morningside's southern edge was just "three minutes' walk" from the northeast corner of Central Park. Because the comparative street levels presented something of a problem in the connection between their entrance gates, even a tiny parkway could not be considered.

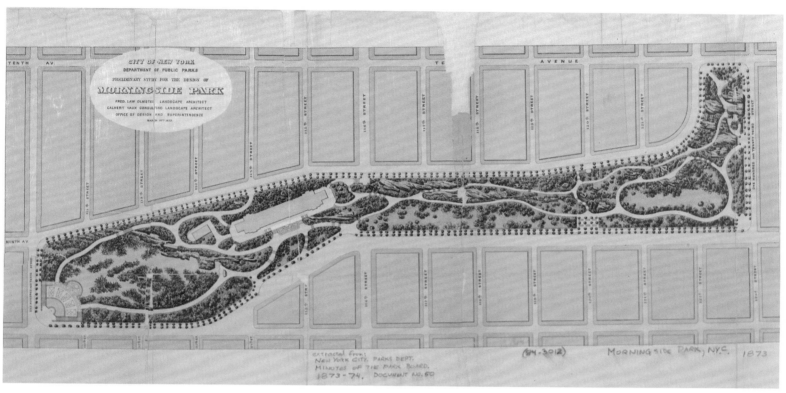

*Olmsted, Vaux and Co., Morningside Park, New York, 1873.* Revised general plan.

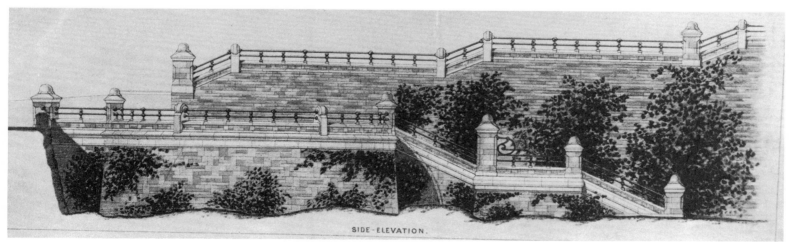

*Olmsted, Vaux and Co., Jacob Wrey Mould, Morningside Park, New York.* Embankment and stairway design.

Olmsted and Vaux succeeded in Buffalo where in New York
they could not. Here they designed a park and parkway
system, approaching their ideal of public park grounds
designed for a variety of individual recreational uses,
connected by 200-foot-wide, tree-lined parkways which in
themselves could convey something of a park-like atmosphere
to those living in neighborhoods nearby. Indeed, a parkway
would even convey the anticipation of a park at its terminus.
Delaware Park was the park itself, with pastoral scenery and
trees screening out the city, stretches of greensward and a
lake, for which swans were imported from Hamburg, as in
Central Park. The choice of the park site in north Buffalo was
a considered one, between two large adjacent green areas,
Forest Lawn Cemetery and the grounds of the State Insane
Asylum, intending to preserve for Buffalo an extensive,
permanent rural area. Additionally, Parkside, a suburb of
"sylvan character," adjoined the park on its north and east
sides. The three public grounds are precisely described in the
Buffalo Park Reports (p. 153).

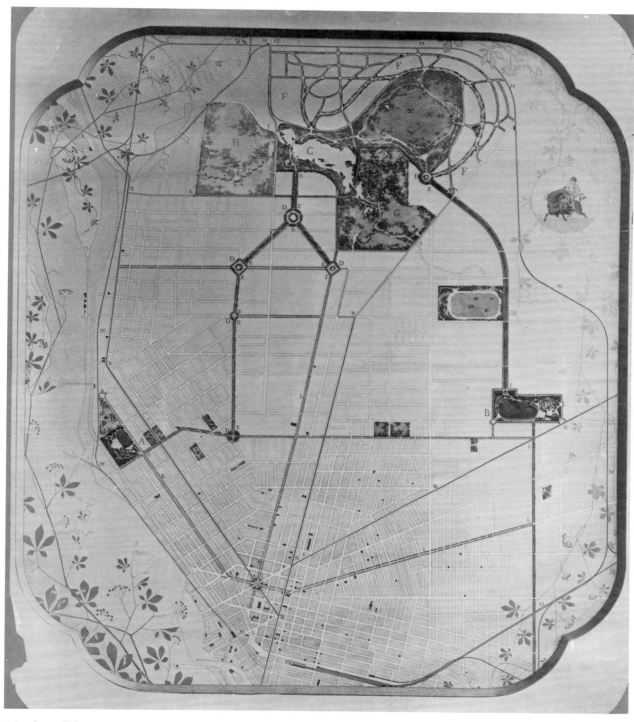

*North Buffalo Map, 1876.*

This 1876 map, of which a later version became known as "Olmsted's Sketch Map of Buffalo," was the basis for a clear description of the early park system approved and executed by the City of Buffalo beginning in 1868. Successive Olmsted firms expanded the system substantially in later years.

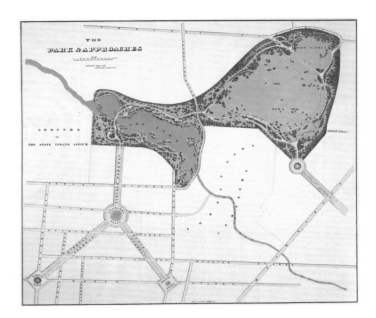

*The Park.*

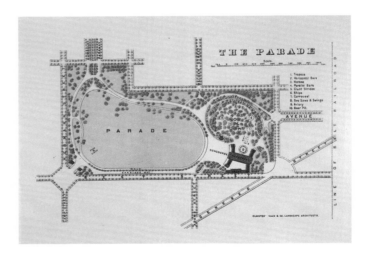

*The Parade.*

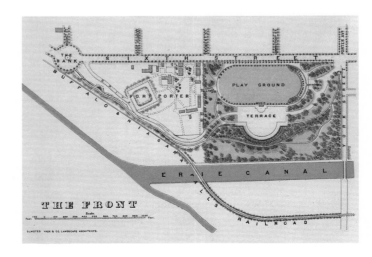

*The Front.*

"The Park, 3½ miles north of the City Hall, a ground designed to be resorted to solely for quiet rural enjoyment. The more notable features are a grand sweep of undulating turf, one hundred and fifty acres in extent, and containing a goodly number of large, well-grown trees, a body of water of forty-six acres, an open grove suited to picnics, and closer woods offering wilder and more secluded rambles. Area, 350 acres."

"The Parade, two and one-half miles easterly from the City Hall, a smooth gently-sloping lawn designed for military drills, parades, attractive out-door sports, and popular festivities. At the easterly end, a small natural grove and a commodious refectory afford ample opportunity for shade, rest and refreshment. Area, 56 acres."

"The Front, one and one-half miles northerly from the City Hall, a ground in which the use is secured forever to the public of the crest of a steep bluff, from 50 to 60 feet above the level of Lake Erie, which commands a broad prospect over the lake, and an interesting view of the Niagara River and Canadian Frontier. In the summer and autumn months it is fanned by a cool westerly breeze, almost constantly blowing from the lake, which, in warm days is grateful and refreshing to visitors and healthful to invalids. Its area is about 50 acres, including the adjoining military post, which is also open to the public."

*Plan for the Refectory, The Parade, 1871.*

The largest park structure Vaux ever designed was the Refectory for Buffalo's Parade. Only the front pavilion and a portion of the adjoining rear wing were built of this very ambitious structure.

*The Refectory, The Parade, 1876.*

Vaux's "chalet"-style Refectory pavilion overlooked the parade ground and grove. It was over 270 feet long and 50 feet wide, and could comfortably shelter over 1,000 visitors who came to see the drills and festivities. "Its elevated site will also afford a fine outlook over the city, and the distant hills of Chautauqua are brought prominently into view." It was dedicated on July 4, 1876, burned in August 1877, and reerected for another grand opening on Memorial Day in 1879, but at half its original size. It no longer exists. Vaux built other buildings in this rustic style at about the same time in Central and Prospect parks.

The Tower at the edge of Delaware Park's lake clearly had its genesis in Central Park's Greensward Presentation Study Number 4 (pp. 108–109). Here was the same prospect, an elevated resting place with water view.

*The Tower, Delaware Park.*

*The Boathouse, Delaware Park, 1875.*

The Boathouse also housed a refectory on its upper story, which served refreshments to be taken out on the open deck where one could view lake activities and park scenery. In winter boats were slung overhead for storage, and the lower dock area was flooded for ice skating and curling.

Seating for those awaiting pedal-driven transport was carved and colored in a manner reminiscent of Vaux's detailing at his earlier Central Park Boathouse. Ochres, tans and yellows in larger areas were customarily set off by blues, reds and dark browns in the details.

*Seating at Boat Landing, Delaware Park.*

*Delaware Park, ca.* 1868. Watercolor, artist unknown.

*The Parade, ca.* 1868. Watercolor, artist unknown.

Olmsted's original Buffalo Sketch Map was mounted together with a hand-lettered explanation of the plan and a series of small watercolor vignettes showing landscapes and structures, some completed, some proposed. These, among them, show the Tower in Delaware Park and the Refectory in the Parade. Although formally labeled "artist unknown," they closely resemble Vaux's watercolor technique as seen in "after" scenes rendered for the Central Park competition and later Central Park bridge watercolors.

*Vaux and Withers, Congress and Columbian Springs Pavilions, Saratoga Springs, New York, 1876.*

When the *New York Daily Tribune* reported on Saratoga's season in July 1878, it noted that the "light and graceful buildings designed by Vaux and Withers of New York" were admirably suited for the evening festivals in Congress Park. The park itself was completed in 1875 according to plans by Frederick Law Olmsted and his then associate, Jacob Weidenmann. The next year, the Congress and Columbian Springs Pavilions, actually a continuous structure housing both natural springs, were completed by Vaux and Withers and opened to the public.  Gaslighting throughout the park and pavilions served for festive evening events—like music from the bandstand on the island in the park's artificial lake—clearly intended to draw crowds away from Newport or even those contemplating Europe. When three or four bands from the large hotels combined as one to make music in Congress Park, "The scene in the evening" writes Ticknor's 1877 Guide, on the occasion of one of the grand concerts, "is remarkably brilliant."

*Congress Park Plan.*

*Congress Spring Pavilion.* Park entrance.

*Congress Spring Pavilion*. Serving bar, dipper boys and patron.

The pavilion structures display High Victorian timber and wood construction at its most decorative and expressive. Although little expense was spared to make fine pavilions where the waters were free, other available enjoyments, such as the casino across the street, could make a Saratoga visit costly.  The stained-glass panels behind the Congress Spring bar would have had their counterpart in the colonettes, beams, arches, pendants and filigree, with major

*Congress Spring Pavilion.* Promenade to the Cafe.

elements in ochres and browns and details picked out in reds, bright blues and greens. While access to the park and its facilities cost a nominal fee, anyone could enter the pavilions without charge directly from Congress Street or Broadway and partake of the waters, either at the bar or, while seated, served by one of the dipper boys.

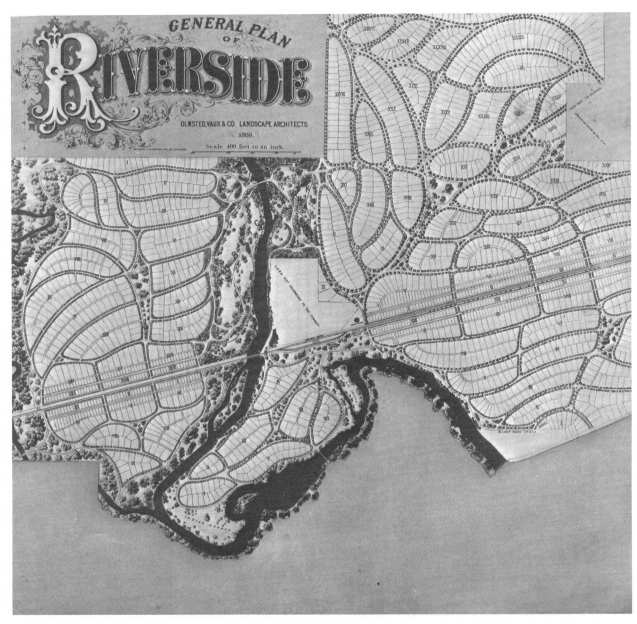

*Olmsted, Vaux and Co., General Plan for Riverside, Illinois, 1868.*

In 1868, a banner year for the firm, Olmsted, Vaux and Co. was engaged by the Riverside Improvement Company to lay out an entire suburban village at the edge of the Des Plaines River, 12 miles from Chicago. The designers were to be paid in house lots. The preliminary report was followed by the actual plan in 1869. Some good progress was made, with an illustrated brochure appearing in 1871, the year, unfortunately, of the Great Chicago Fire in which the Riverside Company's office was destroyed. In the Panic of 1873 the company went bankrupt. It turned out to be a troublesome and unprofitable venture for Olmsted and Vaux, but their plan was basically completed, becoming in time an exemplar of suburban town planning. It has in fact been held up for singular praise over the years by the nation's planning community and has perhaps never been matched for quality and intelligence. The 1871 brochure showed three houses designed by Vaux among the illustrations of landscape scenes, major structures and improvements.

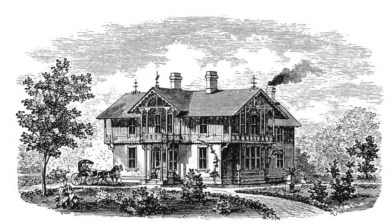

Residence of John C. Dore, Esq., situated on Fair Bank Road, Riverside. Olmsted, Vaux & Co., Architects.

"The house is a low Swiss cottage, the upper story overhanging the lower, with the upper balconies in unexpected places, giving a very picturesque appearance.

"The situation is a very fine one, the Church with its broad grounds on one side—the river and Picnic Island on the other."

"The building is in a plain Gothic style, surrounded by fine grounds, decorated with a summer house, and a swing for the children; while in the rear are the stables, hennery, and the kitchen garden.

"The front veranda commands a fine view of the River, Picnic Island, and the driving on the Fair Bank Road. A beautiful fountain on the front lawn will command attention."

Residence of Geo. M. Kimbark, Esq., situated on Barry Point Road, Riverside. Olmsted, Vaux & Co., Architects.

Residence of E. T. Wright, fronting on Scott's Wood Common, Riverside. Olmsted, Vaux & Co., Architects.

"The house is in a picturesque Gothic style, with steep roof, forming a part of the chamber story.

"There are two verandas, one upon the side towards the common, the other on the lawn. The grounds are large and well shaded with natural growth of fine young forest trees."

The firm's work at Riverside brought Olmsted into contact
with civic leaders and businessmen he had been associated
with as secretary of the Sanitary Commission during the Civil
War. This was in regard to the design of a major park in
Chicago. Vaux, in Chicago on the Riverside job, followed up
on Olmsted's contacts, and in October 1869 he successfully
negotiated for the job of a park and parkway plan for
Chicago's South Park Commission. Their plan, in simple
terms, comprised a two-part park connected by a wide canal.
If their conception had been completed as planned, an
extraordinary series of waterways, lake basins and lagoons
would have enabled one to travel by water from the prairie
edge of the "Lower Division," through the Midway Plaisance
Canal, into the "Upper Division," and out into Lake Michigan.
Again the Great Fire of 1871 intervened, destroying all Park
Commission records and drawings. A later administration
made substantial changes in the plan, not for the better. The
Midway Canal never came into being, but a good deal of the
basic plan was followed, especially that part based on the
preliminary civil engineering recommendations of the
designers. This resulted in the drainage of marshes and
swamps on the site, especially at the lakeshore where the
designers provided a fine, popular promenade. The two
divisions became Washington and Jackson Parks, the latter the
site of the 1893 World's Columbian Exposition whose grounds
Olmsted alone laid out in one of the major undertakings of
his career.

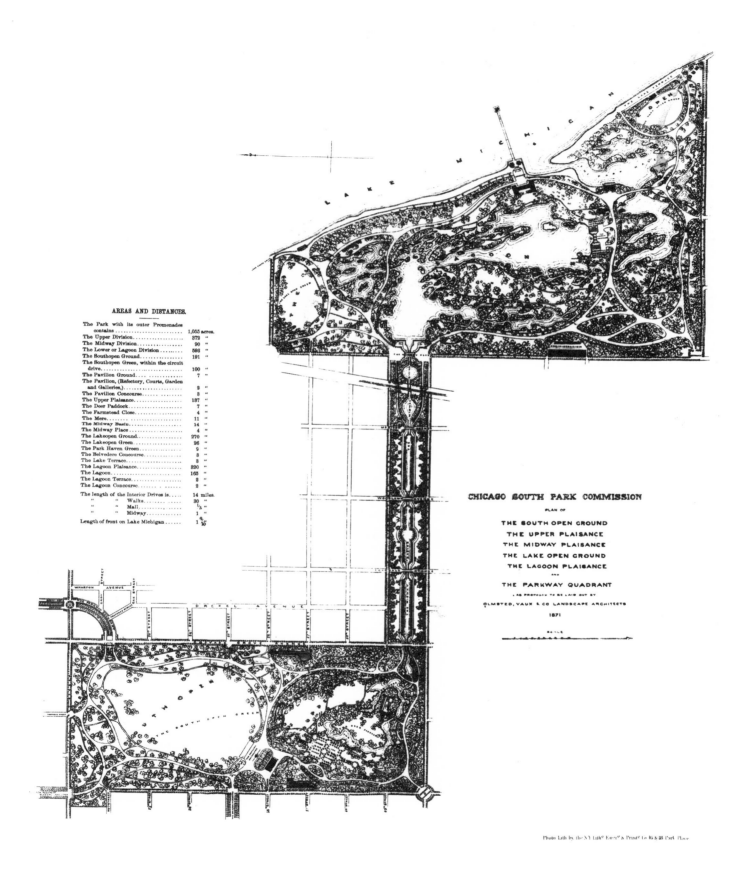

**AREAS AND DISTANCES.**

| | |
|---|---|
| The Park with its outer Promenades contains | 1,055 acres. |
| The Upper Division | 372 " |
| The Midway Division | 90 " |
| The Lower or Lagoon Division | 593 " |
| The Southopen Ground | 191 " |
| The Southopen Green, within the circuit drive | 100 " |
| The Pavilion Ground | 7 " |
| The Pavilion, (Refectory, Courts, Garden and Galleries,) | 2 " |
| The Pavilion Concourse | 3 " |
| The Upper Plaisance | 187 " |
| The Deer Paddock | 7 " |
| The Farmstead Close | 4 " |
| The Mere | 11 " |
| The Midway Basin | 14 " |
| The Midway Place | 4 " |
| The Lakeopen Ground | 270 " |
| The Lakeopen Green | 26 " |
| The Park Haven Green | 9 " |
| The Belvedere Concourse | 3 " |
| The Lake Terrace | 3 " |
| The Lagoon Plaisance | 320 " |
| The Lagoon | 165 " |
| The Lagoon Terrace | 2 " |
| The Lagoon Concourse | 2 " |
| The length of the Interior Drives is | 14 miles. |
| "         "         "      Walks | 30 " |
| "         "         "      Mall | ½ " |
| "         "         "      Midway | 1 " |
| Length of front on Lake Michigan | 1 6/10 " |

**CHICAGO SOUTH PARK COMMISSION**

PLAN OF

THE SOUTH OPEN GROUND
THE UPPER PLAISANCE
THE MIDWAY PLAISANCE
THE LAKE OPEN GROUND
THE LAGOON PLAISANCE

AND

THE PARKWAY QUADRANT

AS PROPOSED TO BE LAID OUT BY

OLMSTED, VAUX & CO LANDSCAPE ARCHITECTS

1871

SCALE

Photo Lith by the N.Y. Lith⁸ Eng⁸ & Print⁸ Co 16 & 18 Park Place

*Olmsted, Vaux and Co., South Park, Chicago, 1871.*

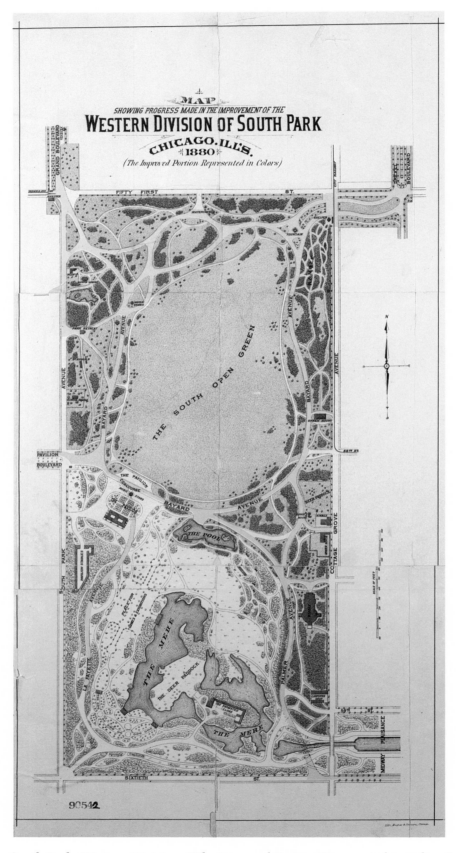

*South Park, Western Division, "The Improved Portion Represented in Colors,"* 1880.

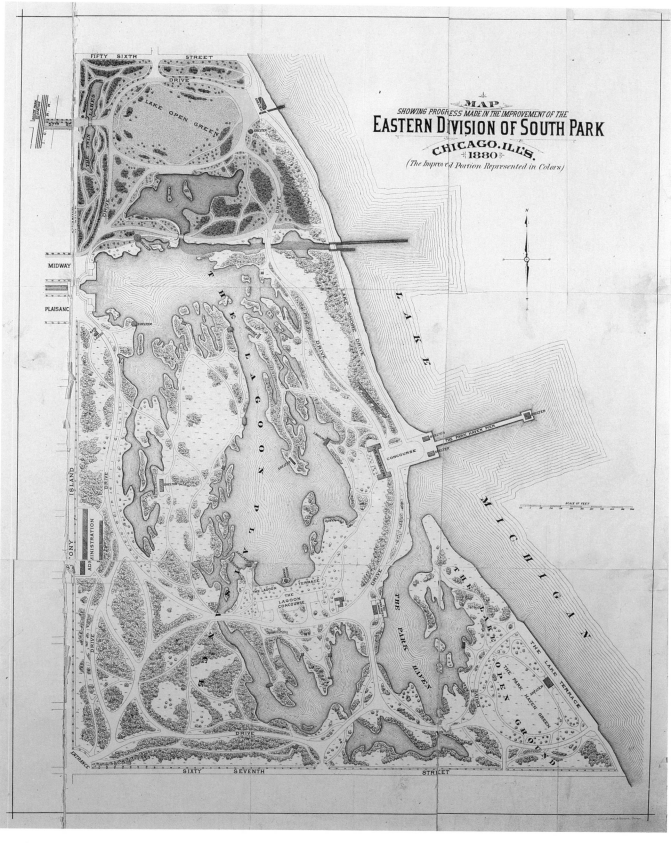

*South Park, Eastern Division, 1880.*

*South Park, Chicago, ca. 1900.*

*South Park, Chicago, ca. 1900.*

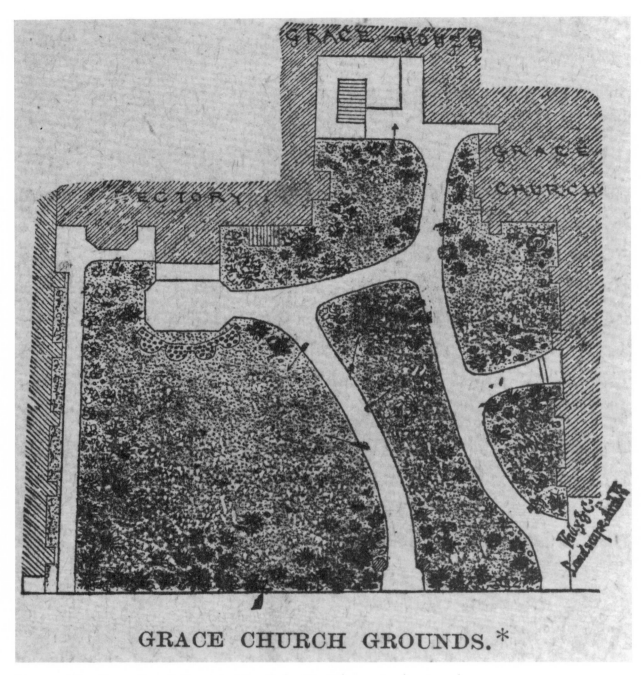

GRACE CHURCH GROUNDS.*

*Vaux and Co., Grace Church Grounds, New York, 1887. Schematic planting plan.*

In his extended article on the Grace Church grounds in *The Churchman* of June 4, 1887, Vaux gives a detailed analysis of his work. After the formation of a "recognizable leading idea," the rationale is followed through. Beyond techniques and plantings suitable for this urban setting, he considers traffic patterns on the grounds, the relationship of landscape to architecture and views from the street into the grounds. On planting: "The California privet was selected as the most useful for masking the fences. No plant thrives better than this privet in smoke and dust, and under the peculiar stress of the city. The most beautiful background effect . . . depended on the use of ampelosis tricuspidata or Japan ivy, which grew freely and rapidly, clinging by fine rootlets close to the stonework of the church and rectory." With characteristic thoroughness he even details certain railing plantings that can be safely lifted away when painting is necessary.

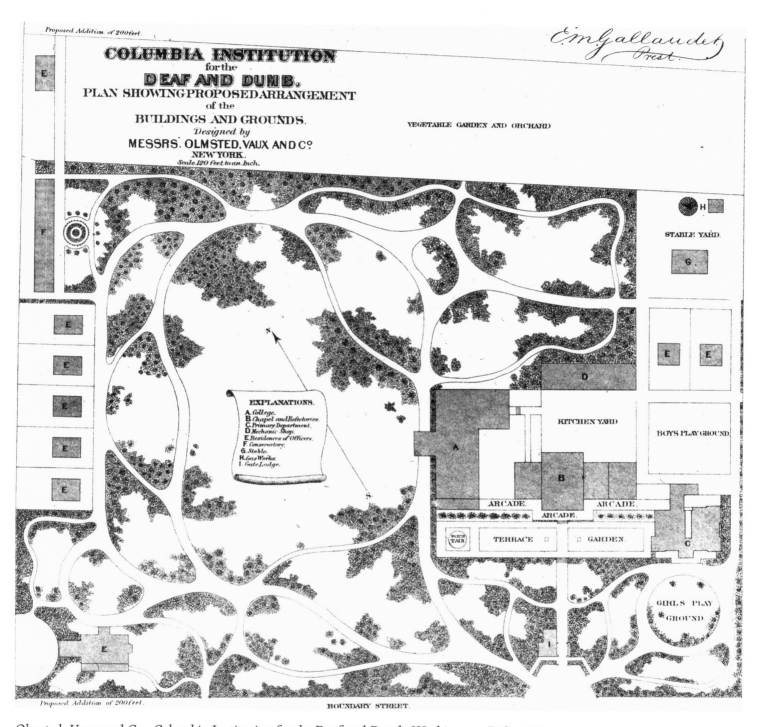

*Olmsted, Vaux and Co., Columbia Institution for the Deaf and Dumb, Washington, D.C., 1866.*

Olmsted's old friend Edward Gallaudet, patron of the Columbia Institution for the Deaf and Dumb, asked him to survey the Washington grounds with an eye toward their improvement. The result was the plan of 1866. Later that year, in regard to building plans, Vaux was in correspondence with the institution, proposing that Frederick Withers visit the site for a "personal examination." The result was Chapel Hall, the main building of the campus and one of Withers' most successful designs. Further correspondence indicates that Vaux, if not involved, was cognizant of the building's progress in design and detailing.

CITY OF FALL RIVER
GENERAL PLAN FOR LAYING OUT THE PARK
AS PROPOSED BY
OLMSTED VAUX & CO. LANDSCAPE ARCHITECTS
MAY 1871.

*Olmsted, Vaux and Co., General Plan for Laying Out South Park, Fall River, Massachusetts, 1871.*

After visiting several areas in Fall River, Vaux wrote to the Committee on Park
Improvement in June 1879 on the advantages of the South Park site, but
recommended that it be part of a comprehensive park system. Of this early plan, just
the Parade and Ball Ground, on the left side, were completed.

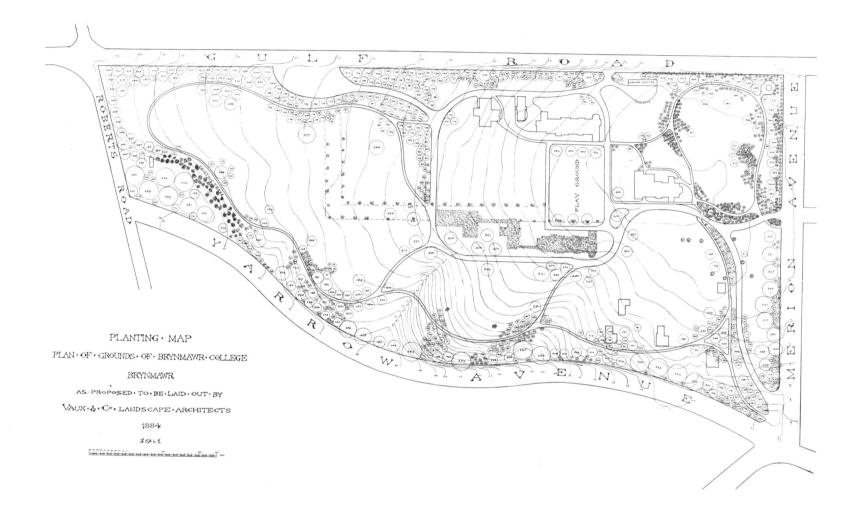

*Vaux and Co., Plan of Grounds of Bryn Mawr College, Bryn Mawr, Pennsylvania, 1884. Planting plan.*

Vaux participated in several partnerships which were often tangential and overlapping. Partners, besides Olmsted, Withers and George K. Radford, the engineer, included Samuel Parsons, Jr., a horticulturist and plantsman, and Louis J. Leeds, a ventilation and heating engineer who was probably the best in the business. Parsons was Vaux's associate in Vaux and Co., which specialized in landscape architecture, while Vaux worked concurrently in building architecture and planning. Jacob Wrey Mould was an associate architect–designer, especially in the Central Park work.

*Vaux and Co., Wilderstein, Rhinebeck, New York,* 1890. Northwest view from the south lawn of the main house.

*Planting Plan for Wilderstein,* 1891.

In April 1890 Vaux brought a surveyor to Wilderstein to make a topographic map of the grounds preparatory to a landscape design for this Rhinebeck estate of New York businessman Robert B. Suckley. In November, Vaux, his son Downing and Samuel Parsons came up to "work up the planting" for the grounds, Parsons writing Suckley afterward to discourage his idea of having evergreens along the roads because of shade and soil conditions. The final result was a landscape with soft lawns and trees grouped in typical Hudson Valley picturesque tradition. Later, drawings were made for a lodge by Vaux and Radford, who also provided plans for and completed some interior changes in the house, which was occupied by Suckley's daughter Daisy until her death in 1991. She bequeathed the entire estate to Wilderstein Preservation, which is now engaged in its restoration.

*Frederick Law Olmsted and Calvert Vaux, Downing Park,*
*Newburgh, New York, 1887. Panoramic view, ca. 1900.*

In 1887, Olmsted and Vaux offered to design a park for the City of Newburgh
without charge if it were named in honor of their mentor, A. J. Downing. The city
accepted, and the park was completed in 1896.

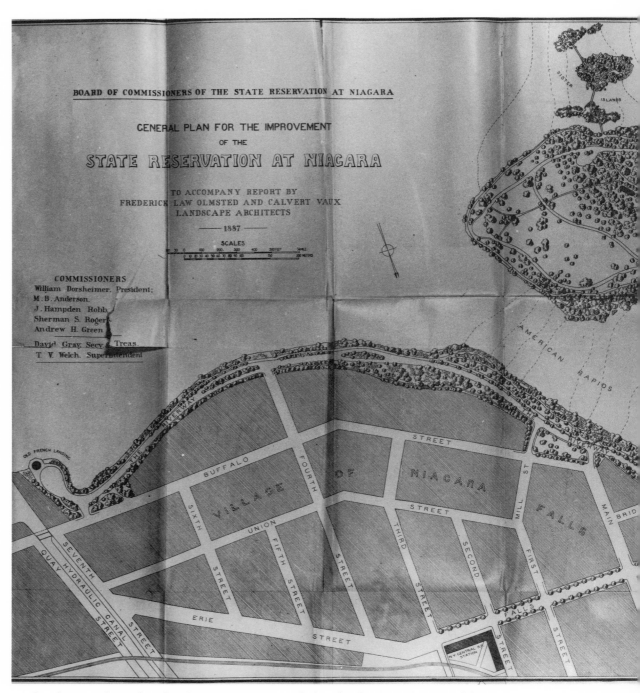

*Frederick Law Olmsted and Calvert Vaux, "General Plan for the Improvement of the State Reservation at Niagara," New York, 1887.*

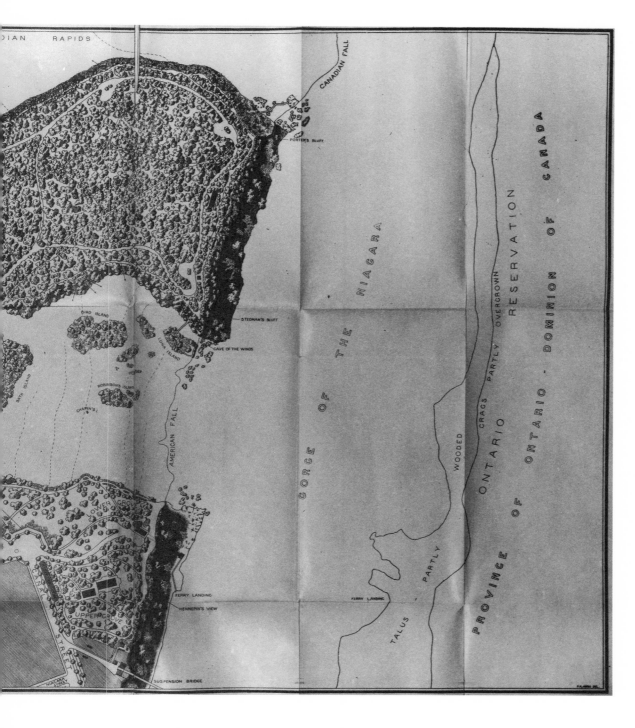

It was only after extensive public and private campaigning over a 20-year period that the Niagara precinct evolved into a "protected" state reservation for public use and enjoyment. Frederic Church and Olmsted were early advocates of the idea. Many others, including an aware international community, joined to lend support, and by 1887 Olmsted and Vaux were commissioned to produce the report and general plan for its improvement. In this the two joined together 15 years after their formal separation. After together devising the comprehensive plan, Olmsted wrote the report, while the actual later implementation and supervision was left to Vaux, who again persevered in the face of changes and modifications directed by the officials then in charge. The work proceeded, Vaux's son Downing and George K. Radford assisting and Samuel Parsons, Jr., later doing landscaping work.

*Grounds for Parliament Buildings, Ottawa, Canada, 1873.*

In 1873 Vaux dispatched a design study to Canada: "Thomas S. Scott, Esq., Chief Architect, Department Public Works, Ottawa. Dear Sir, I send you herewith my study for the arrangement of the grounds and terrace walls in connection with the Government Building, the leading features of the design having been agreed upon prior to your departure from New York." Then, without payment of the full customary fee, the "study" was constructed, becoming a reality. It was not until 1882 and 1883 that Vaux was issued two payments, and only after he had published a "proof" booklet of official correspondence. Vaux's design solution to the change in level of terraces, staircases and curving ramps is elegantly reminiscent of his Central Park Terrace plan, with which it is roughly contemporary. Vaux was later called on to solve another change in level site access when later government buildings were built on either side of the main one, forming a U shape around the forecourt. "I introduced a connecting terrace, with steps, etc. that served to bring the base line of the upper building to the same level as the lower building, and thus did away with the apparent incongruity to the eye." The change in level was a considerable 20 feet.

*Parliament Buildings Grounds.*

*Parliament Buildings Grounds.* Forecourt.

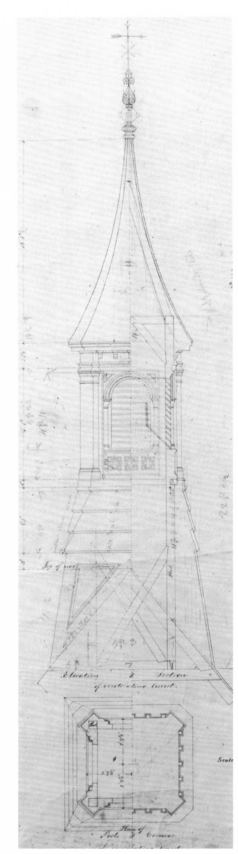

*The Sheppard and Enoch Pratt Hospital.*
Elevation, section and plan of ventilating turret.

# Architecture for the Urban Scene:
## Commercial, Institutional, Humanitarian

CALVERT VAUX reached the height of fame and success in the decade 1865 to 1875. After winning the Central Park competition with Olmsted, as partners they went on to do a series of park and planning projects until 1872, when the partnership ended, Olmsted going on to a growing and successful career in park design, Vaux looking forward to a highly promising future in architecture, while still continuing intermittently as landscape architect for New York City parks. Working again with associates and partners Withers, Mould and Radford, Vaux almost won the competition for the Philadelphia Centenary Exhibition Main Building, and was initially commissioned to design the two major cultural institutions of New York City, the Metropolitan Museum of Art and the American Museum of Natural History. Three major state or private mental institutions in Connecticut, Maryland and New York crossed the drawing boards at the 110 Broadway offices, while a variety of domestic architecture commissions arrived as well. The family Vaux lived in the Stuyvesant Apartments on East 18th Street and had a summer place in Rondout, up the Hudson.

Vaux also began to stand up to the major factors building up against him, especially the new stylistic movements of the day in architecture and the special interest groups trying to dismantle and abuse the parks of his responsibility. The Victorian Gothic to which he was so strongly committed was being superseded by eclectic classic forms, the new symbols in America of success, significance and pride. He chose not to compromise his beliefs, and as commissions waned, toward the end he was able to depend on those who valued his talents and honesty. Major later works in New York included the townhouse for Samuel Tilden, a suspension bridge across Broadway for the Trustees of Trinity Church, and the series of Children's Aid Society buildings for Charles Loring Brace, Olmsted's close friend.

In his two earliest commercial buildings Vaux demonstrated his special capability in construction techniques (to the dismay of many of the craftsmen working on his Hudson Valley houses) by requiring that the interior floor supporting joists rest on corbels built out from the brick or stone walls, not inserted directly into them as was commonly done. Otherwise, in case of a fire burning through the floors, he explains in *Villas and Cottages*, the unsupported joists collapse, acting as powerful levers, and heave over the walls into which they are fastened. If common sense is not convincing, he continues, biblical authority ought to be. He cites the construction of Solomon's temple: "In 1st Kings, C. vi., 6, we are told he made narrowed rests round about, that the beams should not be fastened in the walls of the house."

*Vaux and Withers, Bank of New York, New York, 1856.*

The original Bank of New York stood on the corner of William and Wall Streets, a prime location in lower Manhattan's financial district. Commenting on the solidity of the building and its special security devices, the *Builder* of February 2, 1858, noted, "All the works have been carried out under the superintendence of Mr. Calvert Vaux, architect, from plans approved previously to a dissolution of his partnership with Mr. Withers." The style is difficult to characterize but might be said to contain both French and Italian Renaissance elements. Withers scholars are content to give Vaux full design credit for the building. The officials of the bank were so pleased with their new building, which contained the very latest technological and communications advances, that they voted Vaux a substantial premium above his fee.

DESIGN FOR A PACKING-HOUSE.

*"Design for a Packing-House," New York, 1856.*

The Robins and Co. Packing House was constructed of brick, with brick joist projections on the interior. It was located in lower Manhattan's wholesale meat district on Washington Street. Vaux had earlier designed a house for Robins in Yonkers, New York.

The facades of Milton J. Stone's Commercial Block were of Quincy granite, with columnar granite piers separating the storefronts on the street level. Projecting stone corbels on the interior supported the floor joists. The building has recently been restored, preserving the original facades.

COMMERCIAL BLOCK, COMMERCIAL STREET.

*Commercial Block, Commercial Wharf, Boston, 1854.*

*The Sheppard and Enoch Pratt Hospital, Baltimore, 1861–1895.*

In 1860, Dr. D. T. Brown, superintendent of New York's Bloomingdale Asylum, was selected to provide the experience and direction for the establishment of Baltimore's Sheppard Asylum. Olmsted and Vaux, whose fame had spread and whose services were in demand, had previously worked on the layout of the Bloomingdale Asylum grounds, and Vaux was asked to submit a general plan for the Baltimore facility, in consultation with Brown. The wealthy

*The Sheppard and Enoch Pratt Hospital.* South elevation, rendering by Vaux.

Quaker businessman Moses Sheppard had willed a substantial sum for this purpose, charging his heirs to create "ample apartments . . . for exercise and employment of the patients in such occupations and amusements as may be conducive to their benefit." In 1861 Brown was sent on a professional visit to France and England to observe the latest such facilities, while in December of that year, Vaux was commissioned to provide full working drawings.

Construction proceeded slowly until about 1895, when another Baltimore philanthropist, Enoch Pratt, provided over $1.5 million to the institution with the proviso that the name be changed to The Sheppard and Enoch Pratt Hospital and that the trustees consider care for the "indigent insane at very low rates or absolutely free."

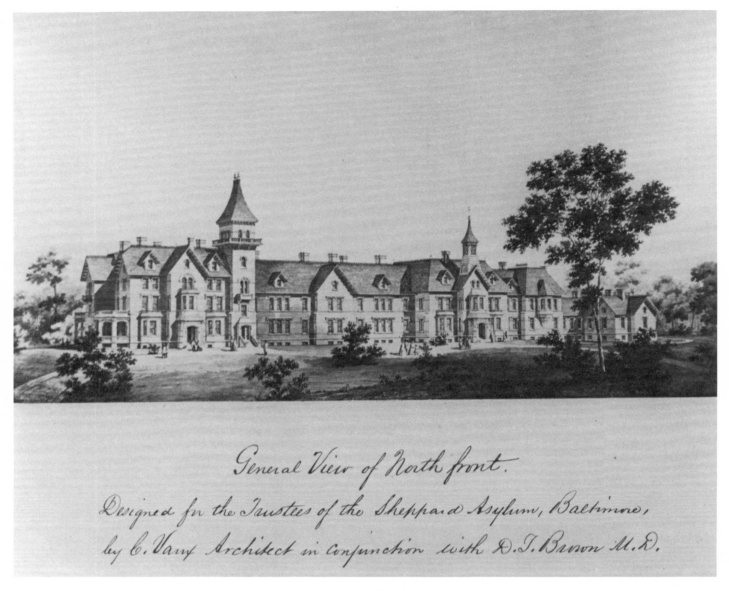

*General View of North front.*

*Designed for the Trustees of the Sheppard Asylum, Baltimore, by C. Vaux Architect in Conjunction with D. J. Brown M. D.*

*The Sheppard and Enoch Pratt Hospital.* General view of north front, rendering by Vaux. As early as 1861 Vaux had completed plans for the north building. Dr. Brown sent Vaux's sketch to the Sheppard Asylum trustees in March of that year.

Sharing in the deep concern that developed in the 1850s and 1860s for the care of the mentally disabled on both moral and medical grounds, the Sheppard trustees determined that theirs be the best possible such asylum. Actual construction began in 1863, the trustee record stating: "Having obtained such a Design for the Hospital Buildings as they considered to be satisfactory, and as meeting the liberal and humane views of the founder. . ." only decided upon after the most careful study, aided by the best professional architectural and medical skill and ability which they could employ. . ." Vaux made superintending visits to Baltimore as brick kilns were built on the grounds and a quarry was opened on the site to provide building stone. Ultimately there came into being the Western and Eastern Divisions, mirror images of each other for men and women, each 230 feet long with 100-foot perpendicular wings. They were complete, from underground water storage cisterns to 90-foot towers and the very latest Edison lighting plant. They were easily Vaux's largest single commission, created in a straightforward, functional, Victorian Gothic style.

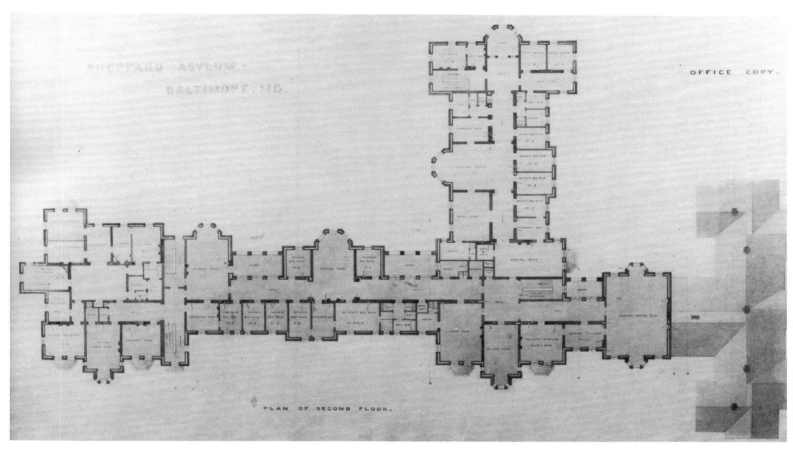

*The Sheppard and Enoch Pratt Hospital.*
Plan of second floor.

Vaux's two divisions are no longer separated; the 100-foot space between them is now occupied by the Central Building whose facades are generally in accord with the original structures. The Vaux buildings, which are carefully preserved, have been designated a National Historic Site.

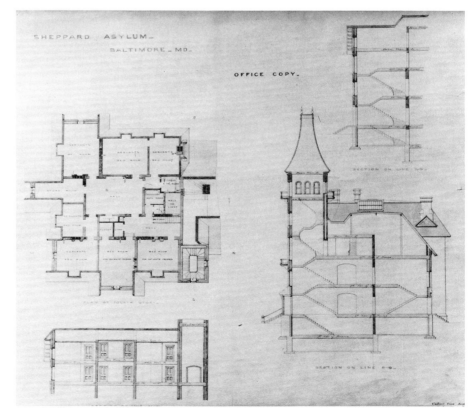

*The Sheppard and Enoch Pratt Hospital.*
Plan and sections.

CENTER AND NORTH WING OF THE RETREAT.

*Vaux, Withers and Co., Retreat for the Insane, Hartford, 1868.* Center and north wing.

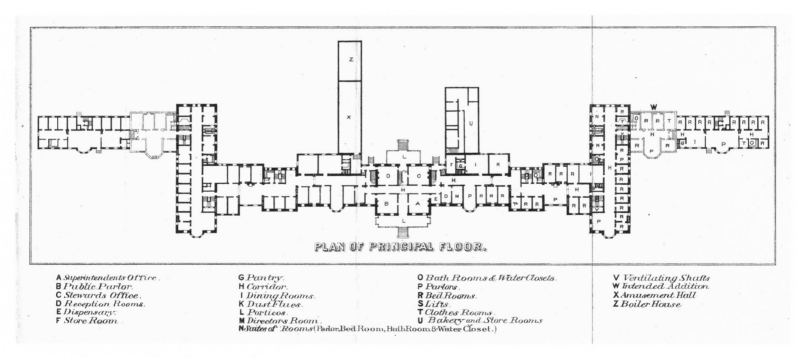

PLAN OF PRINCIPAL FLOOR.

A *Superintendents Office*.
B *Public Parlor*.
C *Stewards Office*.
D *Reception Rooms*.
E *Dispensary*.
F *Store Room*.

G *Pantry*.
H *Corridor*.
I *Dining Rooms*.
K *Dust Flues*.
L *Porticos*.
M *Directors Room*.
N *Suites of Rooms* (Parlor, Bed Room, Bath Room & Water Closet.)

O *Bath Rooms & Water Closets*.
P *Parlors*.
R *Bed Rooms*.
S *Lifts*.
T *Clothes Rooms*.
U *Bakery and Store Rooms*.

V *Ventilating Shafts*.
W *Intended Addition*.
X *Amusement Hall*.
Z *Boiler House*.

*Retreat for the Insane.* Plan of principal floor.

After the Civil War, Vaux and Withers, having re-formed their partnership in New York City, counted two major institutional projects among their commissions. Although done under the firm name, Vaux takes basic design credit for the Hartford Retreat, where Olmsted and Vaux were involved in the design of the grounds, while Withers is credited with the design of the Hudson River hospital. Both were doubtlessly involved in the work on each of these huge building complexes. Dr. John S. Butler, superintendent of the Hartford Retreat, had consulted with Olmsted on the

*Retreat for the Insane.* East view, north wing. The complex is now called The Institute for Living.

*Vaux, Withers and Co., Hudson River State Hospital, Poughkeepsie, New York, 1867.* The original building of what is now the Hudson Psychiatric Center was declared a National Landmark in 1989.

grounds and with Vaux on the new building work needed, and in a letter to Olmsted in 1872, expressing his gratitude, he wrote: "The influence on the patients has been marked, and I have often wished that I could have shown to you and Mr. Vaux some of the cumulative evidences of the good work you have accomplished." Butler may well have had the best talents in the country in landscape design and in institutional planning, given Vaux's earlier work on the Sheppard Asylum.

*Adelbert College, Cleveland, ca. 1882.*

A case for architectural detective work is presented by the Adelbert College building, now part of Case Western Reserve University. Vaux clearly lists "Adelbert College, Cleveland, Ohio," as one of his designs in a series of his buildings that were constructed. The listing is in the Calvert Vaux Papers at the New York Public Library. The university archives, however, contain a set of plans for the building by the architect Joseph Ireland, who had worked in both New York and Cleveland. The Ireland drawings are of interiors and show no exterior elevations. Records or correspondence beyond the above information have not been found. A frequent Vaux entrance theme, though, in both his domestic and especially in his institutional architecture, is comprised of an entry porch with balcony, sometimes supported by columns, a projecting bay above that and a tower, for emphasis, above all.

*Vaux, Withers and Co., Hall-Rice Building, Troy, New York, 1871.*

Lawyer, historian, poet and occasionally chamberlain of Troy, Benjamin Hall's cultural interests clearly extended to architecture when he commissioned this building from Vaux and Withers. Even with towers now removed, it is still something of an all-out demonstration of High Victorian banded style.

*"Messrs. C. Vaux and F. C. Withers, Architects, Study for City Prison and Courts, New York."*

Two months apart in 1875, *The New-York Sketchbook of Architecture* published two different design proposals for the building known as the Jefferson Market Courthouse. In the April *Sketchbook* picture, Vaux's name is given first and the commentary concentrates on provision for the prisoners: "The cells in any prison building should be strong, secure, and entirely unattractive, but not dark or gloomy. The prisoner should certainly have as much sunlight and fresh air as possible: and in the present building, designed for a limited site in a crowded city, the simplest way to add to its light was to add to its height." Vaux's High Victorian design had not been to the taste of the municipal authorities, but this was already history in that the Withers design was under construction.

The June *Sketchbook* drawing gave the name Withers first and pictured the building as ultimately built.

*Third Judicial Courthouse.* Ground floor plan.

*"Messrs. F. C. Withers and C. Vaux, Architects, Court House, Bell Tower and Prison, Third Judicial District, New York."* Photograph, 1905.

Contemporary accounts agree to his authorship, which is easily confirmed by legal documentation of false accusations made against Withers by the stonework contractor. The building in fact came into being against the usual municipal background of political intrigue, cost overruns, accusations, lawsuits and so forth. The design comprised three elements, the courts, prison and fire-watch bell tower. The police court on the ground floor and the civil court above it were separated from the six-tiered jail structure by a courtyard "Entrance for the Black Maria," or prison van. The building is constructed of red brick and Ohio limestone and was declared number 5 on the list of America's ten best buildings in a poll of architects taken in 1895. It is now the Jefferson Market branch of the New York Public Library.

*Suspension Bridge for Trinity Cemetery, New York, 1872.*

*Suspension Bridge for Trinity Cemetery.* Looking south on Broadway.

Between 1872 and 1911 a suspension bridge linked the two halves of Trinity Cemetery on either side of Broadway at 155th Street in Manhattan. The vestrymen of Trinity Church on Wall Street had purchased this upper Manhattan farmland for their rural cemetery in 1842. In the decade of the 1870s and somewhat later, Vaux and three of his partners, Olmsted, Withers and Radford, were at various times involved in the work there, on grounds layout, boundary walls, gates and a keeper's lodge. Radford, a civil engineer from England capable in railway and bridge construction as well as in hydraulics and surveying, was employed by Vaux and Olmsted in their Buffalo and Chicago park work. Although printed contracts for Trinity work

name Vaux alone, or Olmsted and Vaux or Vaux and Withers, it seems probable that Radford, who had earlier observed the construction of Roebling's Cincinnati suspension bridge, may have provided technical advice, although he was working in Buffalo in 1871, when the Trinity bridge was designed.

Vaux's elegant span, with its fine Gothic piers, was demolished in 1911 when Trinity decided that the site for its largest chapel, the Church of the Intercession, and its rectory, vicarage, cloister and tower would occupy the southeast corner of Broadway and 155th Street, the eastern terminus of the bridge.

Vaux and Radford were one of ten finalists in the competition for the Main Building of the Philadelphia Centennial Exhibition of 1876. Of these ten, who were then given a second set of specifications to follow, four final prizewinners were chosen. Vaux and Radford were not among them, having decided not to rework their entry. The four winners had done so, but this, in the words of the competition committee after it was all over, "resulted in giving the awards to some designs that were radically different from the design which the Committee had, since the issue of the specifications, deemed it advisable to adopt, in view of some additional points of great interest that had presented themselves." This statement reflects the extraordinary series of decisions and compromises made at that time. Among these, at one point, was the decision of the executive committee that the Vaux-Radford design was the one to be built, and then they decided it was not to be built. Then portions of it were to be combined with portions of other designs, and so on. In the end all competition schemes were abandoned, and architects in the employ of the exhibition commission and some others chosen by them were simply assigned the design of specific buildings.

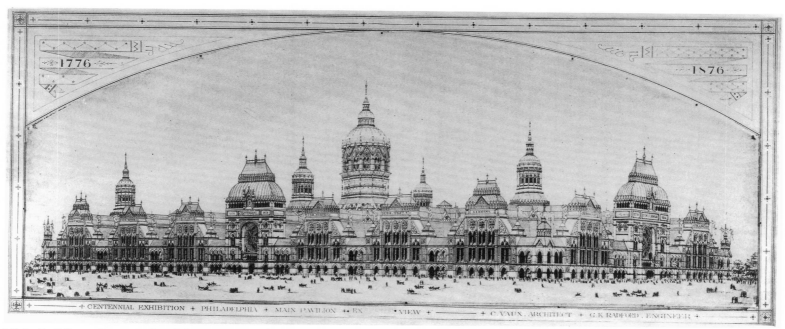

*Main Building, Centennial Exhibition.* Exterior.

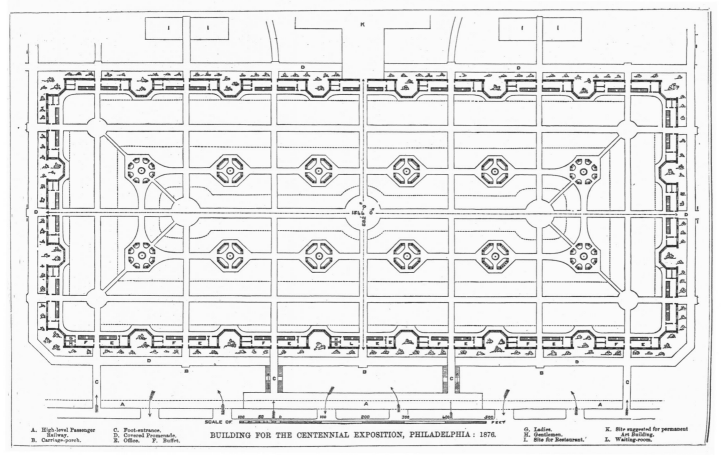

*Main Building, Centennial Exhibition.* Plan.

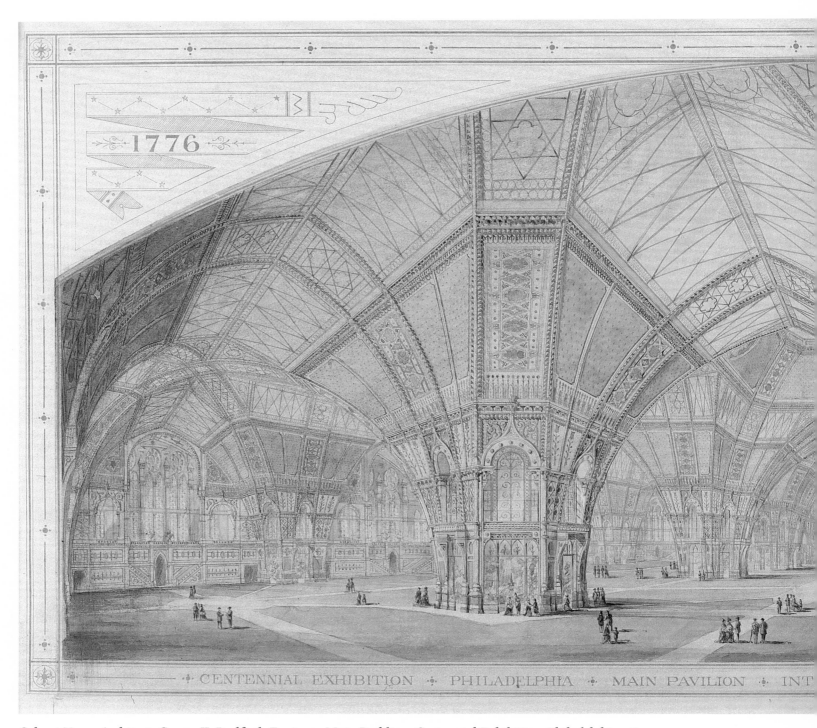

*Calvert Vaux, Architect, George K. Radford, Engineer, Main Building, Centennial Exhibition, Philadelphia, 1872.*

Vaux and Radford's tour de force surely exceeded all previous exhibition buildings in scale and ambition. If built, this stupendous amalgam of architecture, engineering and decoration would have made history, possibly even affecting the course of architecture in the United States, as the Chicago World's Columbian Exposition later did. The design is explained by Vaux: "The various parts of the building are thus included in one grand whole; and the result becomes a spacious hall, adequate to emergencies of the occasion, with long vistas, central and intermediate

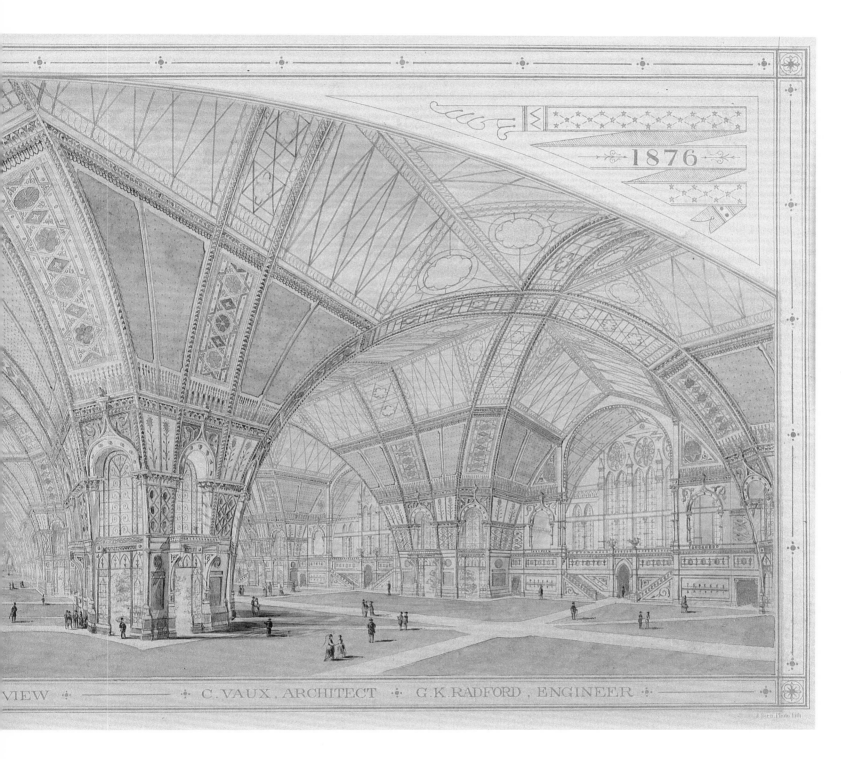

VIEW · ·— · C. VAUX, ARCHITECT · · G. K. RADFORD, ENGINEER · ·—

points of emphasis, direct lines of transit throughout its length and breadth, diagonal lines of communication where really needed, and an entire relief from any appearance of contraction, anywhere." The designers provided for all facilities and exhibits to be serviced by three internal railroad tracks, necessary for an interior counted in today's terms as 5½ football fields long and 2½ wide. The drawing was made by Thomas Wisedell, an English architect who came to America to work in the Vaux office and was later employed by Olmsted in Washington on the drawings for the improvement of the Capitol grounds.

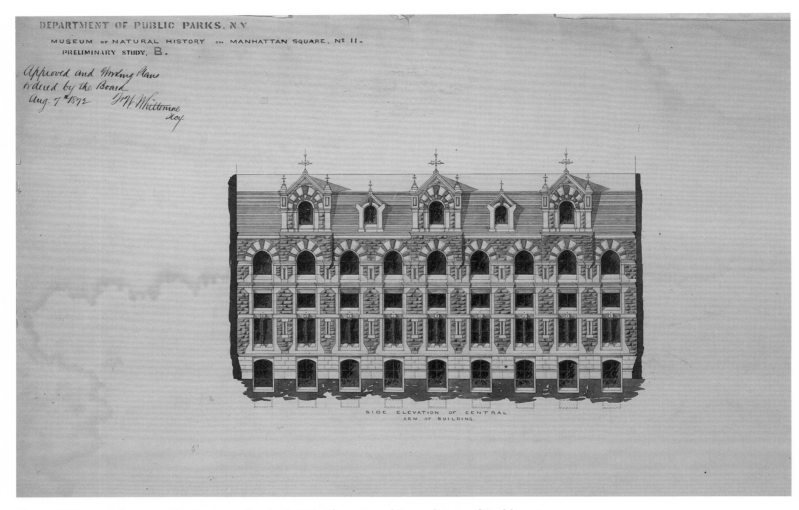

*Natural History Museum, "Preliminary Study B, Side Elevation of Central Arm of Building."*

If completed according to the ambitions of Professor Albert Smith Bickmore and the plans of Vaux and Mould, the American Museum of Natural History would have been the largest building on the North American continent. Ulysses S. Grant laid the cornerstone in 1874 for its first wing, and Rutherford B. Hayes spoke at its dedication in 1878. The building's site, known as Manhattan Square, was located just west of Central Park, to which it once belonged. Vaux and Mould, then "Architects of the Department of Public Parks," oriented the building north and south in accordance with the specifications of Bickmore, who wanted morning and afternoon sun to illuminate the galleries. The carefully detailed facades in Victorian High Gothic style were constructed of red brick and gray granite.

*Calvert Vaux and Jacob Wrey Mould, Natural History Museum, New York, 1874–1878.*

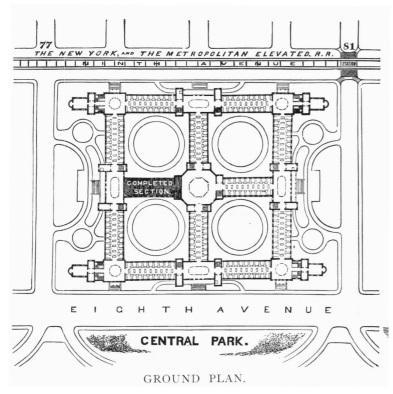

*Natural History Museum.* Ground plan.

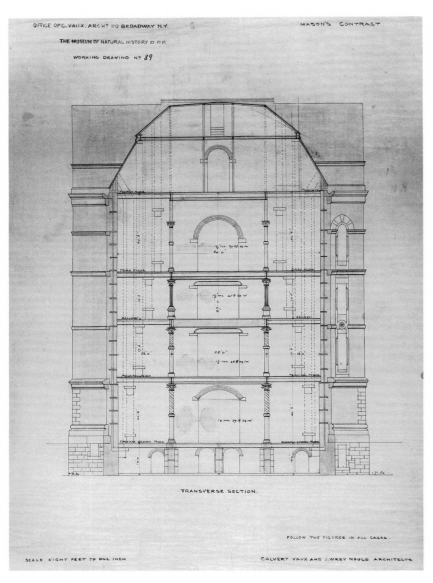

*Natural History Museum.* Working Drawing No. 89,
transverse section.

*Natural History Museum.*
Ethnology and Archaeology, gallery story.
President Hayes at opening ceremonies.

It soon became necessary to protect the galleries from the sun's rays, which were
fading and drying out the museum's valuable specimens. Vaux and Mould were not
destined to build anything else. Major additions by others have almost completely
surrounded their wing so that just one small upper-story segment of their original
exterior is visible from the park area at the western edge of old Manhattan Square.

*Natural History Museum.* Fossils Gallery.

*Natural History Museum.* Bird Hall, principal story.

*Calvert Vaux and Jacob Wrey Mould, The Art Museum, Central Park, New York, 1874–1880.* View looking west
into Central Park from East 81st Street.

The idea of a major encroachment into Central Park would
have been both troublesome and ironic for Calvert Vaux—
troublesome in that he and Olmsted had been expending
much effort in trying to prevent a variety of incursions into
the park; ironic in that when the time came for the erection of
the Art Museum, it was Vaux who was responsible for its
design. The availability of mild, nature-related educational
experiences to enhance a park visit had in fact been

encouraged by Olmsted and Vaux. An art museum had been
spoken of in connection with the Arsenal Building, already on
park ground. Other sites had also been discussed. But an act
of the state legislature in 1868 had authorized a museum on
Central Park grounds. Soon plans for a major art museum
began to emerge from a committee of art patrons, wealthy
businessmen, politicians, men of affairs and influential artists
and architects. This was to replace the galleries on 14th Street

*The Art Museum.* Central Park entrance.

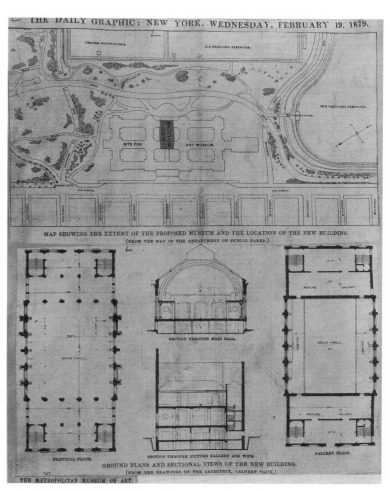

in the Douglas Mansion. The Central Park "Deer Park" was to be the site, just east of the reservoirs. The original building is now completely enveloped by later additions, but one small segment is still visible in an interior gallery, an instructive exhibit, as it were, of fine Victorian Gothic detailing in stone and brick.

*The Art Museum.* Site, plans and sections.

*The Art Museum.* "Main Hall of the Building."

The leading player in the Art Museum process was Andrew Haswell Green, comptroller of Central Park. Green had previously had Vaux and Mould, official park architects, work out plans for what he hoped would be a Park Commission–sponsored museum. Vaux and Mould simply were to be the designers for a structure on park land, whatever the sponsorship. Vaux's first plans were rejected in a report of the "special committee of architects appointed by the Museum to super-intend the building," a less than ideal beginning of what was not to go at all well. The report was signed by Russell Sturgis, James Renwick and Richard Morris Hunt, whose proposal for sets of monumental classical gateways for Central Park had been successfully opposed by Vaux and others. The further process is explained by a museum historian: "When Mr. Vaux changed his plans, the shell of the building was constructed. Even then, the Trustees were compelled to ask for important changes in the interior. Their criticism was not against the building as such, but against its adaptability for the exhibition of their collections. Fortunately, both Mr. Vaux and the Park Commissioners were most cordial in their desire to conform to the wishes of the Trustees. But museum building was a new form of architectural work in America. Thus it was but natural that differences of opinion should occur, even with the heartiest good will of each person."

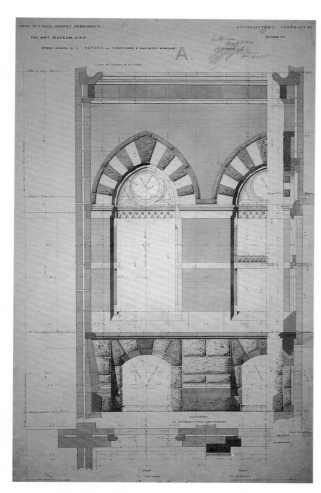

*The Art Museum.* First floor and basement
window details.

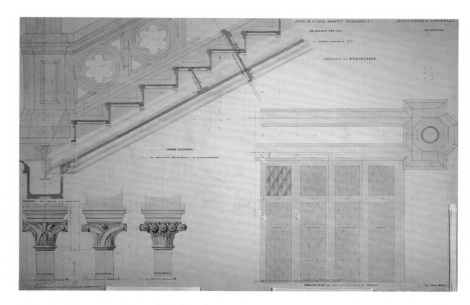

*The Art Museum.* Details of staircases.

GENERAL VIEW OF BUILDINGS — IN COURSE OF ERECTION ON 71ST & 72ND STS. & 1ST AVE. N.Y. — FOR THE IMPROVED DWELLINGS ASSOCIATION

*Vaux and Radford, Buildings for the Improved Dwellings Association, New York, 1882.*

In 1879 legislation was passed in New York calling for improved standards in tenement construction. One year later, several trustees of the Children's Aid Society were among a group that formed the Improved Dwellings Association to sponsor apartment buildings that they hoped would serve as an exemplar for decent tenement housing. Earlier charitable society attempts in housing betterment had been conducted in cities like Boston and Brooklyn. The association commissioned Vaux and Radford, already engaged in work for the Children's Aid Society, to provide the design. When completed it was publicized in pamphlets and pictures, in the hope that the standards it set would be followed.

*Improved Dwellings Association.* Buildings prepared for demolition, 1960.

*Improved Dwellings Association.* Courtyard in 1932. Photo by Berenice Abbott for the federal art series "Changing New York."

PLAN OF BUILDINGS-IN COURSE OF ERECTION-ON 71ST AND 72ND STS AND 1ST AVE.— NEW·YORK
FOR- THE IMPROVED DWELLINGS ASSOCIATION — VAUX & RADFORD ARCH'TS. 1880

*Improved Dwellings Association.* Plan.

Vaux, in an intelligent departure from the norm, planned for the apartments to be entered
from the interior court, accessed from the north and south side streets. Thus court access
to the apartments fronting First Avenue avoided the usual mutual interference on a
commercial street of both apartments and storefronts.

The Children's Aid Society was one aspect of a social reform movement of the day in which Olmsted and Vaux considered themselves participants. Their contribution involved the creation of uplifting and recreational opportunities for the pressured, hardworking lower classes of the city who could not go to the country for relaxation but who could obtain a small measure of relief in the public parks, in an environment of nature's scenery, freely and democratically available to all.

One of Olmsted's closest friends, Charles Loring Brace, helped found the Children's Aid Society to care for New York City's abused and abandoned children. Trained originally as a theologian, Brace was one of the outstanding social reformers of his day, finding his vocation in the exercise of morality and philanthropy combined. After some years of travel and writing, in 1852, at the age of 27, he became head of the society, the first organization in the United States to concern itself with childhood poverty and crime. Brace had previously performed welfare work among immigrants whose unrestricted influx over many years resulted in the crowded slums of New York City. To him, children appeared to experience the most suffering. He directed the society for the rest of his life.

Given the Brace-Olmsted-Vaux relationship, Vaux was chosen by Brace to create a series of shelters and schools for his young charges, and between 1879 and 1892, the firm of Vaux and Radford designed nine facilities for the society in Manhattan and one in Brooklyn, the latter a health home or sanitarium at the oceanside in West Coney Island. They also supervised the construction of several cottages at the society's summer home, in nearby Bath Beach, between 1886 and 1888.

*Vaux and Radford, 44th Street Lodging House for Boys and Industrial School, New York, 1888.*

The reason for the stepped gable theme in several such facades of the society's buildings seems to lie in the 44th Street Lodging House at Second Avenue, the one donated by banker-philanthropist Morris K. Jesup. The society's *46th Annual Report* of 1888 explains: "This house, designed by Mr. Vaux after an old Nuremburg house called the 'Petersen' building, is one of the most picturesque in the city. The high, sharp roof and red tiles, the steep gables, quaint dormer windows and lovely oriole [*sic*] towers, with a graceful clock-tower making a center above, form one of the most admirably effective specimens of architecture which can be seen in any American city. It does great credit to Mr. Vaux's genius, and is in harmony with the generous donor's well-known taste in artistic matters." Deference to a client's wishes may well be read here. Whether or not Vaux decided to continue this design theme on his own or because future clients liked the effect, the stepped gable facade was appropriately reminiscent of the city's Dutch heritage. The facade treatment of bay window–engaged shallow buttresses seems perfectly in accord with the stepped gable. The Second Avenue elevated rail line and the building are long gone.

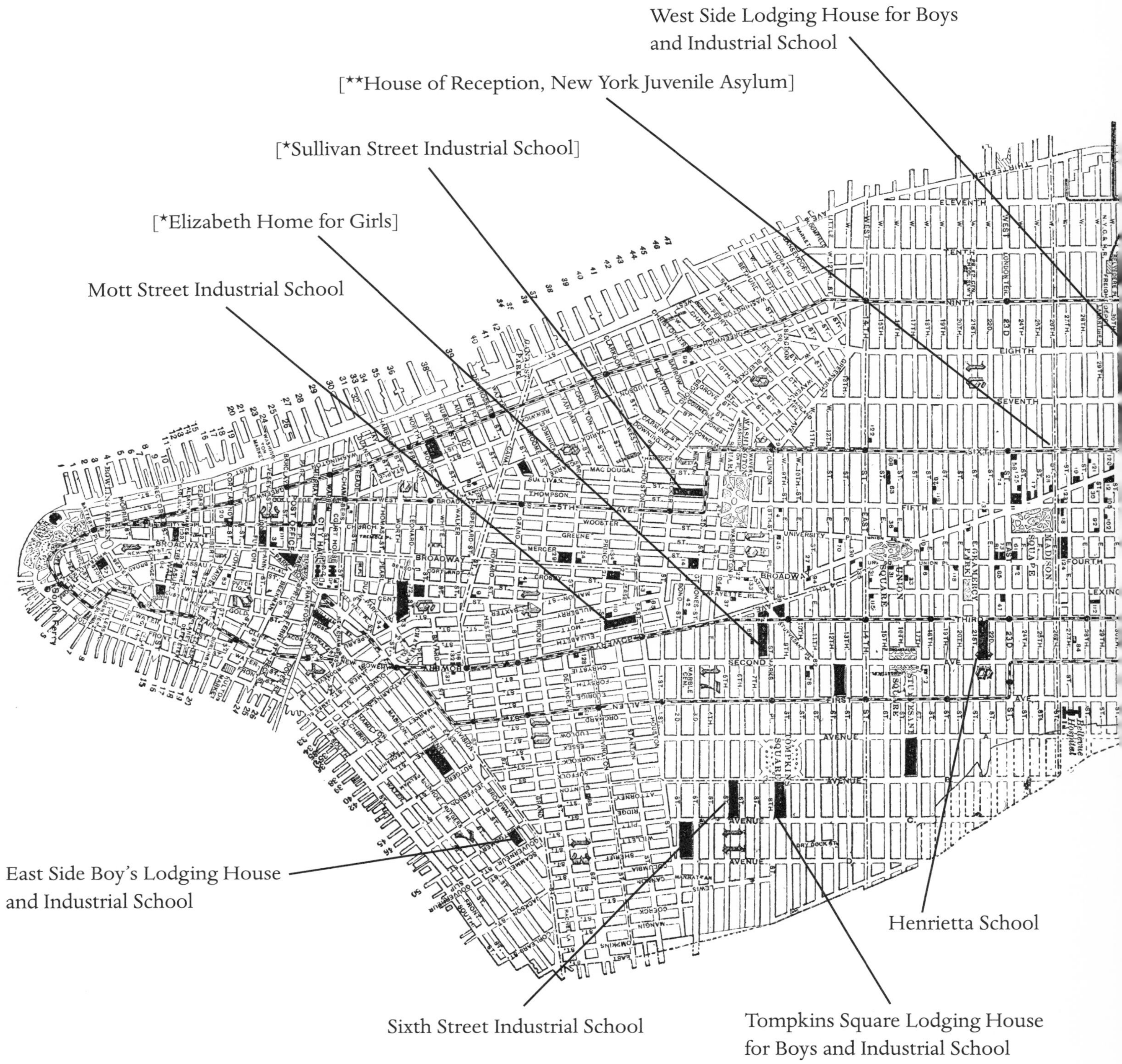

West Side Lodging House for Boys and Industrial School

[**House of Reception, New York Juvenile Asylum]

[*Sullivan Street Industrial School]

[*Elizabeth Home for Girls]

Mott Street Industrial School

East Side Boy's Lodging House and Industrial School

Henrietta School

Sixth Street Industrial School

Tompkins Square Lodging House for Boys and Industrial School

"Stations" of the CHILDREN'S AID SOCIETY in New York City.

*The Elizabeth Home for Girls and the Sullivan Street Industrial School, both completed in 1892, share the general design themes of the previous Children's Aid Society buildings, but are credited to Nicholas Gillesheimer, a partner of Vaux's son Downing. The partnership was located at the same address as Vaux and Radford, 76 Bible House, Astor Place, Manhattan.

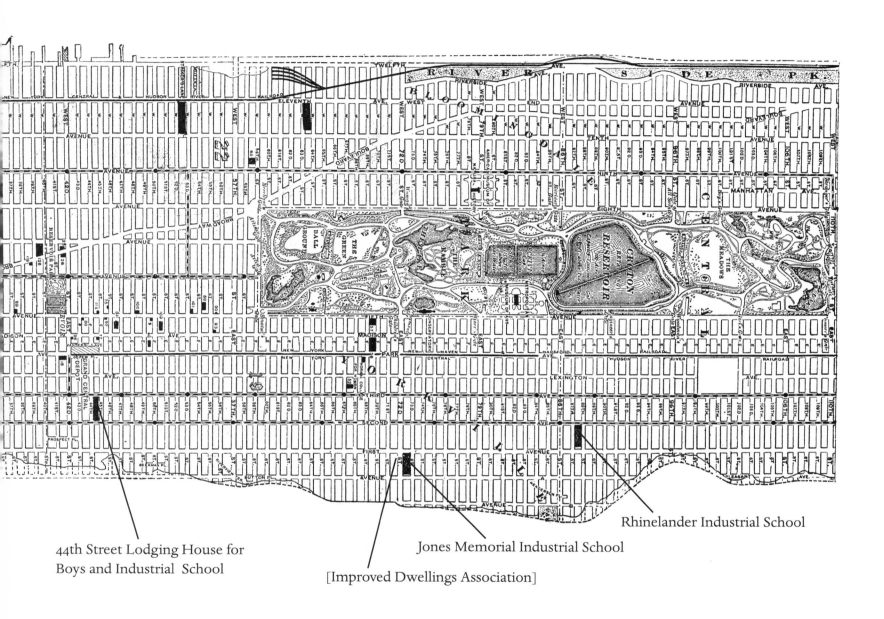

44th Street Lodging House for
Boys and Industrial School

Jones Memorial Industrial School

Rhinelander Industrial School

[Improved Dwellings Association]

**A second charitable organization for which Vaux and Radford did work was the New York Juvenile
Asylum. They remodeled temporary offices for the asylum on West 24th Street and then designed
the new House of Reception on West 27th Street (p. 228). The children dealt with there were subject
to correction.

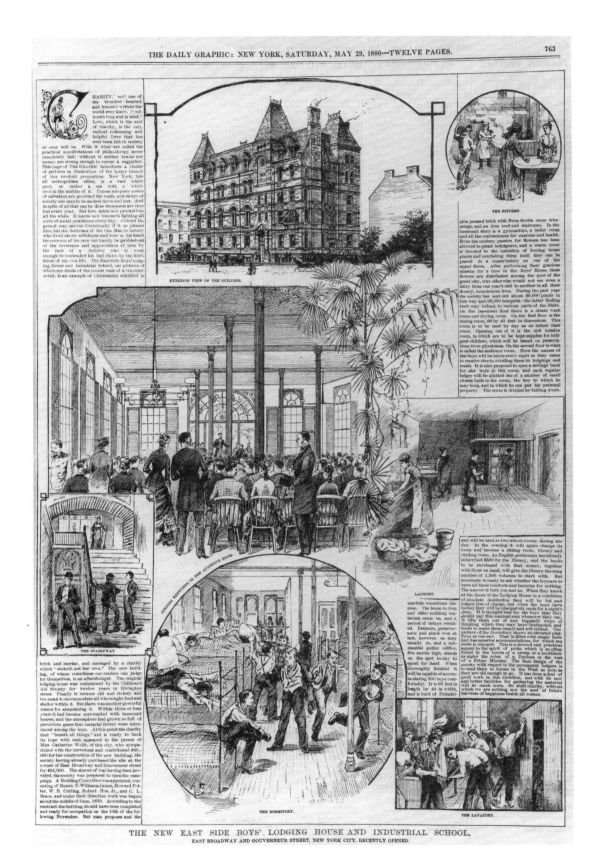

*Vaux and Radford, East Side Boys' Lodging House and Industrial School, New York, 1880.*

*East Side Boys' Lodging House and Industrial School.*

"The East Side Boys' Lodging House and Industrial School . . . is an example of Christianity solidified in brick and mortar, and managed by a charity which 'seeketh not her own,'" wrote *The Daily Graphic*. The society was pleased with Vaux. "He has given us an imposing and picturesque building, presenting a fine harmony of architectural effects from every point of view. In the interior arrangements he has shown much ingenuity and fertility of resources, combining beauty of design with utility and comfort in a very remarkable degree." In functional Gothic style, the building was built of Philadelphia pressed brick and Nova Scotia stone trimming. The fully equipped, five-story building contained a gymnasium, library and even a conservatory, and accommodated 300 boys. "But somebody is ready to ask (asked *The Daily Graphic*) whether the boys are to have all these comforts and luxuries for nothing. The answer is both yes and no. When they knock at the doors of the Lodging House in a condition of absolute destitution they will be fed and lodged free of charge. But when the boys have money they will be charged six cents for a night's sleep." The building was given by Catherine Lorillard Wolfe. Built on East Broadway near Gouverneur and Henry Streets, the building was used for a time as a public school before being demolished.

*Vaux and Radford, West Side Lodging House for Boys and Industrial School, New York, 1882.*

The West Side Lodging House, located on the corner of Seventh Avenue and West 32nd Street, was, the society felt, "one of the most commodious and picturesque buildings which the society has thus far possessed . . . the noble gift of Mr. J. J. Astor." Its Gothic-style facades were built of brick with sandstone trimming, "very beautiful in exterior." John Jacob Astor III appears to have been pleased as well with both the society and Vaux; he later donated another building. The site is now occupied by the Madison Square Garden–Pennsylvania Station complex.

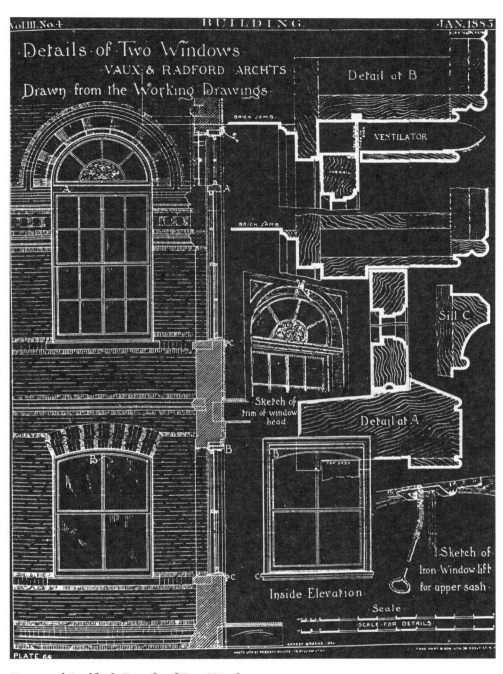

*Vaux and Radford, Details of Two Windows.*

The healthful and efficient functioning of his buildings was a paramount concern of Vaux's. The windows for the West Side building and for others of the society were of a special ventilating sort, devised to allow fresh air in at the top and forcing it far into the room, not allowing it to follow the usual down-draft path along the cold glass of the window's interior. Were a heater to be placed below the window, the column of rising hot air would be "thrown toward the centre of the room" rather than passing out through the open top of any ordinary window.

*Vaux and Radford, Tompkins Square Lodging House for Boys and Industrial School, New York, 1886.*

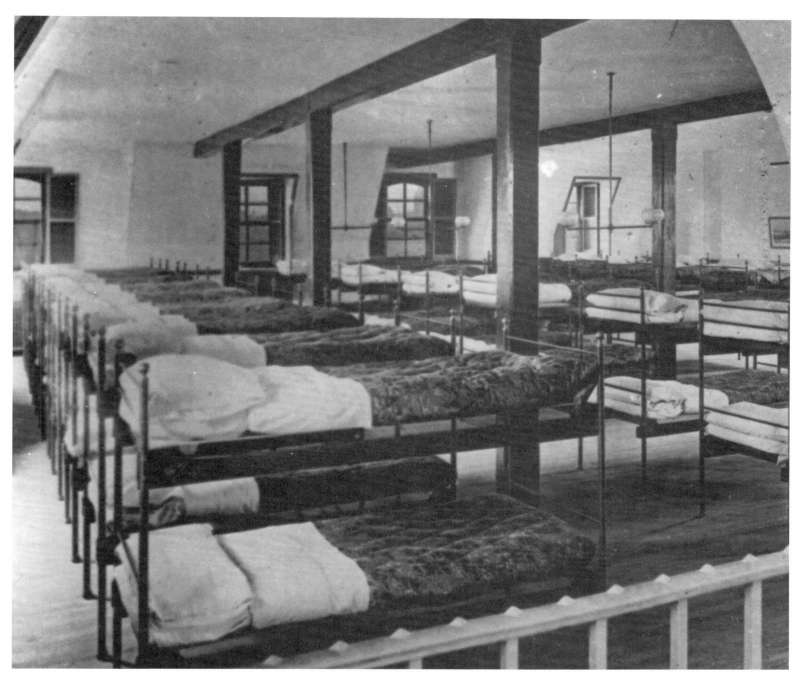

*Tompkins Square Lodging House for Boys.* Dormitory.

The Tompkins Square facility was opened on March 25, 1887, given as the result of the generosity of Mrs. Robert L. Stuart, who provided over $80,000 for its construction. Dormitory accommodations contained "first class beds" of iron with "wire woven mattresses." Besides the double bunks at six cents a night for boys who could pay, the Lodging Houses had single beds at ten cents for boys who had more money, an incentive toward betterment, the society felt. Currently used as residences, the building is located just east of Tompkins Square at East Eighth Street.

*Vaux and Radford, Sixth Street Industrial School, New York, 1891.*

The Sixth Street School was given by Mrs. William Douglas Sloane. It is located on East Sixth Street between Avenues B and C and presently serves as a municipal social service center.

*Vaux and Radford, Rhinelander Industrial School, New York, 1890.*

*Rhinelander Industrial School.* North elevation.

The Rhinelander School, with eight schoolrooms, was given by the Misses Rhinelander, who also provided for playground space on three sides of the building. They had been assisting the activities of the society for 20 years and continued their generous support well after the erection of the school. The original drawing of the front facade is just one of an existing series of 13 made by the architects; the firm's name can just be discerned at the lower right. The building is on East 88th Street between First and Second Avenues and now serves primarily as a youth center.

*Vaux and Radford, Jones Memorial Industrial School, New York, 1890.*

JONES MEMORIAL
INDUSTRIAL SCHOOL
C··A··S
73RD ST NEW YORK.

*Jones Memorial Industrial School.* Plans.

The Jones family were especially generous in that they provided not only a playground in connection with their building, but an endowment toward its continuing support. The school was built on East 73rd Street, east of First Avenue, not far from the Improved Dwellings Association apartments. It was demolished in 1965.

*Vaux and Radford, Mott Street Industrial School, New York, 1890.*

*Mott Street Industrial School.* "Patriotic Election in Mott Street Industrial School: 'One Flag.'" Photo by Jacob A. Riis.

The Mott Street, or 14th Ward, Industrial School, was the second building donated by John Jacob Astor III, in memory of his wife, Charlotte. This was an Italian immigrant neighborhood whose children, the society noted, would not eat the oatmeal and milk prepared for their repast, preferring instead bread dipped in coffee. Children here were taught sewing, drawing, kitchen gardening and probably lessons in nutrition. The building now contains residences.

HOUSE OF RECEPTION OF THE NEW YORK JUVENILE ASYLUM 106 W 27ᵀᴴ ST N.Y. CITY.

*House of Reception.*

*Vaux and Radford, House of Reception, New York Juvenile Asylum, New York, 1890.*

"The new House of Reception . . . has been found, by actual experience, to be particularly well adapted to the purposes for which it has been erected—the reception of children and their temporary detention, as required by the Asylum Charter; the place from which they are finally returned to their friends, or from which they depart to Western homes; the place where the business meetings of the Board of Directors and its several committees are held." The *37th Annual Report of the New York Juvenile Asylum* in 1889 also noted the responsibilities of the board of directors toward their charges. The committee on buildings and repairs of the asylum was headed by Andrew H. Green, the former comptroller of Central Park and a law partner of Samuel J. Tilden. Built on West 27th Street, it has been demolished.

*Vaux and Radford, Chapel, Tifereth Israel Cemetery, Cypress Hills, New York, 1885.*

The one-room chapel of red brick with stone accents is located on Long Island in the cemetery of the Spanish and Portuguese Synagogue of New York City. Vaux also designed the entrance gate to the cemetery. The chapel was restored in 1962.

*Vaux and Radford, Children's Aid Society, Health Home, Brooklyn, New York, 1884.*

*Arnot-Ogden Memorial Hospital.* Front hall.

The Children's Aid Society's Health Home, or Sanitarium, was built on a prime seaside site of four and a quarter acres between Fort Hamilton and Coney Island donated by Mr. A. B. Stone. Mr. D. Willis James provided funds for the building, erected for the care of sick children and ailing infants who could come there with their mothers. The home's wide piazzas and porches were fully open to the sun and ocean breezes. It was closed in 1921 and later demolished.

*Vaux and Radford, Arnot-Ogden Memorial Hospital, Elmira, New York, 1888.*

The 25-bed hospital, funded by a contribution of $75,000 by Marianna Arnot Ogden in memory of her husband, opened on December 20, 1888. The first patient arrived four days later. Both men's and women's wards had sun rooms and piazzas attached. Five private patients' rooms were located on the upper floors. Drawing initially on Vaux and Radford's expertise in the field, the hospital, one of the first organized medical facilities in New York State's Southern Tier, has evolved into a major medical center, the original building having been replaced in 1951.

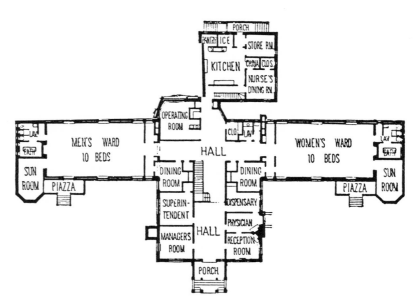

*Arnot-Ogden Memorial Hospital.* Plan.

# Chronology

| | |
|---|---|
| 20 Dec. 1824 | Born, London |
| 1833–1838 | Attends Merchant Taylors' School |
| 1839 | Apprenticed to architect Lewis Nockalls Cottingham |
| 1847 | On death of Cottingham, continues work with his son, Nockalls Johnson Cottingham |
| 1850 | Engaged by A. J. Downing as architectural assistant; arrives in United States |
| 1851 | Becomes Downing's partner, Newburgh, N. Y. |
| 28 July 1852 | Downing dies; undertakes completion of Downing-Vaux commissions |
| 1853 | Forms partnership in Newburgh with Frederick Clarke Withers of Downing's staff |
| 4 May 1854 | Marries Mary Swan McEntee (sons, Calvert Bowyer, b. 1855, Downing, b. 1856; daughters, Julia, b. 1858, Marian, b. 1864) |
| May 1856 | Moves to New York; partnership with Withers dissolved |
| 24 Oct. 1856 | Becomes naturalized American citizen |
| 1857 | Publishes *Villas and Cottages, A Series of Designs for Execution in the United States* |
| 1858 | Wins Central Park design competition with "Greensward" plan, submitted with Frederick Law Olmsted. Olmsted appointed architect-in-chief; Vaux, consulting architect (see below for Central Park chronology) |
| 1860–1861 | Partnership with Withers in New York |
| 1863 | Travels to Europe on official parks survey |
| 1863–1864 | Partnership with Lewis W. Leeds, heating and ventilation engineer |
| 1864 | Publishes second edition of *Villas and Cottages* |
| 1864–1865 | Partnership with Withers |
| Jan. 1865 | Develops initial design scheme for Prospect Park, Brooklyn, N.Y. |
| Nov. 1865 | Persuades Olmsted to return from California to join him in final design and construction of Prospect Park; Olmsted, Vaux and Co. formed |
| 1866–1871 | Partnership with Withers |
| 1868 | Designs Riverside, Ill., town plan with Olmsted |
| 1872 | Partnership with Olmsted dissolved |
| 1874 | Partnership with George K. Radford; designs first building for [American] Museum of Natural History with Jacob Wrey Mould |
| 1879 | Designs first building for [Metropolitan] Museum of Art with Mould |
| 1879–1892 | Designs series of Children's Aid Society facilities, Vaux and Radford, architects |
| 1880–1884 | Vaux and Co. formed; Samuel Parsons, Jr., associate and 1887–1895 partner |
| 19 Nov. 1895 | Dies, Brooklyn, N. Y. |

CENTRAL PARK CHRONOLOGY

| | |
|---|---|
| 30 Apr. 1857 | First Board of Commissioners for Central Park appointed |
| 11 Sept. 1857 | Olmsted appointed superintendent of Central Park |
| 28 Apr. 1858 | Olmsted and Vaux's "Greensward" plan wins the Central Park design competition |
| 17 May 1858 | Board of Commissioners of the Central Park appoint Olmsted architect-in-chief of the park; Vaux appointed consulting architect |
| 10 Apr. 1862 | Olmsted and Vaux jointly appointed landscape architects to the board [of Central Park Commissioners] |
| 14 May 1863 | Olmsted and Vaux resign |
| Feb. 1866 | Olmsted and Vaux reappointed landscape architects to the board |
| 30 Nov. 1870 | Olmsted and Vaux resign |
| 23 Nov. 1871 | Olmsted and Vaux appointed landscape architects advisory to the board |
| 29 May 1872 | Vaux appointed landscape architect and general superintendent; Olmsted appointed temporary board commissioner |
| 24 Oct. 1872 | Vaux appointed consulting landscape architect Olmsted appointed landscape architect |
| 4 June 1873 | Vaux resigns as consulting landscape architect |
| 19 Nov. 1881– | |
| Jan. 1883 | Vaux serves as landscape architect to the City of New York |
| Jan. 1888– | |
| 19 Nov. 1895 | Vaux serves as landscape architect to the City of New York |

# Listing of Works

THE FOLLOWING LIST combines the designs in both editions, 1857 and 1864, of *Villas and Cottages*. Vaux added seven new designs in the 1864 edition to make a total of 39 formal examples, but deleted the names of several of the clients mentioned in the first edition. The listing below combines the available information from both editions, including all names of clients, names of clients later discovered, and first names when initials only were given. When two design numbers are shown, as for example 26/31, the first refers to its sequence in the 1857 edition, the second to that of 1864. Besides the formal presentation of drawings, plans and descriptions of the numbered house designs, Vaux included dozens of additional drawings of houses, estate outbuildings such as coach houses and stables, numerous exterior and interior details, furniture designs and an occasional site plan. These are listed following the numbered designs, page numbers in 1857/1864 sequence. Collaborative works are noted by (D. & V.) for Downing and Vaux and (V. & W.) for Vaux and Withers. The listing under Architectural Designs includes all 39 formal designs in *Villas and Cottages;* those marked "study" were not built.

GIVEN THE RANGE AND VARIETY of Calvert Vaux's creative production, it was deemed best to form several categories of his work. Even so there are overlapping entries, as for a work comprising both a building and its grounds. Rather than separating the entry into architecture and landscape categories, architecture is given precedence, as for example, "Edwin Booth House and Grounds," and the work is listed under Architectural Designs. Overlapping is somewhat a concern where the sorting process is still to be undertaken, in that designs that are known to be Olmsted's alone, as for example the College of California at Berkeley plan, are credited to Olmsted, Vaux and Co. which entity in turn is credited with Vaux's house designs in their Riverside, Illinois, town plan and with Vaux building designs in their park work. However, major works by Withers that are very clearly his own are excluded, even though done under the Vaux, Withers partnership, although, interestingly, occasional drawings of Withers' work show lettering that appears to be in Vaux's hand. Design credit is further complicated by works such as the James Walker Fowler house, where the title block on the original drawings gives only the name of Vaux while the credit note in *Villas and Cottages* indicates the design is by Vaux and Withers. Because of the loss of the great bulk of Vaux's papers, including his professional correspondence as well as letterbooks which are known to have existed, these listings should not be considered complete. In this regard, except when specifically known, dates given are beginning dates for a work, although some elasticity must be assumed in various cases, especially in the earlier examples. Several unrecorded Vaux works have come to light during the preparation of this publication, and more are expected to emerge in the future. Occasional listings under Landscape Architecture Designs refer only to a preliminary survey and subsequent plan of work submitted in a formal report.

ARCHITECTURAL DESIGNS

| | |
|---|---|
| 1850 | Springside, Matthew Vassar House (study), Poughkeepsie, N.Y. (with A.J. Downing) |
| 1851 | Algonac, Warren Delano House, Newburgh, N.Y. (with A.J. Downing) |
| 1851 | F.J. Betts House (study), Newburgh, N.Y. (with A.J. Downing) |
| 1852 | Francis Dodge House, Washington, D.C. (with A.J. Downing) |
| 1852 | Robert P. Dodge House, Washington, D.C. (with A.J. Downing) |
| 1852 | Dr. William A.M. Culbert House, Newburgh, N.Y. (with A.J. Downing) |
| 1852 | S.D. Dakin House (study), Hudson Valley location. (with A.J. Downing) |
| 1852 | William L. Findlay House, Newburgh, N.Y. (with A.J. Downing) |
| 1852 | E.S. Hall House (study), Millville, Mass. |
| 1852 | David Moore House, Newburgh, N.Y. (with A.J. Downing) |
| 1852 | Daniel Parish House, Newport, R.I. (with A.J. Downing) |
| 1853 | Monument for a Mr. Buchanan, Newburgh, N.Y. (with F.C. Withers) |
| 1853 | John W. Burt House (study), Mountain Park [Llewellyn Park], West Orange, N.J. (with F.C. Withers) |
| 1853 | Design for a Square House (study). (with F.C. Withers) |
| 1853 | Design for a Roomy Country House, Orange County, N.Y. (with F.C. Withers) |
| 1853 | Thomas Earle House (study), Worcester, Mass. (with F.C. Withers) |
| 1853 | The Point, Lydig M. Hoyt House, Staatsburg, N.Y. |
| 1853 | Leonard H. Lee House, Cornwall, N.Y. (with F.C. Withers) |
| 1853 | Rev. Edward J. O'Reilly House, Newburgh, N.Y. (with F.C. Withers) |
| 1853 | Nathan Reeve House (study), Newburgh, N.Y. (with F.C. Withers) |
| 1853 | Daniel Ryan House (study), Newburgh, N.Y. |
| 1853 | A Suburban House with a Curvilinear Roof (study), Worcester, Mass. (with F.C. Withers) |
| 1853 | Idlewild, Nathaniel P. Willis House, Cornwall, N.Y. |
| 1854 | R.L. Case House, Newburgh, N.Y. |
| 1854 | III Commercial Block, Commercial Wharf, Boston, Mass. |
| 1854 | Design for a Villa for Matthew Vassar (study), Poughkeepsie, N.Y. |
| 1854 | James Walker Fowler House (study), Newburgh, N.Y. (with F.C. Withers) |
| 1854 | C.H. Rogers House, Ravenswood, L.I., N.Y. |
| 1854 | Alexander Wright House, Goshen, N.Y. |
| 1855 | Halsey Stevens House, Newburgh, N.Y. (with F.C. Withers) |
| 1855 | Henry H. Chamberlain House, Worcester, Mass. (with F.C. Withers) |
| 1855 | Dr. de la Montagnie House, Fishkill Landing, N.Y. |
| 1855 | Jervis McEntee Studio, Rondout, N.Y. |
| 1855 | M.J. Robins House, Yonkers, N.Y. |
| 1856 | John W. Burt House, [Llewellyn Park], West Orange, N.J. (with F.C. Withers) |
| 1856 | Bank of New York, New York, N.Y. (with F.C. Withers) |
| 1856 | Federico L. Barreda House, Newport, R.I. |
| 1856 | John A.C. Gray House, New York, N.Y. (with F.C. Withers) |
| 1856 | Thomas Powell House Alteration, Newburgh, N.Y. |
| 1856 | Robins and Co. Packing House, New York, N.Y. (with F.C. Withers) |
| 1857 | William E. Warren House, Newburgh, N.Y. |
| 1857 | George E. Howard House, Springfield, Mass. |
| 1857 | Parisian Buildings for City Residents (study), New York, N.Y. |

| 1858 | Peter C. Brooks, Jr., House, West Medford, Mass. |
| 1859 | Levi P. Stone House, [Llewellyn Park], West Orange, N.J. |
| 1860 | Ammadelle, Thomas E. B. Pegues House, Oxford, Miss. |
| 1860 | Francis Tomes House, Greenwich, Conn. |
| 1861 | House for Anonymous Client, Fordham, Highbridge, N.Y. |
| 1861–1895 | Sheppard Asylum, Baltimore, Md. |
| 1862 | Ashcroft, Stephen H. Hammond House, Geneva, N.Y. |
| 1863 | A. T. McClintock House, Wilkes-Barre, Pa. (with F. C. Withers) |
| 1865 | Eugene A. Brewster House, Newburgh, N. Y. (with F. C. Withers) |
| 1865 | Charles Kimball Townhouse, Brooklyn, N. Y. (with F. C. Withers) |
| 1865 | Study for a Public Museum and Library. (with F. C. Withers) |
| 1865 | Richard Blachford House (study). |
| 1866 | Rev. Henry Field House, New York, N.Y. (with F. C. Withers) |
| 1867 | Hudson River State Hospital and Grounds, Poughkeepsie, N. Y. (with F. C. Withers and F. L. Olmsted) |
| 1867 | John James Monell House, Beacon, N.Y. (with F. C. Withers) |
| 1867 | Edwin L. Godkin House, New York, N. Y. |
| 1868 | Retreat for the Insane, Hartford, Conn. (with F. C. Withers) |
| 1868–1870 | J. Donald Cameron House, Harrisburg, Pa. (with F. C. Withers) |
| 1869 | Margaret H. Frothingham House, New York, N.Y. (with F. C. Withers) |
| 1869 | Clovercroft, Mrs. Fanny B. Godwin House, Roslyn, N. Y. |
| 1869 | George B. Grinnell House, New York, N.Y. (with F. C. Withers) |
| 1870 | George B. Grinnell House, Alterations, New York, N. Y. |
| 1870 | Olana, Frederic E. Church House, Hudson, N.Y. (with F. C. Withers) |
| 1871 | E. T. Wright House, Riverside, Ill. (with F. L. Olmsted) |
| 1871 | Geo. M. Kimbark House, Riverside, Ill. (with F. L. Olmsted) |
| 1871 | John C. Dore House, Riverside, Ill. (with F. L. Olmsted) |
| 1871 | Edward Gleason House, New York, N.Y. (with F. C. Withers) |
| 1871 | Hall-Rice Building, Troy, N. Y. |
| 1872 | Trinity Cemetery Suspension Bridge, New York, N.Y. (with F. C. Withers) |
| 1872 | David Bonner House, New York, N.Y. (with F. C. Withers) |
| 1872 | B. F. Joslin House, New York, N.Y. (with F. C. Withers) |
| 1872–1878 | [American] Museum of Natural History, New York, N. Y. (with J. W. Mould) |
| 1873 | Main Pavilion Design, Centennial Exhibition, Philadelphia, Pa. (with G. K. Radford) |
| 1874 | Jefferson Market Courthouse, New York, N. Y. (with F. C. Withers) |
| 1874 | Henry Baldwin Hyde House, Islip, L. I., N.Y. |
| 1874 | C. H. McCormick House (study), Chicago, Ill. |
| 1874–1880 | [Metropolitan] Museum of Art, New York, N. Y. (with J. W. Mould) |
| 1876 | Charles Irving Brace House, Dobbs Ferry, N.Y. |
| 1876 | George J. Bull House, Worcester, Mass. |
| 1879 | Thomas W. Whittredge House, Summit, N.J. |
| 1880 | James Morse House, Cotuit, Mass. |
| 1880 | Raphael Pumpelly House, Newport, R.I. |
| 1880 | Addition to the Bank of New York, New York, N. Y. (with G. K. Radford) |
| 1880 | East Side Children's Aid Society Boys' Lodging House and Industrial School, New York, N.Y. (with G. K. Radford) |

1881        Samuel J. Tilden House, New York, N.Y. [now the National Arts Club]. (with
            G. K. Radford)

1881–1889   Trinity Cemetery Gatehouse and Grounds, New York, N.Y. (with G. K. Radford
            and S. Parsons, Jr.)

1882        Improved Dwelling Association Model Tenement, New York, N.Y.
            (with G. K. Radford)

1882        Adelbert College, Cleveland, Ohio.
            [now part of Case Western Reserve University]

1882        West Side Children's Aid Society Lodging House for Boys and Industrial School,
            New York, N.Y. (with G. K. Radford)

1882–1883   Edwin Booth House and Grounds, Middletown, R.I.

1884        Health Home, Children's Aid Society, Brooklyn, N.Y. (with G. K. Radford)

1885        R. S. Bowne House, Flushing, N.Y.

1885        Chapel, Tifereth Israel Cemetery, Cypress Hills, N.Y.

1886        Harlem River Bridge Design (study), New York, N.Y. (with G. K. Radford)

1886        Tompkins Square Children's Aid Society Lodging House for Boys and Industrial
            School, New York, N.Y. (with G. K. Radford)

1888        44th Street Children's Aid Society Lodging House for Boys and Industrial School,
            New York, N.Y. (with G. K. Radford)

1888        Arnot-Ogden Memorial Hospital, Elmira, N.Y. (with G. K. Radford)

1888        Jones Memorial Children's Aid Society Industrial School, New York, N.Y.
            (with G. K. Radford)

1890        Mott Street Children's Aid Society Industrial School, New York, N.Y.
            (with G. K. Radford)

1890        New York Juvenile Asylum, New York, N.Y. (with G. K. Radford)

1890        House of Reception, New York Juvenile Asylum, New York, N.Y.
            (with G. K. Radford)

1890        Rhinelander Children's Aid Society Industrial School, New York, N.Y.
            (with G. K. Radford)

1890        Henrietta Children's Aid Society Industrial School, New York, N.Y.
            (with G. K. Radford)

1890–1892   Samuel D. Coykendall House, Rondout, N.Y. (with G. K. Radford)

1891        Sixth Street Industrial School, New York, N.Y. (with G. K. Radford)

1894        Luna Island Bridge, State Reservation at Niagara, N.Y.

n.d.        G. T. Headly House, Hudson, N.Y.

## LANDSCAPE ARCHITECTURE DESIGNS

1858–1876   Central Park, New York, N.Y. (with F. L. Olmsted)

1860        Hillside Cemetery, Middletown, N.Y. (with F. L. Olmsted)

1860        Edward K. Collins Estate, New Rochelle, N.Y. (with F. L. Olmsted)

1861        Bloomingdale Asylum Grounds, White Plains, N.Y. (with F. L. Olmsted)

1862        Retreat for the Insane, Hartford, Conn. [now Institute of Living]. (with F. L.
            Olmsted)

1866        Columbia Institution for the Deaf and Dumb, Washington, D.C. [now Gallaudet
            University]. (with F. L. Olmsted)

1866        College of California, Berkeley, Calif. [now University of California, Berkeley
            campus]. (with F. L. Olmsted)

| | |
|---|---|
| 1866 | Free Institute of Industrial Science, Worcester, Mass. [now Polytechnic Institute]. (with F. L. Olmsted) |
| 1866 | Agricultural College, Orono, Maine [now University of Maine, Orono campus]. (with F. L. Olmsted) |
| 1866–1873 | Prospect Park, Brooklyn, N.Y. (with F. L. Olmsted) |
| 1867 | Parade Ground for Kings County, Brooklyn, N.Y. (with F. L. Olmsted) |
| 1867 | Fort Greene Park, Brooklyn, N.Y. (with F. L. Olmsted) |
| 1867 | Walnut Hill Park, New Britain, Conn. (with F. L. Olmsted) |
| 1867 | Seaside Park, Bridgeport, Conn. (with F. L. Olmsted) |
| 1868 | Eastern and Ocean Parkways, Brooklyn, N.Y. (with F. L. Olmsted) |
| 1868–1876 | Buffalo Park System: Delaware Park, The Parade and The Front, Buffalo, N.Y. (with F. L. Olmsted) |
| 1871 | Buffalo State Hospital Grounds, Buffalo, N.Y. (with F. L. Olmsted) |
| 1871 | Tompkins Park, Brooklyn, N.Y. (with F. L. Olmsted) |
| 1871 | South Park, Fall River, Mass. (with F. L. Olmsted) |
| 1871–1873 | South Park, Chicago, Ill. (with F. L. Olmsted) |
| 1873, 1887 | Morningside Park, New York, N.Y. (with F. L. Olmsted and S. Parsons, Jr.) |
| 1873–1879 | Parliament Buildings Grounds, Ottawa, Canada. |
| 1877–1885 | Riverside Park, New York, N.Y. (with F. L. Olmsted and S. Parsons, Jr.) |
| 1879 | Greystone, Samuel J. Tilden Estate, Yonkers, N.Y. |
| ca. 1880 | Dr. G. P. Davis Grounds, Hartford, Conn. |
| 1884 | Bryn Mawr College Grounds, Bryn Mawr, Pa. |
| 1885 | Grant's Tomb Site, Riverside Park, New York, N.Y. (with S. Parsons, Jr.) |
| 1886 | Grace Church Grounds, New York, N.Y. |
| 1887 | Downing Park, Newburgh, N.Y. (with F. L. Olmsted) |
| 1887–1895 | State Reservation at Niagara Falls, N.Y. (with F. L. Olmsted) |
| 1888 | Riverside Cemetery, Trenton, N.J. |
| 1888 | Berkeley Oval, New York, N.Y. |
| 1888 | High Bridge Park, New York, N.Y. (with S. Parsons Jr.) |
| 1888 | Academy Avenue Park, Middletown, N.Y. |
| 1889 | The Clearing, Wisner Estate, Summit, N.J. [now Reeves-Reed Arboretum] |
| 1890 | Wilderstein, Rhinecliff, N.Y. (with D. Vaux and S. Parsons, Jr.) |
| 1891 | Isaac Gale Johnson Grounds, Bronx, N.Y. |
| 1894 | New York University Grounds, Bronx, N.Y. |
| 1894 | Corlears Hook Park, New York, N.Y. (with S. Parsons, Jr.) |
| 1894 | St. Johns Park, St. Johns, Newfoundland, Canada. |
| 1895 | New York Botanical Garden, Bronx, N.Y. (with S. Parsons, Jr.) |
| 1895 | Mulberry Bend Park, New York, N.Y. (with S. Parsons, Jr.) |
| n.d. | East River Park, New York, N.Y. (with S. Parsons, Jr.) |
| n.d. | Wesleyan Seminary Grounds, Macon, Ga. |
| n.d. | Cemetery, Macon, Ga. |

TOWN PLANS

| | |
|---|---|
| 1868 | Riverside, Ill. (with F. L. Olmsted) |
| 1871 | Tarrytown Heights, N.Y. (with F. L. Olmsted) |

SELECTED PARK STRUCTURE DESIGNS

*Central Park, New York, N.Y.*

| | |
|---|---|
| 1858 | Numerous masonry, iron and wood bridges |
| 1858 | Numerous rustic shelters, arbors and boat landings |
| 1859–1860 | Water [Bethesda] Terrace |
| 1864 | Casino |
| 1867 | Ball Players House |
| 1867–1872 | Belvedere |
| 1868 | Mineral Springs Pavilion |
| 1869 | Offices of Administration (with J. W. Mould) |
| 1870 | Dairy |
| 1872–1876 | Boathouse |
| 1888 | Greenhouses (with G. K. Radford) |

*Prospect Park, Brooklyn, N.Y.*

| | |
|---|---|
| 1867 | Swiss Thatched Cottage |
| 1867 | East Wood Arch |
| 1867 | Endale Arch |
| 1868 | Meadowport Arch |
| 1868 | Nethermead Arches |
| 1869 | Dairy |
| 1870 | Lullwood Bridge |
| 1871 | Cleft Ridge Span |
| 1872 | Concert Grove House |
| 1874 | Concert Grove Pavilion |
| 1890 | Terrace Bridge (with G. K. Radford) |

*Kings County Parade Ground, Brooklyn, N.Y.*

| | |
|---|---|
| 1869 | Lodge and Shelter |

*Fort Greene Park, Brooklyn, N.Y.*

| | |
|---|---|
| 1870 | Shelter |

*Delaware Park, Buffalo, N.Y.*

| | |
|---|---|
| 1875 | Boathouse |
| 1875 | Tower |
| 1875 | Boat Landing Seating |

*The Parade, Buffalo, N.Y.*

| | |
|---|---|
| 1876 | Refectory |

*Congress Park, Saratoga Springs, N.Y.*

| | |
|---|---|
| 1876 | Congress and Columbian Springs Pavilions |

# Bibliography

*Note:* The Calvert Vaux Papers at the New York Public Library consist of approximately 100 items, including correspondence with Olmsted, Central Park Comptroller Andrew Haswell Green and James S. T. Stranahan, an extended report to Green on Central Park plantings by Ignaz Pilat, business letters, a holograph copy of his Fort Green [*sic*] or Washington Park report, newspaper clippings, his listing of major works and positions held, four drawings and a portrait photograph. By far the greatest single body of original Vaux material is found in the Olmsted Papers collection at the Library of Congress. The exchange of correspondence between Vaux and Olmsted consists of many dozens of letters of professional and personal content beginning in the early 1860s and extending throughout their careers. There are also letters to each other's family members.

Formal reports on park design progress and other matters by the Olmsted and Vaux firm are contained in the annual reports and other official park documents of the Boards of Park Commissioners or Departments of Parks published by the cities of New Britain and Walnut Hill, Conn.; Chicago, Ill.; Fall River, Mass.; and Brooklyn, Buffalo, Newburgh and New York, N. Y. The firm itself occasionally printed reports for private clients.

CALVERT VAUX AS AUTHOR OR COAUTHOR

Vaux, Calvert. "American Architecture," *The Horticulturist,* viii (February, 1853) 168–172.
———. "Brooklyn Park, Report on the Boundaries," Brooklyn, 1865, mss. 1–17, Avery Library, Columbia University.
———. and Samuel Parsons, Jr. *Concerning Lawn Planting.* New York: Orange Judd Co., 1881.
———. et al. "The Fraternity Papers, 1869–1877," mss., 7 vols., New-York Historical Society.
———. *General Plan for the Improvement of Morningside Park.* New York: Evening Post Job Printing Office, 1887.
———, "Hints for Country House Builders," *Harper's New Monthly Magazine,* xi (November, 1855) 763–778.
———, "Landscape Gardening," *Encyclopaedia Americana, Supplement to the Encyclopedia Britannica,* 9th ed. New York: J. M. Stoddart, 1886, iii, 562–564.
———, et al. *Official Correspondence in Reference to the Plan for the Arrangement of Public Grounds in Front of the Parliament Buildings at Ottawa, Dominion of Canada, C. Vaux, Architect, 1873–79.* New York: G. P. Putnam's Sons, 1879.
———, Papers. Rare Books and Manuscripts Division, New York Public Library, Astor, Lenox and Tilden Foundations. [See also Olmsted correspondence, Papers of Frederick Law Olmsted, Manuscript Division, Library of Congress.]
———, "Parisian Buildings for City Residents," *Harper's Weekly,* i (December 19, 1857) 809–810.
———, "A Philosophical Emperor," *Popular Science Monthly,* xi (August, 1877) 461–469.
———, "Should a Republic Encourage the Arts?" *The Horticulturist,* vii (February, 1852) 73–77.
———, "Street Planning in Relation to Architectural Design," *Proceedings of the Architectural League from Organization to January, 1889,* (March 4, 1889) 135–146.
———. *Villas and Cottages: A Series of Designs Prepared for Execution in the United States.* New York: Harper and Brothers, 1857. Rev. ed. 1864, repr. 1867, 1874. Reviews in *The Horticulturist,* xii (March–April, 1857) 368; *Harper's New Monthly Magazine,* xiv (March, 1857) 554; *Crayon,* vi (March, 1857) 169. Repr. 1857 ed., New York: Da Capo Press, 1968; 1864 ed., New York: Dover Publications, 1970, 1991.

————, Letters to Fletcher Harper, January 24, 1855, Harper and Brothers, New York; January 29, 1855, Newburgh, N.Y., The Pierpont Morgan Library, New York.

————, ["Mr. Vaux's Part in It, The Central Park Plan," *New York Daily Tribune*, xxxvii (February 19, 1878) 5.]

————, [Godkin, E. L., "Mr. Godkin Replies to Mr. Vaux," *New York Daily Tribune*, xxxvii (February 20, 1878) 5.]

————, [Godkin, E. L., and Owen F. Olmsted, "The Central Park Plan, Mr. Vaux's Share in It Equal to Mr. Olmsted's," *New York Daily Tribune*, xxxvii (February 21, 1878) 5.]

————, ["Mr. Vaux Wishes to Withdraw His Letter about Mr. Godkin," *New York Daily Tribune*, xxxvii (February 22, 1878) 5].

————, "Grant's Tomb Memorial Site," *The New York Times*, xxxiv (August 10, 1885) 1.

CALVERT VAUX AS COAUTHOR WITH FREDERICK LAW OLMSTED

Olmsted, Frederick Law, and Calvert Vaux. *Description of a Map Accompanying a Model of Clay as a Plan for the Central Park in the City of New York.* New York: J. F. Baldwin, 1858.

————. *Description of a Plan for the Improvement of the Central Park "Greensward"* New York, 1858. Repr., New York: Sutton, Bowne and Co., 1868.

————. *General Plan for the Improvement of the Niagara Reservation.* Niagara Falls, N.Y.: Gazette Book and Job Office, 1887.

————. *Two Letters to the President on Recent Changes and Projected Changes in the Central Park.* [New York]: Printed by order of the Executive Committee [Board of Commissioners, Department of Public Parks, New York City], 1872.

Olmsted, Vaux and Company. *Preliminary Report to the Commissioners for Laying Out a Park in Brooklyn; Being a Consideration of Circumstances of Site and Other Conditions Affecting the Design of Public Pleasure Grounds.* Brooklyn, N.Y.: 1866.

————. *Preliminary Report upon the Proposed Suburban Village of Riverside, near Chicago.* New York: Sutton, Bowne and Co., 1868.

BOOKS, 19TH CENTURY

*Annual Reports.* New York: Children's Aid Society, 1879–1895.

*Annual Reports.* New York: Juvenile Asylum, New York: 1889–1892.

Bremer, Frederika. *The Homes of the New World.* Trans. Mary Howitt. 2 vols. New York: Harper and Brothers, 1854.

Bullock, John. *The Rudiments of Architecture and Building for the Use of Architects, Builders, Draughtsmen, Machinists, Engineers and Mechanics.* New York: Stringer and Townsend, 1855.

*Catalogue of the Museum of Medieval Art Collected by the Late L. N. Cottingham, F.S.A. Architect.* London: Henry Shaw, 1851.

Cook, Clarence. *A Description of the New York Central Park.* New York: F. J. Huntington and Co., 1869.

Cottingham, Lewis N. *Plans, Elevations, Sections, Details and Views with Mouldings, Full Size, of the Chapel of King Henry VII at Westminster Abbey.* 2 vols. London: Priestly and Weale, 1822.

————. *The Smith and Founder's Directory, Containing a Series of Designs and Patterns for Ornamental Iron and Brasswork.* London: 1824.

————. *Working Drawings for Gothic Ornament, selected and composed from the best examples, consisting of capitals, bases, cornices, &c., with a Design for a Gothic Mansion.* [London:] Priestly and Weale, [1830].

*Description of the Designs for the Improvement of Central Park.* New York: Board of Commissioners of Central Park, 1858.

Downing, Andrew Jackson. *The Architecture of Country Houses; Including Designs for Cottages, Farm Houses and Villas, with Remarks on Interiors, Furniture, and the Best Modes of Warming and Ventilating.* New York: D. Appleton and Co., 1850.

———. *Cottage Residences; or a Series of Designs for Rural Cottages and Cottage Villas, and their Gardens and Grounds Adapted to North America.* 2nd ed. New York and London: Wiley and Putnam, 1844.

———. *Rural Essays.* Ed. George William Curtis. New York: Leavitt and Allen, 1857.

———. *A Treatise on the Theory and Practice of Landscape Gardening Adapted to North America.* New York: C. M. Saxton and Co., 1841.

Lamb, Martha J., ed. *The Homes of America.* New York: D. Appleton and Co., 1879.

Lossing, Benson John. *The Hudson, from the Wilderness to the Sea.* New York: Virtue and Yorston, 1866.

———. *Vassar College and Its Founder.* New York: C. A. Alford, 1867.

Morse, James H. *Diary, 1866–1911.* New York: The New-York Historical Society. Mss.

Oakey, Alexander F. *Home Grounds.* New York: Appleton, 1881.

Olmsted, Frederick Law. *Walks and Talks of an American Farmer in England.* New York: George P. Putnam, 1852.

Olmsted, Frederick Law, Jr., and Theadora Kimball, eds. *Forty Years of Landscape Architecture, Being the Professional Papers of Frederick Law Olmsted, Senior.* 2 vols. New York and London: G. P. Putnam's Sons, 1922, 1928. Repr., Cambridge, Mass.: MIT Press, 1973.

*Riverside in 1871, With a Description of Its Improvements.* Chicago. The Riverside Improvement Company, 1871.

Robinson, Charles J., ed. *A Register of the Scholars Admitted into Merchant Taylors' School, from A.D. 1562 to 1874, Compiled from Authentic Sources and Edited with Biographical Notices.* 2 vols. Lewes: Farncombe and Co., 1882, 1883.

Silliman, B., Jr., and C. P. Goodrich, eds., *The World of Science, Art and Industry Illustrated from Examples in the New York Exhibition, 1853–54.* New York: Putnam, 1854.

Schuyler, Montgomery. *American Architecture Studies.* New York: Harper and Brothers, 1892. *American Architecture and Other Writings,* rev. ed. Ed. William H. Jordy and Ralph Coe. 2 vols. Cambridge, Mass: Belknap Press of Harvard University, 1961.

Staunton, Howard. *The Great Schools of England.* London: Sampson Low, Son, and Marston, 1865.

*The Central Park: Photographed by W. H. Guild, Jr., with Description and a Historical Sketch,* by Fred B. Perkins, New York: 1864.

Truefitt, George. *Architectural Sketches on the Continent.* London. J. Masters, 1847.

Weidenmann, Jacob. *Beautifying Country Homes.* New York: Orange Judd Co., 1870.

Wheeler, Gervase. *Rural Homes or Sketches of Houses Suited to American Country Life with Original Plans, Designs, etc.* New York: Charles Scribner, 1852.

Willis, Nathaniel P. *Out-doors at Idlewild; or, the Shaping of a Home on the Hudson.* New York: Charles Scribner, 1855.

Withers, Frederick Clarke. *Church Architecture.* New York: A. Bicknell, 1873.

## PERIODICALS, 19TH CENTURY

"The American Museum of Natural History, New York," *American Architect and Building News,* i (August 12, 1876) 261.

"Belvedere," *Building,* iv (May 22, 1886) plate 21.

"Central Park," *Harper's Weekly,* i (September 5, 1857) 563.

"Central Park," *Harper's Weekly,* i (November 28, 1857) 576–577.

"Central Park, New York, Competition," *The Builder,* xvi (October 2, 1858) 660.

Colvin, A. M., "Sale of the Cottingham Museum," *The Builder,* ix (November 22, 1851) 742.

"Courthouse, Bell Tower, Prison," *American Architect and Building News,* iii (June 15, 1878) 209.

"Design for a Marine Villa," *The Horticulturalist,* viii (February, 1853) 190.

"Designs for the Proposed Centennial Exposition Building," *New-York Sketchbook of Architecture,* ix (September, 1874) 1–6.

"The Downing Monument," *The Horticulturalist,* xi (November, 1856) 286.

Elliot, Charles W., "About Barns," *Putnam's Monthly, a Magazine of American Literature, Science and Art,* v (June, 1855) 629–631.

"House at Worcester, Mass., Residence of Dr. Bull," *American Architect and Building News,* i (April 8, 1876) 117.

"House in Gramercy Park, New York," *American Architect and Building News,* xxxiii (September 5, 1891) 155.

Magonigle, H. Van Buren, "A Half Century of Architecture," *Pencil Points,* xiv (November, 1933) 474–479.

"New Boys Lodging House, New York," *American Architect and Building News,* xvi (November 29, 1884) 259.

"New Harlem River Bridge," *Building,* v (July 31, August 7, 1886) 49–51, 61.

Parsons, Samuel, Jr., "Interesting Facts in Regard to the Inception and Development of Central Park," *Transactions of the American Society of Landscape Architects,* (1899–1908) 105–110.

"Residence of R. S. Bowne, Esq., at Flushing, Long Island," *Building,* iv (February 13, 1886) 76.

Richards, Addison T., "Idlewild, The Home of N. P. Willis," *Harper's New Monthly Magazine,* xvi (January, 1858) 145–156.

Schuyler, Montgomery, "Concerning Queen Anne, Recent Building in New York," *Harper's Magazine,* lxvii (September, 1883) 557–578.

Vaux, Downing, "Historical Notes," *Transactions of the American Society of Landscape Architects,* (1899–1908) 81–83.

## BOOKS, 20TH CENTURY

Adamson, John William. *English Education 1789–1902.* London and New York: Cambridge University Press, 1964.

Barlow, Elizabeth. *Frederick Law Olmsted's New York.* Illustrative portfolio, William Alex. New York: Praeger Publishers in association with the Whitney Museum of American Art, 1972.

Beveridge, Charles E., and David Schuyler, eds. *Creating Central Park, 1857–1861.* Baltimore: Johns Hopkins University Press, 1983.

Braceland, F. J. *The Institute of Living, 1822–1872.* Hartford: Connecticut Printers. 1972.

Bullock, Orin M., Jr. *The Restoration Manual.* Norwalk, Conn.: Silvermine Publishers, 1966.

Burchard, John, and Albert Bush-Brown. *The Architecture of America: A Social and Cultural History.* Boston: Little, Brown and Co., 1961.

Burnham, Alan, ed. *New York Landmarks: A Study and Index of Architecturally Notable Structures in Greater New York.* Middletown, Conn.: Wesleyan University Press, 1963.

Chadwick, George F. *The Park and the Town: Public Landscape in the 19th and 20th Centuries.* New York: Frederick A. Praeger, 1966.

Clark, Kenneth. *The Gothic Revival, an Essay in the History of Taste.* 3rd ed. [Printed in Great Britain by Butler and Tanner Ltd., Frome and London:] John Murray, 1962.

Clarke, M. L. *Classical Education in Britain, 1500–1900*. Cambridge: Cambridge University Press, 1959.

Condit, Carl W. *American Building Art: The Twentieth Century*. New York: Oxford University Press, 1961.

———. *The Chicago School of Architecture*. Chicago: University of Chicago Press, 1964.

Corbitt, Kevin D., ed., "The Letters of Vaux, Withers and Company, Architects, Calvert Vaux and Frederick Clarke Withers to Edward Miner Gallaudet, President of the Columbia Institution for the Deaf (now Gallaudet University), 1866–1880." Unpublished ms., Gallaudet University, 1989.

Cromley, Elizabeth C. *Alone Together: A History of New York's Early Apartments*. Ithaca, N. Y.: Cornell University Press, 1990.

Downing, Antoinette F. and Vincent J. Scully, Jr. *The Architectural Heritage of Newport, Rhode Island, 1640–1915*. 2nd rev. ed. New York: Clarkson N. Potter, 1965.

Draper, F. W. M., *Four Centuries of Merchant Taylors' School, 1561–1961*. London: Oxford University Press, 1962.

Fein, Albert. "The American City: The Ideal and the Real," in Edgar Kaufman, Jr., ed., *The Rise of an American Architecture*. New York: Metropolitan Museum of Art, 1970.

———. ed. *Landscape into Cityscape*. Ithaca, N. Y.: Cornell University Press, 1967.

Forbush, B. *The Sheppard and Enoch Pratt Hospital, 1853–1970*. Philadelphia: J. B. Lippincott Co., 1970.

Frederickson, George M. *The Inner Civil War, Northern Intellectuals and the Crisis of the Union*. New York: Harper and Row, 1965.

Gifford, Don, ed. *The Literature of Architecture, The Evolution of Architectural Theory and Practice in Nineteenth-Century America*. New York: E. P. Dutton and Co., 1966.

Graff, M. M. *Central Park–Prospect Park, A New Perspective*. New York: Greensward Foundation, Inc., 1985.

Hitchcock, Henry Russell. *Architecture of the Nineteenth and Twentieth Centuries*. Baltimore: Penguin Books, 1958.

———. *Early Victorian Architecture in Britain*. 2 vols. New Haven: Yale University Press, 1954.

Howe, Winifred E. *A History of the Metropolitan Museum of Art*. New York: Metropolitan Museum of Art [printed at the Gilliss Press], 1913–1946.

Kleeman, Rita Halle. *Gracious Lady, the Life of Sara Delano Roosevelt*. New York and London: D. Appleton–Century Co., 1935.

Kouwenhoven, John. *The Columbia Historical Portrait of New York*. Garden City, N.Y.: Doubleday and Co., 1953.

Kowsky, Francis R. *The Architecture of Frederick Clarke Withers and the Progress of the Gothic Revival in America after 1850*. Middletown, Conn.: Wesleyan University Press, 1980.

Lancaster, Clay. *Prospect Park Handbook*. New York: Greensward Foundation, Inc., Long Island University Press, 1972.

Loth, Calder, and Julius Trousdale Sadler. *The Only Proper Style, Gothic Architecture in America*. Boston: New York Graphic Society, 1975.

Maas, John. *The Gingerbread Age, A View of Victorian America*. New York: Rinehart and Co., 1957.

Matzdorf, David W. "Calvert Vaux: 1824–1895." Unpublished thesis, Architectural Association, London, 1977.

Mumford, Lewis. *The Brown Decades, A Study of the Arts in America, 1865–1895*. New York: Harcourt, Brace and Company, 1932. 2nd rev. ed., New York: Dover Publications, 1955.

————, ed. *Roots of Contemporary American Architecture.* New York: Reinhold Publishing Corp., 1952.

Myles, Janet. "L. N. Cottingham, 1787–1847. Architect, His Place in Gothic Revival." Unpublished dissertation, Leicester Polytechnic, 1989.

Parsons, Mabel, ed. *Memories of Samuel Parsons.* New York: G. P. Putnam's Sons, 1926.

Pumpelly, Raphael. *My Reminiscences.* 2 vols. New York: Henry Holt and Co., 1918.

Reed, Henry Hope, and Sophia Duckworth. *Central Park, A History and a Guide.* New York: Clarkson N. Potter, 1967.

Reps, John William. *The Making of Urban America: A History of City Planning in the United States.* Princeton, N. J.: Princeton University Press, 1965.

Roberts, Howard. *Survey of London; Southbank and Vauxhall.* Vol 23. London: London County Council and London Survey Commission, 1951.

Roper, Laura Wood. *FLO—A Biography of Frederick Law Olmsted.* Baltimore: Johns Hopkins University Press, 1974.

Rossiter, Henry P., ed. *M. and M. Karalik Collection of American Water Colors and Drawings.* Boston: Museum of Fine Arts, 1962.

Schuyler, David, and Jane Turner Censer, eds. *The Years of Olmsted, Vaux & Company.* Baltimore: Johns Hopkins University Press, 1992.

Scully, Vincent J., Jr. *The Shingle Style: Architectural Theory and Design from Richardson to the Origins of Wright.* New Haven: Yale University Press; London: Geoffrey Cumberlege, Oxford University Press, 1955.

Sherman, Frederick Barreda. *From the Guadalquivir to the Golden Gate.* Mill Valley, Calif.: Hall and Smith Co., 1977.

Sigle, John David. "Calvert Vaux, An American Architect." Unpublished thesis, University of Virginia, 1967.

————, *Papers, American Association of Architectural Biographers.* Vol. 5, *Bibliography of the Life and Works of Calvert Vaux.* Charlottesville: Press of the University of Virginia, 1968.

Stevenson, Elisabeth. *Park Maker: A Life of Frederick Law Olmsted.* New York: Macmillan, 1977.

Tatum, George Bishop. "Andrew Jackson Downing, Arbiter of American Taste, 1815–1852." Unpublished dissertation, Princeton University, 1950.

————, and Elisabeth Blair MacDougall, eds. *Prophet with Honor: The Career of Andrew Jackson Downing, 1815–1852.* Washington, D. C.: Dumbarton Oaks Colloquium on the History of Architecture, xi, 1987.

Upjohn, Everard M. *Richard Upjohn, Architect and Churchman.* New York: Columbia University Press, 1939.

White, Norval, and Elliot Willensky, eds. *AIA Guide to New York City.* New York: New York AIA Chapter, 1967. Rev. eds., 1978, 1988.

## PERIODICALS, 20TH CENTURY

Schuyler, David, "Belated Honor to a Prophet: Newburgh's Downing Park," *Landscape,* 31, no. 1 (Spring, 1991) 10–17.

"Calvert Vaux, Designer of Parks," *The Park International* (September, 1920), 138–143.

"Central Park's Bethesda Terrace and Its Restoration," *Antiques,* cxxxiii, no. 4 (April, 1988) 888–899.

Craig, James, "Beginning of Central Park," *New York Telegram and Evening Mail* (November 10, 1924) 4.

"Curators for Future Restorers: Applying the Approach to a Central Park Monument," *Architecture: The AIA Journal,* 77, no. 11 (November, 1988) 134–135.

Downs, Arthur C., "Downing's Newburgh Villa," *Association for Preservation Technology Bulletin,* iv, nos. 3–4 (1972) 1–113.

Dunning, Brian, "Pioneer of the Weekend Cottage," *Country Life,* cxxxiv (October 10, 1963) 894–897.

"Exhibit Marks Centennial of Landscape Architects: Works of Frederick Law Olmsted," *Architectural Record,* cxxxvii (March, 1965) 332.

Fein, Albert, "Parks in a Democratic Society," *Landscape Architecture,* lv (October 1964) 24–31.

"A Green Room at the Heart of the City," *Architectural Digest,* 48, no. 12 (November, 1991) 26–32.

Hubbard, Theodora Kimball, "Riverside, Illinois, A Residential Neighborhood Designed over Sixty Years Ago, Selected from the Papers of Frederick Law Olmsted, Sr.," *Landscape Architecture,* xxi (July, 1931) 256–291.

Israels, Charles H., "New York Apartment Houses," *Architectural Record,* ii (July, 1911), 476–508.

Kowsky, Francis R, "Municipal Parks and City Planning: Frederick Law Olmsted's Buffalo Park and Parkway System," *Society of Architectural Historians Journal,* xlvi (March, 1987) 49–64.

Lancaster, Clay, "Central Park, 1851–1961," with an introduction by James Thrall Soby, "Vernal Mood," *Magazine of Art,* xliv (April, 1951) 122–128.

Landmark Preservation Commission of the City of New York, Scenic Landmark Designations: *Central Park, Prospect Park, Riverside Park and Drive, Eastern Parkway, Ocean Parkway.*

Leech, Robert W., "The First Dilemma," *Landscape Architecture,* 77, no. 11 (January–February, 1987) 62–65.

Menhinick, Howard K., "Riverside Sixty Years Later," *Landscape Architecture,* xxii (January, 1932) 109–117.

"New Life for a Historic Tile Ceiling?," *Architectural Record* 180, no. 1 (January, 1992) 38–39.

"Olana," *The Society of Architectural Historians Newsletter,* x (November, 1966) 3.

Pattee, Sarah Lewis, "Andrew Jackson Downing and His Influence on Landscape Architecture in America," *Landscape Architecture,* xix (January, 1929) 79–83.

Proctor, John Clagett, " The Tragic Death of Andrew Jackson Downing and the Monument to His Memory," *Columbia Historical Society Records,* xxvii (1925) 248–261.

"Reassessing the Art of Landscape Design," *Architectural Record,* 174, no. 10 (September, 1984) 69–75.

"The Rehabilitation of Bethesda Terrace: The Terrace Bridge and Landscape, Central Park, New York," *Association for the Preservation of Technology Bulletin,* xviii, no. 3 (1986) 24–39.

"Return to Splendor: Oriental Pavilion, Prospect Park, Brooklyn, New York," *Architectural Record,* 77, no. 8 (July, 1989) 10–13.

"Samuel Parsons, A Minute of Life and Service," *Transactions of the American Society of Landscape Architects,* 1922–1926, 92–94.

"Saving Sandstone: Bethesda Terrace Restoration, Central Park, New York City," *Architectural Record,* 174, no. 6 (May, 1986) 130–137.

Scully, Vincent J., Jr. "American Villas, Inventiveness in the American Suburb from Downing to Wright," *The Architectural Review,* cxv (March, 1954) 163–179.

———, "Palace of the Past: Frederick Church's Olana at Hudson, New York," *Progressive Architecture,* xlvi (May, 1965) 184–189.

Steese, Edward, *"Villas and Cottages* by Calvert Vaux," *Society of Architectural Historians Journal,* vi (January–June, 1947) 1–12.

Stewart, John J., "Notes on Calvert Vaux's 1873 Design for the Public Grounds of the Parliament Buildings in Ottawa," *Association for the Preservation of Technology Bulletin,* viii, no. 1

(1976) 1–27. [Dennis Steadman Francis, "Further Notes on Calvert Vaux," ibid., no. 3 (1976) 81–82.]

Tishler, William H. "Frederick Law Olmsted, Prophet of Environmental Design," *American Institute of Architects Journal,* xliv (December, 1965) 31–35.

Van Ingen, W. B., "Central Park—As It Was in the Beginning," *New York Times Magazine,* (December 24, 1922) 14.

"Vaux Redux: Exhibition Review," *Metropolis,* 8, no. 10 (November, 1989) 27.

"Who They Were: Calvert Vaux," *Old House Journal,* xix, no. 6 (November–December) 18–20.

BIOGRAPHICAL NOTICES AND OBITUARIES

"Calvert Vaux," *American Architect and Building News,* 1 (November 1895) 23.

"Calvert Vaux (Vawks)," in James Grant Wilson and John Fiske, eds., *Appleton's Cyclopedia of American Biography.* New York: D. Appleton and Co., vi (1889) 269.

"Calvert Vaux," *Harper's Weekly,* xxxix (November 30, 1895) 1130.

"Calvert Vaux," *The National Cyclopedia of American Biography.* New York: James T. White and Co., ix (1899) 332.

"Calvert Vaux," *New York Herald Tribune* (November 22, 1895), 1.

"Calvert Vaux," *Scientific American,* lxxiii (November 30, 1895) 339.

"Calvert Vaux (1824–1895)," in Daniel Cott Gilman, Harry Thurston Peck, and Frank Moore Colby, eds. *The New International Encyclopedia.* New York: Dodd Mead and Co., xx (1904) 30. Reprinted in *Society of Architectural Historians Journal,* vi (January, 1947) 1.

"Calvert Vaux Missing," *The New York Times,* xlv (November 22, 1895) 1.

"Calvert Vaux Was Drowned," *The New York Times,* xlv (November 22, 1895) 1.

Cust, Lionel Henry. "Lewis Nockalls Cottingham," *Dictionary of National Biography.* London: Oxford University Press, 1950.

"George Truefitt Retires," *Building News* (August 1, 1890) 167.

Hamlin, Talbot Faulkner, "Frederick Clarke Withers," *Dictionary of American Biography.* New York: Charles Scribner's Sons, xx (1938) 435.

Howland, Henry E., "Calvert Vaux," *Reports, Constitution, By Laws and List of Members of the Century Association for the Year 1895.* New York: The Century Association, 1896, 18–19.

Hubbard, Theodora Kimball, "Frederick Law Olmsted," *Dictionary of American Biography.* New York: Charles Scribner's Sons, xiv (1934) 24–28.

Keller, Herbert Anthony, "Andrew Jackson Downing," *Dictionary of American Biography.* New York: Charles Scribner's Sons, v (1930) 417–418.

"The Late George Truefitt, Retired Fellow," *Royal Institute of British Architects Journal* (August 30, 1902) 461.

McNamara, Katherine, "Calvert Vaux," *Dictionary of American Biography.* New York: Charles Scribner's Sons, xix (1936) 237–239.

Miller, Wilhelm, "Calvert Vaux," *Standard Cyclopedia of Horticulture.* New York: Macmillan, iii (1915) 1601.

"Mr. and Mrs. Calvert Vaux," *New York Social Register* (November, 1889). New York: Social Register Association, 1890.

Murray, John, "Lewis Nockalls Cottingham," *A Biographical Dictionary of English Architects, 1660–1840.* London: 1954, 153–154.

Withey, Henry F., and Elsie Rathburn Withey, "Calvert Vaux," *Biographical Dictionary of American Architects (Deceased).* Los Angeles: New Age Publishing Co., 1956.

# Appendix

PARISIAN BUILDINGS FOR THE CITY RESIDENTS BY CALVERT VAUX, *Harper's Weekly,* December 19, 1857, pp. 809–810.

AT A MEETING of the Institute of American Architects, held some time since, the idea of erecting in New York buildings for city residents on the European plan, was brought forward for discussion, and a paper, illustrated by a design, was read by Mr. Vaux, one of the members.

The subject seems to be one of marked popular interest, and we therefore give this week an outline of the paper read at the meeting, and several engravings that will enable our readers to comprehend the leading features of the particular plan submitted for examination.

In all the large American cities at the present time, and in New York especially, there is a constantly increasing demand in the way of house accommodation, for a more liberal supply of convenience and comfort than has been considered necessary by most persons till within the last few years. This desire seems to progress even faster than the extraordinary prosperity of the people. The mechanic nowadays shares with the millionaire his taste for the luxuries of privacy, fresh air, water, and light; and the wish to occupy, together with the capacity to appreciate, a commodious residence, is widely spread among all classes.

It is certainly well that this desire should exist, and it ought, doubtless, to be responded to by professional architects as far as possible, inasmuch as it is the duty of science and art to popularize as well as to discover, and to assist in developing, in an economical form, all those refinements of convenience that education teaches us are healthful and agreeable. The present position of matters—at any rate in New York—does not seem to be entirely satisfactory. The area of the city is limited, and the population, for many reasons, growing larger and larger every year, the available building sites have continued increasing in value, till the mere interest on the purchase money of an ordinary city lot, without any house on it, would in any European city be considered an exorbitant rent for the house and lot together.

If buildings could be erected at an extremely reasonable cost, this would in a measure compensate for the high price to be paid for the land they occupy; but this, we are all aware, is not the case. Wages are high, and the outlay necessary for building and fitting up even a small house renders a high rental necessary, if the investment is to be at all remunerative. This matter of burdensome rent is a growing evil in New York, and is well known to be so. Strenuous efforts have, indeed, been made to economize space by reducing the width of the lots, and it is not uncommon now to see two houses built on a space of twenty-five feet—thus making each residence to consist of long rooms that are very thin, narrow passages that are very dark, and crowded stairways that are very uncomfortable; still the rent is materially reduced by this process, and such houses readily find occupants, who are willing to pay a high price and live, as it were, on a ladder, rather than give up the advantages of a convenient situation. This whole difficulty can, of course, be avoided by taking a house at some considerable distance from the city; and the facilities for suburban residences are fortunately always on the increase; still, although many may live agreeably in this way, the great majority of those who have to work for their living in a large city will naturally seek for accommodations within an easy distance of the scene of their labors.

There are, we know, several other methods of obtaining a residence in a city like New York. Thus, a family may live at a hotel or in a boarding-house, but the ceaseless publicity that ensues, the constant change, and the entire absence of all individuality in the everyday domestic arrangements, will always render this method of living distasteful, as a permanent thing, to the heads of families who have any taste for genuine home comforts, whether they happen to belong to this continent or the other. In some cases, two or more parties make arrangements to hire a house together, and this is a tolerably satisfactory plan, if the residents are suited to each other; but it seems to offer no advantages that might not be more completely obtained if the suites of apartments were entirely separated and complete in themselves.

In Europe, extensive buildings several stories high are frequently arranged with all the rooms required for a family grouped together on one level, or nearly so, and approached through one hall door from a public staircase; and this *Continental plan*, as it is called, seems to possess so many advantages, that it deserves more attention than has hitherto been accorded to it in America. As yet it is little more than its title indicates, a *Continental plan*, so far as New York is concerned; for it has hardly taken any root here, except in the inadequate shape of what are known as tenement houses, and this limited development of its capabilities is naturally calculated to deter rather than induce property owners to invest their capital in this style of building.

In the Scotch cities the advantages obtained by having separate suites of rooms under the same roof were recognized and acted on many years ago, and numbers of such buildings were carried up eight or ten stories high; but there seems a practical disadvantage in this extreme loftiness of the building, that would render it unadvisable to try any experiment of the sort in New York. Two or three flights of easy stairs may be readily surmounted, and the freedom from dust and noise obtained by those who might live in the third or fourth stories, would be found to compensate, in a great measure, for the trouble of traversing an extra flight or two of stairs; and thus people of about the same standing in society could, in all probability, be readily induced to occupy comfortable apartments as high as the fourth floor, but beyond this, the extra labor would soon be considered excessive, and the much cheaper rooms would attract a lower class of tenants than those likely to occupy floors nearer the level of the street: this would, in all probability be thought very disagreeable in an American city, although accepted as a matter of course in Edinburgh. The same objection holds good in many of the French and German buildings arranged on this plan, and although they offer models for imitation in most respects, this difficulty will, in all probability have to be avoided if the idea is to be successfully developed here.

It is not uncommon to find the larger and more elegant European establishments built round an open court. They are thus made to occupy, for the most part, ground at a considerable distance behind the most valuable frontage that faces on the main street; but such a plan does not seem practicable here, not only on account of the peculiar plan of the city, but because every family that owns or rents a house wishes to have the principal parlor command a view of the street; and American ladies, who are in the habit of spending the greater part of their time in their own apartments, think it far more lively and cheerful to look out on a busy thoroughfare than on a monotonous quadrangle, however elegantly it may be decorated. The suites facing the court would not, therefore, be so readily rented, and it consequently seems desirable in New York to abandon this feature if possible.

It is not at all uncommon in the European buildings on this plan to find the public staircase in the middle of the house, and although ample in dimensions, somewhat restricted in its supply of light and air. Indeed, as a general rule, the public approaches are allowed to be of secondary importance, and the agreeable effect of the rooms themselves, when arrived at, is possibly enhanced thereby; but a different plan must be adopted if the idea is to be suited to New York needs, the public staircase, which is the unusual feature to which we have to be accustomed, must be made light, airy, and elegant; and if possible, lighter, airier, and more elegant than any other part of the house, or a prejudice will be likely to be excited on entering the premises against the whole effect, and this it is all-important to avoid.

In London the subject has attracted a good deal of attention, and some very handsome buildings have been put up; but the price of ground is so comparatively moderate, even in very eligible situations, that a frontage on the main avenue of fifty or sixty feet is given to each suite of apartments without the rental being exorbitant.

A large frontage is of course desirable, and for extensive and costly suites of rooms absolutely necessary. It is not thought advisable, however, in the study submitted, to show what may be done with a fine open site, but rather to take the ordinary dimensions of two 25 x 100 feet city lots, and exhibit a method of arranging suites of rooms for families on these restricted dimensions, so that each suite of apartments may have its parlor facing on the street, and also a sufficient number of rooms for the accommodation of a family of moderate size.

On one side of the basement which would be partially above ground, but of which no plan is shown, a set of rooms, consisting of parlor and bedroom, with bath-room, etc, is provided; these would be adapted to the wants of a single gentleman, needing only such attendance as could be furnished by the housekeeper who would occupy the rooms on the other side of the basement, and who, it is proposed, should take general charge of the building, keep the stairways clean, receive messages, etc.; the rear of the basement would be occupied by cellarage for the tenants. Each one having a roomy, well-lighted cellar, for coal, etc.; convenient of access to these cellars, a lift, communicating with the kitchens of each set of rooms, is provided, this lift being also intended to take baskets of clothes to and from the different stories and a large drying room that is planned over the kitchen-block, immediately under the roof.

Above the basement the suites of apartments correspond in all respects one with the other; the public staircase is planned in the centre of the block, facing the street, and lighted with large windows every story. The hall of each tenant opens from a landing on this staircase, and is furnished with a glazed inner and a solid outer door. From this hall is an entrance to the parlor, one to the dining-room, and one to the kitchen wing and bedrooms.

Behind the dining-room is an open well for light. By arranging the plan of bedrooms on a somewhat higher level than the parlors several advantages are obtained; for the bedroom passage and the kitchen being nine feet high, while the parlors and bedrooms are twelve feet high, the additional three feet can, by a difference of level, be so placed that it may be arranged for closet room, at a convenient height for use both from the bedroom and kitchen floor, and it also allows of a passage to the bedrooms that does not pass the kitchen door at all, which is desirable for the sake of privacy; the pantry is proposed to be about six feet six inches in height, and thus a housekeeper's pantry of available dimensions can be planned over it without encroaching on the next floor.

A dust shaft is introduced, that may be used both from the bedroom and kitchen level, on each suite. A well-house for light and ventilation is arranged where it will be of the most advantage to the passage to bedrooms and to the bath-rooms; the bedroom passage is purposely diverted from a straight line, so as to avoid the uninviting appearance of a long, narrow corridor, and three bedrooms are grouped at the extreme end of the lot, where they will get the best light and be most quiet and retired. The dining-room pantry has closets and a sink, and the kitchen is provided with range, sink, boiler, wash trays; kitchen closets, storeroom, coal closet, and servants' bedroom up a few steps from the kitchen level, and this completes the accommodation offered.

The rooms are of moderate size, and it is conceived that a set of apartments of this sort would be found all-sufficient for a large number of families living in New York, and paying higher rents than these suites would command for small, ill-planned, and disagreeably situated houses, that are found very uncomfortable to live in. It is proposed that the staircase should be fire-proof, and it is thought that the situation chosen and style of finish used ought to be such that the rents might average about $450 for a set of rooms on the principal floor, $400 for the second story, $350 for the third, $300 for the fourth, and $200 for the basement. It is conceived that if the plan were carried out on this scale in an agreeable situation, not too far up town, it would at once become a highly remunerative investment for the outlay incurred.

THE CENTRAL PARK EXHIBITION OF THE UNSUCCESSFUL PLANS
FOR CENTRAL PARK, *The New-York Daily Times,* May 13, 1858, p. 10.

ALL THE PLANS RECEIVED by the Commissioners for the Central Park are now on exhibition at No. 637 Broadway. They ought to attract general attention,—not only on account of their intrinsic interest, but because the admission fund is to be distributed among the unsuccessful competitors and forms the only compensation for their labor.

The index to the printed matter sent in with the plan for competition, mentions thirty-three plans. One of these proves not to be a plan for the Park, and two of those sent in (Nos. 8 and 18) are colored, so that the competitors are reduced to thirty. Two other plans have been sent in, not for competition (Nos. 34 and 35), of which the last deserves attention. The inception and execution of a park of large dimensions is in this country an undertaking involving many difficulties and much labor. It was not known to the Commissioners or to the public what talent or skill or cultivation existed in this country for the proper designing and carrying out of the work, and it was very desirable that the work should be undertaken, if possible, by some of our own countrymen, who would of course understand our needs and capacities better than any outsider. The leading idea in the mind of almost any European would be to provide ample drives and rides for the upper classes, while here, on the contrary, it should be to provide not only for them, but more amply for the recreation and amusement of the laboring masses, who could not easily get beyond the heated brick walls and the hard contact of the pavement.

The Commissioners issued proposals with specific requirements in August, fixing the time for receiving the plans as the 1st of January, 1858, this was afterward extended to March 1, and then to April 1. On the 2d of February, the Board required from designers estimates for the cost of each item of work, the curious result of which we shall show in a comparative table, at the close of our article.

The designers have had every difficulty to contend with; the topographical surveys were not performed by the Commission in time to be of much use; they were difficult of access; the photographic map furnished was worthless; the Winter season was unfavorable for out-of-door work; the time allowed was too limited for thorough study and elaboration. Yet, with all disadvantages, a high degree of taste, skill and knowledge has been brought into activity by the competition, which will be felt throughout the country.

Ten at least of these designs, however, inadequate they may appear upon a flat piece of paper, would make Central Park a beautiful and creditable work, and any one of them would improve greatly in its execution. We believe, however, that the Commissioners will

fail lamentably if they attempt to combine the leading features of the plans they have
selected. Minor details may be incorporated into any one of them, but the great features of
each cannot be carved and pieced without injury. Of the designs chose, Nos. 33 and 26 are
the most marked and positive in ideas and treatment. In both we find that unity or central
character, so essential to any good design and a high degree of skill and bold dealing with
the subject. However grand the straight main avenue of No. 26, terminated by the hall or
theater, might be upon another field, we cannot see that is in harmony with the character of
the grounds of the Central Park. These grounds are exceedingly broken and picturesque
and require a decided and picturesque, though to some degree an artificial treatment. This is
found in No. 33. The sweeping lines of the grand drive fall in naturally into their places, the
lakes are in harmony with the surface lines, while the art required is shown in the charming
promenades near the central and along the eastern side of the reservoirs, and in the ride
around the wall of the new reservoir. The public should bear it in mind that these reservoirs
cannot be made into lakes, however crooked the walls may be built. A high wall, crowned
with a fence, elevates the surface of the water above all the surrounding lands, and hides the
water from view and it is only by some contrivance like this ride, that it can be seen at all,
except at one or two points. It is a serious question whether an artificial work like this
reservoir is not marred by the attempt to make it a natural piece of water, but it is too late
to change it, and the disaffected must therefore growl in silence. We may be allowed to
indulge a hope that the Commissioners will agree to proceed with the work at once, for
they will be able to get no better plan in its leading features than No. 33. With regard to two
other plans selected, we do not find in them the decided merit discovered by the Board; they
lack individuality, and while they include many things and many ornaments, we see little to
select from them which will combine with No. 33. Had we been of the Commission we
should have selected better, of course, we should have seem some value in No. 32 and No. 17
and No. 12 and No. 14 and No. 22 and No. 28 and No. 25 and No. 16 and No. 29. We also ask
especial attention to the small and beautifully worked plan No. 35 which unfortunately was
not prepared for competition.

   Nearly all of the designers have yielded to the imperative demands of the ground, for
we find in most of the plans one main tour or drive around the whole park; various degrees
of skill and perception being shown in laying it down. We find in three cases a strait [*sic*]
avenue projected along the whole extent of the Fifth Avenue, and on a level with it; in two
of the plans a strait [*sic*] central avenue; in six of them the drives winding about in great
agony; in a large number a collection and confusion of desirable and undesirable structures
and ornaments. In more than half the designs the parade ground is laid down between the
present reservoir and the Fifth Avenue, while in very few of the designs is there shown that
masterly use of trees and woods which must make the charm and riches of the Park. We do
find this conspicuous in a few, as in Nos. 17, 33, 15, and 16. In No. 17 particularly, is displayed
much knowledge and fine feeling. Evergreens, as the most skillful designers have at once
perceived, are in harmony with the rough and rocky nature of the ground, and will serve to
heighten these natural effects, and to give a peculiar and striking character to the Park. The
artists of Nos. 17 and 33 have both struck upon a happy thought—an evergreen Winter drive
along the low grounds west of the reservoirs, and nearly all the best artists agree upon
laying the woods along the western border, and on their high grounds. America is rich in
beautiful trees, and we should not be sorry to see some portion of the Park devoted to them
where they could be shown both massed and singly. Still, we must ask for the best park
effects however they are to be had, and in producing these, the two leading features must be

wood and lawn. Some fine open spaces and glades may be preserved, and the parade ground whether used as such or not, should be secured as a broad lawn. We are doubtful about the supply of water for the lakes, as projected, in our hot, dry Summer but shall hope everything; but we are sure the water, wood and lawn should be the chief attractions of this Park, and we trust the Commissioners and the employees will neglect all structures and fancy works for a long while to come and devote their energies and their money to the production of these, making them accessible, of course, by means of a few drives and walks. To produce any of these in perfection, drainage (which ought to have been vigorously carried out during the Winter) and trenching are the first requisites, and should be proceeded with at once. The memoir accompanying No. 29 is very full and thorough on these, and will be valued by the Board. Road making is to become a serious business in the Park work, and is a point which requires much inquiry and consideration. The cost of macadamizing fifty foot roads (as projected on No. 9) is estimated by the designers to be $1,400,000. As the entire fund is but $100,000 over this the commissioners ask, "What are we to do!" in view of the fact that most of the designs contemplate drives from sixty to one-hundred feet wide. We are aware of our temerity, but we respectfully suggest that while an avenue of that width is a fine thing a picturesque and rural drive, winding among rocks and trees and over suspension bridges, 60 to 100 feet wide, is rather preposterous. But as we take it for granted that this thing is now decided upon at whatever cost, we can only pray that the hearts of the Commissioners may be softened. Few of the designers have contemplated the possible future, when that long stretch of two and a half miles must be compassed by butchers' carts and milkmen, when pork and timber even must cross it on drays; what then is to happen at the crossings of the main drives, and along those meandering lanes projected by most. The designers of Nos. 12 and 33 seem to have had the difficulty before their eyes, and to to have attempted to resolve it one by fencing in the cross streets, the other by sinking them below the level of the park. The latter plan is the most thorough, if it can be accomplished in a sightly and comfortable manner. Let us see one done in that way as early as may be to test the question.

Now that we have borne our testimony and relieved our minds, Gentlemen of the Commission our only desire is that you will reduce your numbers (either by "death or resignation" as your Charter contemplates) to five, and proceed with the work of making the Central Park.

As it was impossible without surveys and measurements to compute the cost of the work, the following table will serve to show some of the Commissioners the value of the guesses which the unfortunate designers felt bound to make in accordance with the resolutions of Feb. 2:

DESIGNERS' ESTIMATES OF ITEMS OF COST

| No. | Draining | Roads and Walks | Trees and Planting |
|---|---|---|---|
| 33 | $30,000 | $246,454 | $219,000 |
| 32 | 80,000 | 600,000 | 300,000 |
| 31 | 52,000 | 286,000 | 60,000 |
| 30 | 37,500 | 415,000 | 300,000 |
| 29 | 18,075 for the tile. | — | — |
| 28 | 59,175 | 436,724 | 100,000 |
| 27 | 60,000 | 304,714 | 200,000 |
| 25 | 21,900 | 500,000 | 250,000 |
| 23 | 90,000 | 158,000 | 200,000 |
| 22 | 145,000 | 265,000 | 250,000 |

| No. | Draining | Roads and Walks | Trees and Planting |
|---|---|---|---|
| 21 | 30,000 | 207,065 | 180,000 |
| 19 | 13,725 | 742,649 | 18,500 |
| 18 | 500 | 316,800 | 600 |
| 17 | 28,500 | 701,750 | 130,000 |
| 16 | — | 220,000 | 135,000 |
| 15 | 16,760 | 432,830 | 26,200 |
| 14 | 25,000 | 84,000 | 147,200 |
| 10 | — | 389,439 | — |
| 9 | 11,000 | 315,000 | 12,000 |
| 7 | — | 100,250 | — |
| 6 | 3,600 | 192,540 | 16,000 |
| 3 | — | — | 65,000 |
| 1 | — | — | 75,000 |

| | | | | |
|---|---|---|---|---|
| Draining Highest | $145,000 | lowest | $ | 500 |
| Roads and Walks | 742,649 | lowest | | 84,000 |
| Trees and Planting | 300,000 | lowest | | 600 |

THE CENTRAL PARK, *The New-York Daily Times,* May 29, 1858, p.4

EVERYBODY EXPECTED that as soon as the Commissioners of the Central Park had decided upon the plan they intended to carry out, they would set to work and carry it into effect at once. We do not hear of their doing so. They selected Messrs. Olmsted and Vaux's design, and the last thing we have heard of it is a string of proposed modifications in it, which will, if adopted, possibly make a good plan, but certainly not Design No. 33, which got the prize, and very probably an *olla podrida,* without unity or harmony, or any other good quality except variety, will be the result. We have never been admirers of patchwork, and admire patchwork parks as little as any patchwork we know of. We cannot, for the life of us, see why a design for a park should be modified to death any more than a design for a building. If enthusiastic admirers of Egyptian or Gothic architecture were allowed to introduce their modifications into a design for a Greek building, the result would be curious perhaps but not beautiful. However, we are content to leave these matters in the hands of the Commissioners. We only ask to have them settled at once. It is impossible for the architect to go on with the work, unless he has the whole scheme in his mind from first to last, so as to make all details and all stages of it subservient to the final effect. If he is liable to be stopped short every week by fresh changes suggested by the Board of Commissioners, it would be just as well to parcel it out in lots amongst the thirty-three candidates and let each follow his own fancy in his little division. The thing is just now in that stage in which it is the easiest thing in the world to botch it, and nothing is so well adapted to bring about this result as the intervention of numerous cooks.

There has been some fuss made in one of two quarters about the fact that Mr. Olmsted, who is not an engineer, has been substituted in the general supervision of the whole work for Mr. Viele, who is an engineer. In the first place, this contention about whether a man can write engineer after his name or not, is the silliest of trifling. The comparative merit of the plans is the proper test of his fitness, and not the place in which he graduated. Mr. Olmsted's plan has received the approval of the Commissioners as well as of the public, in addition to which his career as Superintendent has been successful. He has long been a practical farmer.

He has traveled over Europe, and paid close attention to the parks and gardens of the Old World. Mr. Viele has, we believe, never seen a park in his life, and has devoted no special attention to the subject.

In the next place, the idea that a military or civil engineer is the proper person to lay out a park is the climax of absurdity. No park was ever laid out by any man simply because he was an engineer, and none of the best parks were laid out by engineers at all. Versailles was designed by an architect, and Crystal Palace Gardens in London, which rank next them in beauty, were laid out by Sir Joseph Paxton, a gardener. It is no part of an engineer's business to perform the duties of a landscape gardener, and his education, to a great degree, unfits him for it. He has been taught to study naked use; the landscape gardener's aim is to produce beauty. The notion that Brunel or General Sir John Burgoyne would be the fittest men to lay our ornamental grounds, would excite great laughter in Europe; and even here, where there has been less experience on the subject, nobody is ass enough to suppose such a thing except the *Herald*. There is just one job on the Central Park for which Mr. Viele's services will be required, and that is the tunneling of the transverse roads, and this we hope he will get. That he could construct a good redoubt, or canal or railroad, we don't in the least doubt, and wish him every success in the practice of his profession.

# List of Illustrations and Sources

# Index

A. J. Downing memorial, The Mall, Washington, D. C.